INSTITUTE OF JEWISH STUDIES

MANCHESTER

SCRIPTA JUDAICA

EDITED BY A. ALTMANN

I

ISAAC ISRAELI

Cum priuilegio Pontificis maximi Leonis deci
mi: ⁊ Francisci christianissimi Francorum regis.

Omnia opera ysaac in hoc volumine con
tenta: cum quibusdam aliis opusculis:

Liber de definitionibus.
Liber de elementis.
Liber dietarū vniuersaliū: cum cōmēto petri hispani.
Liber dietarum particularium: cum cōmento eiusdem.
Liber de vrinis cum commento eiusdem.
Liber de febribus.
Pantechni decem libri theorices: et decem practices: cum tractatu de gradibus medicinarum constantini.
Viaticum ysaac quod constantinus sibi attribuit.
Liber de oculis constantini.
Liber de stomacho constantini.
Liber virtutum de simplici medicina constantini.
Compendium megatechni Galeni a constantino compositum.

Cum tabula ⁊ repertorio omnium operum
et questionum in cōmentis contentarum:

THE TITLE-PAGE OF *OMNIA OPERA YSAAC*, LYONS, 1515

SCRIPTA JUDAICA · I

ISAAC ISRAELI

A NEOPLATONIC PHILOSOPHER OF THE EARLY TENTH CENTURY

His Works translated with comments and an outline of his Philosophy

BY

A. ALTMANN
Director, Institute of Jewish Studies, Manchester

AND

S. M. STERN
Fellow of All Souls College, Oxford

OXFORD UNIVERSITY PRESS
1958

Oxford University Press, Amen House, London E.C.4
GLASGOW NEW YORK TORONTO MELBOURNE WELLINGTON
BOMBAY CALCUTTA MADRAS KARACHI KUALA LUMPUR
CAPE TOWN IBADAN NAIROBI ACCRA

PRINTED IN GREAT BRITAIN

ACKNOWLEDGEMENTS

THE authors wish to acknowledge the courtesy they received from the British Museum, the Bodleian Library, the Cambridge University Library, the Montefiore Endowment Committee of the Spanish and Portuguese Congregation in London, the Sassoon Library in Letchworth, the Leningrad State Public Library, the Biblioteca Comunale in Mantua, the Biblioteca Palatina in Parma, and the Library of the Aya Sofiya in Istanbul. Manuscripts in the possession of these libraries were used in the preparation of the present volume. Special thanks are due to the John Rylands Library and the Manchester Central Library for their unfailing kindness in helping to secure photographic reproductions of some of the most important among those manuscripts. Dr. D. A. Rees and Mr. R. Pring-Mill have kindly helped with the correction of the English style of Part I, Dr. S. Lauer with the preparation of the index, and Dr. R. Walzer with proof-reading.

The editor of the 'Scripta Judaica' series, of which this is the first volume, is grateful to the Delegates of the Clarendon Press for undertaking its publication. Funds made available to the Institute of Jewish Studies by the Conference on Jewish Material Claims against Germany, Inc., New York, were used towards reducing the price of the copies of the volumes in the series.

CONTENTS

PART I

TEXTS WITH COMMENTS

PART II

THE PHILOSOPHY OF ISAAC ISRAELI

(*by* a. altmann)

A. The Downward Way

ABBREVIATIONS

Armstrong, *Architecture*	A. H. Armstrong, *The Architecture of the Intelligible Universe in the Philosophy of Plotinus*, Cambridge, 1940.
BDef.	*Book of Definitions*, translated in ch. I of this work; quoted according to the sections of the translation (to which the sections of the re-edition of the Hebrew version also correspond).
BEl.	*Book on the Elements*, quoted according to the pages of ed. S. Fried, Drohobycz, 1900. An excerpt from the book, corresponding to Fried, pp. 51–60, is translated in ch. V of the present work; the pages of ed. Fried are given in the margin.
BSpirit	*Book on Spirit and Soul*, translated in ch. III of the present work; quoted according to the sections of the translation (to which the sections of the re-edition of the Hebrew version also correspond).
BSubst.	*Book of Substances*, translated in ch. II of the present work; quoted according to the numbers of the fragments and the folios of the manuscript (given in the margin). (The numbers of the fragments and the folios are also indicated in the edition of the Arabic text.)
CAG	*Commentaria in Aristotelem Graeca*, published by the Berlin Academy.
Ghāyat al-Ḥakīm	Ps.-al-Majrīṭī, *Ghāyat al-Ḥakīm* (*Aim of the Wise*), ed. H. Ritter, Leipzig–Berlin, 1933. (For some details concerning the book see below, pp. 7–8.)
Guttmann, *Israeli*	J. Guttmann, *Die philosophischen Lehren des Isaak b. Salomon Israeli*, Münster, 1911 (cf. below, p. xv).
Ibn Ḥasdāy	Ibn Ḥasdāy's *The Prince and the Ascetic*, chs. xxxii–xxxv of which form a philosophical excursus and are reproduced from a Neoplatonic treatise to which the name 'Ibn Ḥasdāy's Neoplatonist' is applied (see below, pp. 95 ff.).
Ikhwān (al-Ṣafā')	'The Sincere Brethren.' 'The Epistles of the Sincere Brethren' (for which see below, p. 150) are quoted according to the Arabic original, Cairo, 1928, and the German translation of F. Dieterici, which consists of various volumes with separate titles: *Naturanschauung und Naturphilosophie der Araber*, Leipzig, 1876; *Anthropologie der Araber*, Leipzig, 1871; *Die Philosophie der Araber im X. Jahrhundert.* (1) *Einleitung und Makrokosmus*, Leipzig, 1876; (2) *Mikrokosmus*, Leipzig, 1879; *Die Lehre von der Weltseele*, Leipzig, 1872.
al-Kindī	The edition of al-Kindī's philosophical treatises by M. Abū Rīda; *Rasā'il al-Kindī al-Falsafiyya*, Cairo, 1950–3 (two vols.; the pages refer to vol. i).

Mant. 'Mantua text', or 'Chapter on the Elements', translated in ch. IV of the present work; quoted according to the sections of the translation (to which the sections of the edition of the Hebrew version also correspond).

pseudo-Empedocles The fragments of the Neoplatonic *Book of the Five Substances* attributed to Empedocles; ed. D. Kaufmann, in *Studien über Salomon Ibn Gabirol*, Budapest, 1899. (Also referred to as 'Kaufmann Fragments'.) Other fragments attributed to Empedocles are contained in al-Shahrastānī's *Religions and Sects*, quoted after the edition of Cureton. (Cf. also p. 70, n. 1.)

al-Shaykh al-Yūnānī 'The Greek Master.' Arabic texts based on Plotinus go under this name; they have been collected by F. Rosenthal, 'Aš-Šayḫ al-Yūnānī and the Arabic Plotinus Source', *Orientalia*, xxi (1952), 461–92 (quoted as i); xxii (1953), 370–400 (quoted as ii); xxiii (1954), 42–66 (quoted as iii). (Also referred to as 'The Arabic Plotinus'.)

Steinschneider, *HebrÜb.* M. Steinschneider, *Die hebräischen Übersetzungen des Mittelalters*, Berlin, 1893.

Theology of Aristotle The excerpts from the *Enneads* of Plotinus, in Arabic, going under the name of the *Theology of Aristotle*. The vulgate version is quoted according to the ed. of F. Dieterici, Leipzig, 1882. (There is another edition by ʿA. Badawī, Cairo, 1955.) There is also an interpolated version (referred to as the Long Version, or as *LTheol.*), discovered by A. Borisov in three Leningrad manuscripts and corresponding to the Latin version, printed in Rome, 1519. The extracts printed by A. Borisov, *Izvestiya Akademiyi Nauk SSSR*, 1933, pp. 755–68, are referred to as *LTheol.*, ed. Borisov. Book X, sections 1–7, of the Long Version are derived from Ibn Ḥasdāy's Neoplatonist, cf. below, pp. 95 ff.

Vajda, *Commentaire* G. Vajda, 'Le Commentaire kairouanais sur le "Livre de la Création" ', *Revue des études juives*, cvii (1946–7), 99–156, cx (1949–50), 67–92, cxii (1953), 5–33, quoted according to volume and page of the journal. The study contains an edition and an analysis of the commentary on the *Sēfer Yĕṣīrā* (*Book of Creation*) (an old gnostic text, re-interpreted in successive epochs according to the ideas of the epoch), by Dūnash ibn Tamīm, a disciple of Israeli.

Yĕṣīrā Commentary Dūnash ibn Tamīm's commentary on the *Book of Creation*; cf. the preceding item.

INTRODUCTION

THE present volume offers an English translation of the philosophical treatises of Isaac ben Solomon Israeli, the earliest Jewish Neoplatonist, comments on the texts, and a survey and appraisal of Israeli's philosophy.

The following are the philosophical works of Israeli studied in the present volume. (We have left aside his medical works, though a study of them might bring to light here and there some passage relevant to philosophy.)

The first text included is that of the *Book of Definitions*, which is extant in medieval Latin and Hebrew translations, only a portion of it having survived in the Arabic original.

The fragments of the *Book of Substances* are extant in an Arabic manuscript in the possession of the Leningrad State Public Library (a short portion also in a manuscript of the British Museum), and were published for the first time by one of the joint authors.

The short *Book on Spirit and Soul* has been translated from the only available Hebrew version (except for a short passage extant in the original Arabic).

The *Chapter on the Elements* is translated from a Hebrew version of the Arabic original, preserved in a manuscript of the Biblioteca Comunale di Mantova (Mantua) and erroneously ascribed to Aristotle. It was first edited by one of the joint authors.

The only philosophical work by Israeli not included in this volume is the rather lengthy *Book on the Elements* which is extant in Latin and Hebrew versions and available in S. Fried's edition. It has been omitted both on account of its size and of the large amount of extraneous matter irrelevant to philosophy proper contained in it. Its contents, in so far as they have a bearing on Israeli's philosophy, have been taken into account in Part II. Moreover, an extract which has special philosophical importance is included in translation.

The results of our investigations into Israeli's sources can be summarized as follows. He has two principal sources. The one is al-Kindī,[1] whose influence pervades the *Book of Definitions*. Israeli is indebted to al-Kindī in some of the topics of the introductory section, such as the four types of inquiry and the definitions of philosophy (§§ 1–2, cf. also § 3); and in such important doctrines as those concerning the intellect (§ 4), the soul (§ 5), and *creatio ex nihilo* (§§ 42–43). Al-Kindī's influence is apparent, moreover, in a variety of details: in the use of different terms for heavenly and sublunar bodies (§ 7) and in a large number of miscellaneous definitions (§§ 11, 13, 14, 18, 25, 26, 30, 33, 36, 37, 39, 40, and 41). The other source is a lost pseudo-Aristotelian treatise, which we were able to reconstruct in the course of our studies, and for which we suggest the name 'Ibn Ḥasdāy's Neoplatonist' (cf. below, pp. 95 ff.). This treatise determined Israeli's doctrine of the chain of emanation, the nature of the intellect, and the return of the soul to its lofty origin. The influence of this Neoplatonic treatise is discernible in all Israeli's writings: in the Mantua text, where it is expressly quoted; in the *Book of Substances*, where its main theses are discussed at length; in the *Book on Spirit and Soul*, where its doctrines are supported by biblical quotations; and in a lesser degree also in the *Book of Definitions* (§§ 2 and 5). Unfortunately, Israeli's biography does not enlighten us about his philosophical studies or about the way in which he acquired his knowledge of the philosophy of al-Kindī and the Neoplatonist (cf. below, p. xxiii).

It will not be amiss to sum up the influence of Israeli upon later philosophical literature (the considerable fame which he acquired among Muslims, Jews, and Christians as a medical writer need not receive more than a passing mention in this context).[2] In Muslim

[1] For al-Kindī, the first great Islamic philosopher (first half of the ninth century), see Tj. de Boer's article 'al-Kindī' in the *Encyclopaedia of Islam* (out of date); M. Guidi and R. Walzer, *Studi su al-Kindī I* (Reale Accademia Nazionale dei Lincei, ser. vi, vol. vi, fasc. v), Rome, 1940; H. Ritter and R. Walzer, *Studi su al-Kindī II* (ibid., ser. vi, vol. viii, fasc. i), Rome, 1938; R. Walzer in *Oriens*, 1950, pp. 4–11. We have gained quite new insight into al-Kindī's philosophy since the discovery by H. Ritter of a manuscript in Istanbul containing numerous works by him. For an edition of his works see Abbreviations, s.v. al-Kindī.

[2] For his writings on medicine cf. M. Steinschneider, *HebrÜb.*, § 479; id., *Die arabische Literatur der Juden*, Frankfurt, 1902, § 28; C. Brockelmann, *Geschichte der arabischen Litteratur*, Leiden, 1937 ff., i. 271, Suppl. i. 421; cf. also L. Leclerc, *Histoire de la médecine arabe*, Paris, 1876, i. 409–12; G. Sarton, *Introduction to the History of Science*, Baltimore, 1927, i. 639 ff. Cf. also P. Erlangen, *Isaac*

writings, the only trace of Israeli's philosophy which we have been able to detect is the quotation in the *Ghāyat al-Ḥakīm*, a work written in eleventh-century Spain (see below, p. 8). Among the Jewish Neoplatonists of Spain he seems to have been generally known. Moses ibn Ezra (*c.* 1060–1139) used the *Book of Definitions* without naming it (see below, p. 7), and referred expressly to a lost treatise of Israeli's (see below, pp. 107–8). There are striking similarities between certain doctrines of Israeli and the Neoplatonic elements in Joseph ibn Ṣaddīq (d. 1149) which strongly suggest Israeli's influence (see below, pp. 30, 44, 73–74, 117). How far Solomon ibn Gabirol, the greatest among the Jewish Neoplatonists, is indebted to Israeli is a question which still requires detailed investigation. Among the earlier Jewish theologians of the East, Saadya Gaon was acquainted with Israeli's thinking, and may owe his concept of 'rational laws' partly to Israeli (see below, p. 217). On the other hand, a more strictly Aristotelian philosopher of the rank of Maimonides had, naturally enough, little sympathy with the somewhat primitive Neoplatonism of Israeli. In his well-known letter to Samuel ibn Tibbōn, in which other Neoplatonic writings also fall under his strictures, he describes Israeli as being 'only a physician'.[1] The rising tide of Aristotelianism was, however, unable to obliterate interest in Neoplatonic writings like Israeli's, which had a profoundly spiritual appeal. In the thirteenth century David Qimḥī, the celebrated Bible commentator, urged Abraham ibn Ḥasdāy, the author of *The Prince and the Ascetic* and translator of al-Ghazālī's *Balance of Action*, to render into Hebrew Israeli's *Book on the Elements*, a request which was fulfilled. In his preface, Ibn Ḥasdāy

Judaeus, Leben, Werke und Bedeutung für Hali Abbas und die medizinische Schule von Salerno, Tübingen thesis, 1922; H. Friedenwald, *Manuscript Copies of the Medical Works of Isaac Judaeus*, New York, 1929 (we have not seen the last two works). The Spanish version of the *Book of Fevers* has been published by J. Llamas, *Isḥāq Israeli, Tratado de las Fiebres, Edición de la versión castellana*, Madrid–Barcelona, 1945. In these works, and especially in those by Steinschneider, there will also be found indications about Israeli's fame as a physician among Muslims, Jews, and Christians (to whom his works were available mainly in the Latin translations made by Constantine the African).

[1] 'The *Book of Definitions* and the *Book on the Elements* by Isaac Israeli are also futile and vain, because he, too, was only a physician'—*Pĕ'ēr ha-Dōr*, Amsterdam, 1765, fol. 28^{v}; *Qōbheṣ*, Leipzig, 1859, ii. 28; ed. A. Marx, in *Jewish Quarterly Review*, 1934–5, p. 378.

speaks with great admiration of Israeli's philosophy, and regrets the fact that his work had fallen into oblivion amongst Jews who did not know Arabic. Falaqēra (*c.* 1225–95) was likewise an ardent admirer of Israeli. Later Hebrew authors also quote Israeli, more especially his *Book on the Elements.*[1]

Of great importance is Israeli's influence on the circle of Jewish mystics in Gerona, who became acquainted through him with the concept of first matter and first form or wisdom and the scheme of emanations outlined in the pseudo-Aristotelian source mentioned above. It is by no means certain that in quoting pseudo-Aristotle from the Mantua text they knew that it was Israeli's treatise they had before them, but this in no way diminishes the fact that the Neoplatonic doctrine concerned owed its transmission to Israeli (see below, pp. 130–2).

The Latin schoolmen were acquainted with the *Book of Definitions* and the *Book on the Elements*, both of which were translated by Gerard of Cremona. The first, especially, was quite popular: it was extensively used by Gundissalinus in the twelfth century[2] and by various authors, including Albert the Great and Thomas Aquinas, in the thirteenth.[3]

Part I of the present book contains the translation of the texts and comments upon them. The reader's indulgence is asked for some unevenness in the commentary: while some points have been elaborated fully (maybe even too fully), there are problems which are not perhaps sufficiently elucidated. It is this second shortcoming which we especially regret; it is due partly to the present state of knowledge of early Islamic philosophy and partly to our desire

[1] The passages of the Hebrew authors are collected by Fried, pp. 43–45. Fried's views concerning the indebtedness of various Jewish philosophers to Israeli (ibid., pp. 55–75) are, however, ill-founded.

[2] See Gundissalinus, *De Divisione Philosophiae*, ed. L. Baur, Münster, 1903, pp. 5–9.

[3] The passages of Albert in which Israeli is quoted are collected by J. Guttmann, *Die Scholastik des 13. Jahrhunderts in ihren Beziehungen zum Judentum und zur jüdischen Literatur*, Breslau, 1902, pp. 55–60, those of Thomas in the same author's *Das Verhältniss des Thomas von Aquino zum Judentum und zur jüdischen Literatur*, Göttingen, 1891, p. 15. For Vincent of Beauvais see *Die Scholastik &c.*, pp. 129–30, for Bonaventura, ibid., p. 139, for Roger Bacon, ibid., p. 150, for Nicholas of Cusa, ibid., p. 172. Cf. also the Comments on *BDef.*, § 24.

not to postpone unduly the publication of the present volume. Part II contains a survey of Israeli's philosophy. The subject has been treated previously in Jacob Guttmann's *Die philosophischen Lehren des Isaak b. Salomon Israeli*, Münster, 1911 (in the series 'Beiträge zur Geschichte der Philosophie des Mittelalters', ed. C. Baeumker). But as a result of the discovery of fresh texts, and in the light of the researches undertaken in this volume, Guttmann's account has had to be considerably revised.[1]

[1] The same is true of the shorter sketches in the standard histories of Jewish philosophy: Julius Guttmann, *Die Philosophie des Judentums*, Munich, 1933, pp. 96–102, and G. Vajda, *Introduction à la pensée juive du moyen âge*, Paris, 1947, pp. 65–68.

BIOGRAPHICAL NOTE

THE meagre biographical notes provided by the extant sources prove of little help for an elucidation of Israeli's philosophical background and training. Yet it would seem advisable to pass them in review in order to obtain some indication of the principal data of his life.[1]

One of the fundamental texts for Israeli's biography is the article about him in the *Generations of the Physicians* by Ibn Juljul, an Andalusian author of the second half of the tenth century (ed. F. Sayyid, Cairo, 1955, p. 87). The substance of Ibn Juljul's account has been known for a long time from the reports of later authors (see below), but the original text has been recovered only lately. It reads as follows:

Isḥāq ibn Sulaymān the Israelite. A native of Egypt, he began his career as an oculist. He emigrated to al-Qayrawān, became a companion and disciple of Isḥāq ibn 'Imrān,[2] and served as a physician of 'Ubayd Allāh the Shī'ite.[3] He was a physician with a ready tongue who was well acquainted with the arrangement of speech and the disposition of discourse.[4] He lived to an age of over a hundred, never married, and had no children.

[1] The uncertainties and contradictions in the accounts of Israeli's life have given rise to much discussion, to hypotheses and counterhypotheses, among those writing about him. Many of the views which have been put forward were intrinsically unacceptable, others were put out of court by fresh evidence. I thought it superfluous to enter into the labyrinth, and based my discussion on the primary evidence (some of which is new). I have quoted the names of certain scholars for valid arguments advanced by them, but passed over in silence evidently incorrect suggestions. Those curious to acquaint themselves with the whole discussion can do so with the help of the bibliographical references in this note.

[2] Isḥāq ibn 'Imrān, nicknamed 'swift poison', an eminent physician who came from Baghdad to the Aghlabid court in al-Qayrawān, finally quarrelled with the amīr Ziyādat Allāh and was executed. For him see Brockelmann, op. cit. [p. xii, n. 2], i. 266, Suppl. i. 417.

[3] 'Ubayd Allāh al-Mahdī, the founder of the Fāṭimid dynasty in North Africa, reigned A.H. 297/A.D. 910–A.H. 322/A.D. 934.

[4] Not quite clear, but probably refers to the style of his medical writings; Ṣā'id, however, saw in these phrases a reference to his knowledge of logic and his mastery of various sciences.

He is the author of various works, the like of which had never been written by previous writers, such as his book on urine, which is the most comprehensive work on the subject ever written and by which he gained superiority over all the earlier writers; his book on fevers; and his book on foodstuffs and drugs. He also wrote several books on philosophy, such as the book which bears the title of *Garden of Wisdom* and deals with questions of philosophy and metaphysics; his book on definitions and descriptions; his introduction to logic; ⟨the book on the elements;⟩[1] his book on the theriac.

When he was asked: Would you like to have a child? he answered: No, as I have a much better thing in the *Book of Fevers*—meaning that his memory would survive better through the *Book of Fevers* than through a child.

The next author to give a biography of Israeli is Ṣāʿid of Toledo in the middle of the eleventh century, who devotes a paragraph to him in the chapter on the Jews in his *Generations of the Nations* (ed. Cheikho, Beirut, 1912, p. 88).[2] The paragraph is, however, derived from Ibn Juljul, though the wording is altered.

Among the moderns we mention Isḥāq ibn Sulaymān, a disciple of Isḥāq ibn ʿImrān (known by the nickname *samm sāʿa* [swift poison]). He was a distinguished physician and served as a physician of ʿUbayd Allāh al-Mahdī, ruler of Ifrīqiya. He was besides a scholar in logic and learned in all branches of knowledge. He lived to a very old age, attaining as he did over a hundred years. In the course of this long life he remained unmarried and amassed no goods. He is the author of remarkable works, including a treatise on nutrition, a book on fevers which is unique of its kind, a work on urine, the *Book on the Elements*, a treatise on definitions and descriptions, and, finally, a work entitled *The Garden of Wisdom* dealing with questions of metaphysics. Isḥāq died shortly before the year 320 [= A.D. 932].

The only additional information contained in Ṣāʿid's text is the date of Israeli's death; but it can be assumed with great probability that this stood also in the original text of Ibn Juljul and was omitted by error in the unique extant manuscript.

[1] Not in the text; but as the accounts derived by later authors from Ibn Juljul mention this book, I assume that the words have fallen out by an error in the unique manuscript of Ibn Juljul's work.

[2] Cf. the French translation by R. Blachère, *Ṣâʿid al-Andalusî, Kitâb Ṭabaḳât al-Umam* (*Livre des Catégories des Nations*), Paris, 1935, p. 157.

The biographical article in Ibn Abī Uṣaybiʿa's *Generations of Physicians* (thirteenth century, ed. Müller, Cairo, 1882, ii. 36–37) is partly derived from Ibn Juljul, but other sources were also used. Ibn Abī Uṣaybiʿa repeats the date for Israeli's death (which seems to confirm the assumption that it did occur in Ibn Juljul's original text), and gives as his patronymic Abū Yaʿqūb (which is confirmed by the titles of the *Book of Substances* and of some of the medical works). Ibn Abī Uṣaybiʿa also quotes a second version of Israeli's self-confident utterance: 'I have four books which will keep alive my memory more than children would: the *Book of Fevers*, the *Book of Foodstuffs and Drugs*, the *Book of Urine*, and the *Book on the Elements*.' He then quotes a passage from the *History of the Fāṭimid Dynasty* by the physician Ibn al-Jazzār, a pupil of Israeli,[1] which contains two scenes from the life of Israeli as related by himself. The first shows Israeli, who has just arrived in Ifrīqiya (= modern Tunisia) from Egypt, paying court to the Aghlabid amīr Ziyādat Allāh[2] in his camp in al-Urbus (modern Laribus); this must have occurred in A.H. 295/A.D. 907, during the expedition of Ziyādat Allāh against the rebel Abū ʿAbd Allāh al-Shīʿī, the Fāṭimid emissary, when he made al-Urbus his headquarters.[3] The anecdote is told in order to show the frivolous disposition of the Aghlabid ruler. The second anecdote, about Abū ʿAbd Allāh, who after the capture of Raqqāda, Ziyādat Allāh's capital, availed himself in his turn of the medical services of Israeli, contrasts the frivolity of Ziyādat Allāh with the seriousness of the Fāṭimid general. In the bibliographical section which follows, Ibn Abi Uṣaybiʿa has a few additional

[1] For Ibn al-Jazzār, a very well known physician (said to have died in 395/1004 at the age of about 80), see Brockelmann, op. cit. [p. xii, n. 2], i. 274, Suppl. i. 424. His *History of the Fāṭimid Dynasty* is lost, but there are a number of quotations. (I hope to publish a series of unknown excerpts in a work which I am preparing on the chronicles of the Fāṭimids of North Africa.)

[2] The last ruler of the Aghlabid dynasty of amīrs; reigned from 290/903 until 296/909, the year in which he fled from his capital Raqqāda (a suburb of al-Qayrawān) before the victorious general of the Fāṭimids, Abū ʿAbd Allāh, who was preparing the way for his master, ʿUbayd Allāh al-Mahdī. For the historical background see my article 'Abū ʿAbd Allāh al-Shīʿī', in the *Encyclopaedia of Islam*, 2nd edn.

[3] The expedition of al-Urbus forms the subject of ch. xxv of al-Nuʿmān's chronicle *The Beginnings of the Dynasty* (for which see the article quoted in the preceding note), entitled 'The account of Ziyādat Allāh's expedition to al-Urbus and of his retreat'; thanks to it the date can be fixed as 295/907.

features: he quotes a favourable remark by Ibn Riḍwān concerning the *Book of Fevers*; mentions in addition to the *Book of Urine* an epitome of it; and mentions an *Introduction to the Art of Medicine*, a *Book of Pulse*, and a work on philosophy in eleven books (*mīmar*).[1]

While Ibn Abī Uṣaybiʿa used Ibn Juljul's account, Abraham ibn Ḥasdāy, in the preface to his Hebrew translation of Israeli's *Book on the Elements* (ed. Fried, p. 3), quotes Ṣāʿid's account. He gives, however, 330, instead of the original's 320, as the date of Israeli's death,[2] and adds at the end of the passage:[3]

> And the Mahdī raised him above all his scholars and all his people, and at his command he wrote all his books and composed his treatises. For this very reason he composed them in Arabic, for it is one's duty to fulfil the command of the ruler.

The biographical information in later Hebrew authors such as Isaac Lattes (in A. Neubauer, *Mediaeval Jewish Chronicles*, Oxford, 1895, ii. 233–4) and Gedaliah ibn Yaḥyā, *The Chain of Tradition*, Venice, 1586, fol. 40*a*, is evidently based on Ṣāʿid.

According to Ṣāʿid and Ibn Abī Uṣaybiʿa, who, if our surmise expressed above is correct, took the date from the original text of Ibn Juljul, Israeli died 'shortly before A.H. 320' (literally, 'near to 320'). This figure is, however, contradicted by reports in some Islamic historians. Ibn Ḥammād, in his *History of the Fāṭimid Dynasty* (ed. M. Vonderheyden, Algiers–Paris, 1927, text, p. 15, transl., pp. 28–29), tells us that the death of the caliph ʿUbayd Allāh in 322/934 was precipitated by ignoring the advice given to him by Isaac the Israelite who had warned him against the lethal effect of a certain potion prescribed by Ibn al-Jazzār.[4] Other historians tell a similar story about the circumstances surrounding the death of the third Fāṭimid caliph, ʿUbayd Allāh's grandson, al-Manṣūr,

[1] Here may be mentioned an anecdote told by al-Tamīmī, an Egyptian physician of the end of the tenth century, which shows Israeli in the presence of ʿUbayd Allāh, correcting a mistake committed by a colleague on a point of *materia medica* (see Leclerc, as quoted above, p. xii, n. 2).

[2] In view of the agreement of Ṣāʿid's Arabic text and that of Ibn Abī Uṣaybiʿa, both of which have 320, this must be due to an error.

[3] The addition is obviously a free composition by Ibn Ḥasdāy.

[4] The story cannot be correct as it stands: Ibn al-Jazzār must have been about 7 years old in 322/934, if we accept the dates furnished by his biographers (see p. xix, n. 1).

who died in 341/953. Again we hear that the disregard of advice given by the court physician Isaac Israeli caused the ruler's death; this time it was the sudden transition from the cold to a hot bath which proved fatal. (Cf. Ibn al-Athīr, under the year 341, ed. Tornberg, viii. 373–4; Ibn Khallikān, s.v. Ismāʿīl ibn al-Qayyim, ed. Wüstenfeld, no. 97, transl. de Slane, i. 221; Ibn Khaldūn, Būlāq, 1284, iv. 45–46.)[1] The two stories look suspiciously like two variants of one anecdote, and their value as evidence need not be too highly assessed. On the other hand, the date *c.* 320 seems to rest solely on the authority of Ibn Juljul. There is, however, an argument (already adduced by Fried in the introduction to his edition of the *Book on the Elements*, p. 12) which speaks for a later date. Ibn al-Jazzār, who was a disciple of Israeli (and says that he heard the anecdote quoted above, p. xix, from Israeli himself), died in 395/1009 at the age of about 80; in 320/932 he was only a boy of about 5.

If, then, we assume that Israeli died about 344/955–6 (in which year his pupil Dūnash ibn Tamīm referred to him as no longer alive, see below, p. xxii, n. 1), he must have been born at about 855 if we trust Ibn Juljul's account that he died at an age of over a hundred. We are told that he was of Egyptian origin, and we find him in Egypt in 292–3/905, at the age of about 50 (according to the single autobiographical notice found in Israeli's works, *BDef.*, § 31, below, p. 62). We know nothing about the period of his life which is of especial interest for us in our present context—his formative years. Did he spend the first fifty years of his life in Egypt, and was it there that he received his schooling in philosophy, or did he visit the centres of philosophical studies in the more easterly provinces of the Islamic empire?[2] For the

[1] All these accounts obviously go back to the same source, probably to Ibn Shaddād's *History of al-Qayrawān* (beginning of the twelfth century), which is Ibn al-Athīr's usual source for North African matters. All these passages have already been brought to light by S. Munk, in 'Notice sur Abou'l-Walid Merwan ibn-Djana'h', *Journal asiatique*, ii (1850), 8.

[2] The problem would clearly be solved if it were possible to assume that the Isḥāq ibn Sulaymān mentioned by Ḥunayn ibn Isḥāq is identical with our Isḥāq ibn Sulaymān. Ḥunayn, the great translator of Greek works into Arabic, in his invaluable lists of his translations of the works of Galen (edited by G. Bergsträsser under the title *Ḥunain ibn Isḥāq über die syrischen und arabischen Galen-Übersetzungen*, Leipzig, 1925) says of four of his translations that they

background of Israeli's philosophy the biographical tradition has no clues to offer, and we have to fall back on the internal evidence of his writings (see below).

In 292–3/905 he was still in Egypt according to his own testimony; according to another testimony by himself he was in Ifrīqiya in 295/907, when Ziyādat Allāh was at al-Urbus (see above). This fits very well; but here another hole can be picked in Ibn Juljul's account, according to which Israeli became the disciple of Isḥāq ibn ʿImrān after his arrival in Ifrīqiya. On the basis of Ibn Juljul's own dates, Israeli at his arrival was about 75 years old, so that such a relationship seems absurd. One could, however, resolve the difficulty by treating Ibn Juljul's date for the death of Israeli as erroneous and assuming that Israeli was at the time of his coming to Ifrīqiya about 50 years old. There is, however, another difficulty. According to the biographical tradition Isḥāq ibn ʿImrān was executed by Ziyādat Allāh: now between the coming of Israeli and the end of Ziyādat Allāh's rule there passed less than a year, so that there remains no time in which to place Israeli's discipleship. Again, one could find a way out by assuming that Israeli came to Ifrīqiya earlier, say immediately after 292–3/905, and that he did not present himself to Ziyādat Allāh until 295/907; thus he could have attended Isḥāq ibn ʿImrān for a year or two after his arrival. Fried, on the other hand, has suggested (pp. 15–16) that Israeli had already studied under Isḥāq ibn ʿImrān in Baghdad, Ibn ʿImrān's original home; this is, however, pure conjecture. At any rate, one ought not build too much on the somewhat shaky foundations of Ibn Juljul's account.[1]

were made for 'Isḥāq ibn Sulaymān': viz. the *Book of Mixture* (no. 12); *The Natural Faculties* (no. 13); *The Slimming Diet* (no. 75); and *That the Good Physician is a Philosopher* (no. 103). If the identification were acceptable, this information would open wider vistas for Israeli's contacts with the scholars of Baghdad; unfortunately it is by no means so. It is much more likely that Isḥāq ibn Sulaymān is identical with a Muslim notable of that name, who was for some time governor of Egypt; see M. Meyerhof, 'New Light on Ḥunain b. Isḥāq', *Isis*, 1926, p. 716.

[1] We should not omit to mention the interesting passage in which Israeli's pupil Dūnash ibn Tamīm (for whom cf. Vajda, *Commentaire*, and S. M. Stern, 'A treatise on the armillary sphere by Dūnas ibn Tamīm', *Homenaje a Millás-Vallicrosa*, ii (Barcelona, 1956), 372–82, and the references quoted) refers to Israeli's relations with his great compatriot, Saadya Gaon. It is contained in Dūnash's commentary on the *Sēfer Yĕṣīrā*, written 344/955–6 (see Vajda, *Com-*

It has been explained above (pp. xi–xii) that internal evidence allows us to name the writings of al-Kindī and the treatise of Ibn Ḥasdāy's Neoplatonist as the main influences in Israeli's philosophy. One would like to know the way in which Israeli acquired his knowledge of al-Kindī's philosophy. Was it through the perusal of al-Kindī's works, or, more likely, through personal contact with some of al-Kindī's disciples?[1] We cannot say. Nor do we know if the combination of doctrines derived from al-Kindī with the system of Ibn Ḥasdāy's Neoplatonist was a personal achievement of Israeli or whether he had precursors in that respect. As a matter of fact we know very little about the diffusion of the treatise of the Neoplatonist; we only know that, apart from Israeli, it was used by the author of the longer version of the *Theology of Aristotle*, whose date and environment are, however, unknown. Thus the external circumstances in which Israeli became acquainted with the main sources of his philosophy remain shrouded in mystery; on the other hand, his place in the history of Islamic and Jewish philosophy has been clarified as a result of the researches undertaken in this volume.

mentaire, cvii, p. 20): 'When he [viz. Saadya] lived in al-Fayyūm, before he went to Baghdad, he addressed numerous letters to our city of al-Qayrawān, to our master, Isaac the son of Solomon, of blessed memory, consulting him about problems of the "external sciences" [i.e. philosophical and scientific—in contrast to theological—subjects]. Rabbi Isaac used to show me those letters, though I was only twenty years old, and I pointed out some errors in them, which caused my master great pleasure, on account of my youth.' Saadya left Egypt in the year 905. This passage also shows that Israeli died not later than 344/955–6.

[1] The exact date of al-Kindī's death is not known, but it must have occurred at the beginning of the second half of the ninth century, so that Israeli could hardly have met al-Kindī himself.

PART I

TEXTS WITH COMMENTS

I

THE BOOK OF DEFINITIONS

PRELIMINARY NOTE

FOR this work of Isaac Israeli, the best known of all his philosophical writings, a rich variety of textual evidence is available. A considerable portion of the Arabic original has been recovered and the whole treatise is extant in Latin and Hebrew versions. I shall first give an account of the fragment of the Arabic original, and then of the Latin and Hebrew translations.

(1) *The Arabic original*

The fragment was discovered by H. Hirschfeld among the Genizah manuscripts preserved in the Cambridge University Library (five folios: TS. 8 Ka. 6[2]) and published by him in 'The Arabic portion of the Cairo Genizah at Cambridge', no. vi, *Jewish Quarterly Review*, xv (1902), 689–93 (description of the manuscript: pp. 682–3). The fragment comprises the text from the middle of § 7 to the end of § 43. As the beginning is missing, there is no external indication to identify it; but Hirschfeld, who had previously edited the Hebrew text (see below), recognized the identity of the Arabic text from the contents. His discovery and publication of it are no doubt deserving of praise; unfortunately, however, one cannot help saying that he was a careless editor. The text as printed by him contains many errors due to misreading of the manuscript (only a few errors can be imputed to misprints). In order to relieve the critical apparatus of corrections which do not concern the manuscript tradition but only its editor, I have published the results of my collation in the introduction to my edition of the Hebrew version by Nissim (see below). In the translation I translate from the correct readings of the manuscript without noting in the apparatus Hirschfeld's erroneous text. (On the other hand, emendations to the text of the manuscript are noted in the apparatus.)

The manuscript is written in Hebrew characters, and it can be shown that the manuscript used by Nissim for his translation was also in Hebrew characters (cf. textual note to § 2, ll. 66–67, 93–94). On the other hand, there is an indication that the latter manuscript goes back to an archetype written in Arabic characters: in § 4, l. 42, the Hebrew version has *the genus*, i.e. the manuscript in Hebrew characters on which it was based read *al-jins*. This is a mistake for *al-ḥiss*, 'sense'; such a mistake must go back to a manuscript written in Arabic characters (الحس for الحس—a similar mistake occurs in *BSubst.*, cf. my edition, *Journal of Jewish Studies*, 1956, p. 16).

(2) *The Latin translation by Gerard of Cremona*

The Latin translation made by Gerard of Cremona (1114–87)[1] is available in a critical edition prepared by J. T. Muckle, 'Isaac Israeli, Liber de Definicionibus', *Archives d'histoire doctrinale et littéraire du moyen âge*, 1937–8, pp. 299 ff., based on three manuscripts (Paris, B.N. 14,700 = A; 6443 = C; Vat. Lat. 2186 = B) and the printed edition in *Omnia opera Ysaac*, Lyons, 1515, fols. ii^r–iv^r (= L). This Latin translation, for which the siglum L is used in the critical apparatus (with L^A, &c., standing for the manuscripts used by Muckle, L^L for the Lyons edition), is the most important witness for the restitution of those parts the Arabic original of which is missing; it is markedly superior to Nissim's Hebrew translation. We find variant readings for a certain number of passages, introduced by the words '*in alio*'. These must go back to the translator who either collated different copies of the Arabic original or, more probably, had at his disposal an Arabic manuscript with variant readings in the margin.

[1] The translation is attributed to Gerard in the heading contained in some of the manuscripts and in the list of his translations which accompanies the contemporary 'Vita' (B. Boncompagni, *Della vita e delle opere di Gherardo Cremonese*, Rome, 1851—also in *Atti dell'Accad. pontif. de' nuovi Lincei*, iv. 387–493; K. Sudhoff, 'Die kurze "Vita" und das Verzeichnis der Arbeiten Gerhards von Cremona', *Archiv für Geschichte der Medizin*, 1914, pp. 75–80). For Gerard see, in addition to the preceding, M. Steinschneider, 'Die europäischen Übersetzungen aus dem Arabischen', *Sitzungsberichte der kaiserlichen Akademie der Wissenschaften in Wien*, 1904, pp. 16–27; G. Sarton, *Introduction to the History of Science*, ii. 338–44; L. Minio-Paluello, 'Note sull'Aristotele Latino Medievale', *Rivista di Filosofia Neo-scolastica*, 1951, pp. 102 ff.

Muckle's edition is very useful, but as he did not compare the Latin text with the Arabic original and the Hebrew version, there is room for improvement. Suggestions for it are to be found in the textual annotations.

(3) *The abbreviated Latin version*

The abbreviated Latin version was edited by Muckle, op. cit. (pp. 328–40), from MS. Munich, Lat. 8001; it is anonymous. M. Alonso has put forward the suggestion that it is by Dominicus Gundissalinus ('Traducciones del arcediano Domingo Gundisalvo', *Al-Andalus*, 1947, pp. 295 ff., ch. 7: 'Liber de difinitionibus' de Isḥāq al-Isrā'īlī, pp. 325 ff.). The version is quoted in Gundissalinus's *De divisione philosophiae* (cf. above, p. xiv). According to Alonso's hypothesis, the abbreviated Latin version, by Gundissalinus, is earlier than Gerard's complete translation. As there is, however, a very close relation between the two versions, Alonso suggests that Gerard has made use of it for his own translation. This does not seem, however, very plausible; the epitome is obviously based on the full translation of Gerard; while epitomizing the contents of the work it also smooths out the style of the translation in many passages. Whether the author of the epitome was in fact Gundissalinus himself, or a third person whose work was then used by Gundissalinus, could only be decided by a delicate stylistic examination. At any rate, the use of an epitome of a translation of Gerard by Gundissalinus (both of whom were working in Toledo at the same time) is of some interest for our knowledge of the milieu of the Toledan translators. (The text of the abbreviated version in the unique manuscript is very bad; if read, however, together with the full text, most of the obscurities can be cleared up.)

(4) *The Hebrew translation by Nissim ben Solomon*

Nothing seems to be known of the personality of the translator, as he can hardly be identified with either of the two men with similar names known as writers on philosophy (cf. Steinschneider, *HebrÜb.*, § 224). The style and terminology of the translator are very peculiar, and his translation is awkward and often erroneous; if we did not possess the other versions, it would not always be possible to discern its meaning. J. L. Teicher has put forward the suggestion ('The Latin-Hebrew school of translators in Spain in the twelfth century', *Homenaje a Millás-Vallicrosa*, ii. 416–22) that the translation was made from the Latin, not from the Arabic original, and that it was made in Spain in the twelfth century. I think, however, that the arguments advanced in favour of these views do not withstand a critical examination. I have scrutinized Teicher's argument in detail in the introduction to my edition of Nissim's translation, and as the reader who wishes to form his own judgement can be referred to those pages, there is no need to repeat the rather technical argument here. I have tried to show that the alleged proofs that the Latin translation is the original of the Hebrew version are based on mistaken interpretation of the passages in question, and that, on the other hand, there are several passages in the Hebrew which show that the translator had the Arabic original before him. It is true, however, that there are some instances in which the Hebrew shows an acquaintance with the Latin. Thus we have either to fall back on Guttmann's view, according to which Nissim, while translating from the Arabic, also consulted the Latin version; or ascribe the glosses derived from the Latin version to an interpolator. It may also be admitted that, though the arguments adduced by Teicher in order to prove the twelfth-century date for the translation of Nissim do not hold water, such a date has something to recommend it. The peculiar manner of the translator would find a natural explanation if we assumed that he worked at an early stage of the movement of translation before the standard Hebrew philosophical terminology was elaborated (mainly by the Tibbonids).

The translation has been published by H. Hirschfeld, in *Festschrift zum 80. Geburtstag M. Steinschneiders*, Leipzig, 1896, Hebrew part, pp. 131–42 (with a preface, German part, pp. 233–4). As it was possible, by a comparison with the Arabic original which was discovered in the meantime by Hirschfeld himself and with the other versions, to establish an improved text, I have re-edited it on the basis of the manuscript in the Montefiore Library, which contains the whole text, and the Oxford and Parma manuscripts, which contain the first three paragraphs. The new edition will appear in the *Hebrew Union College Annual*.

(5) *The second Hebrew translation*

A fragment of four folios from a second Hebrew translation was discovered by Borisov among the fragments of Hebrew manuscripts in the Second Firkovitch Collection (Hebrew nos. 388 and 412). He published a few lines, as a sample, in Part III of his article 'Some new fragments of Isaak Israeli's works' (for the bibliographical mystery connected with this article see below, p. 79). The full text of the extant fragments was published by A. Altmann, in *Journal of Semitic Studies*, 1957, pp. 232–42. The extant fragments cover the following parts of the treatise: a fragment of the title; the last words of § 1 and the first half of § 2; the second half of § 3 and the first half of § 4; the second half of § 8 and the first half of § 9. The name of the translator is not known; the translation is composed, in contrast to that of Nissim, in the normal Hebrew philosophical style.[1]

(6) *Quotations by Moses ibn Ezra and the author of the* Ghāyat al-Ḥakīm

I have shown in a note entitled 'Isaac Israeli and Moses ibn Ezra', *Journal of Jewish Studies*, 1957, pp. 83–89, that Moses ibn Ezra (one of the great figures of Spanish Hebrew poetry, second half of the eleventh–first half of the twelfth century) in his philosophico-exegetical work in Arabic, *The Book of the Garden, explaining the meaning of Metaphor and Literal Expression* (*Kitāb al-Ḥadīqa fī Maʿna 'l-Majāz wa'l-Ḥaqīqa*), repeatedly used, without naming it, the *Book of Definitions*, quoting §§ 2, 4, 9, and 42. In that note the passages of *al-Ḥadīqa* are printed (from the manuscript in the Sassoon Library) and confronted with the corresponding texts of the *Book of Definitions*. These quotations of the Arabic text are often valuable, especially for the passages the original Arabic text of which is not otherwise preserved. The results of the collation of Ibn Ezra's quotations are incorporated in the critical apparatus.

The *Aim of the Wise* (*Ghāyat al-Ḥakīm*), the Latin translation

[1] An author of the thirteenth century, Ibn Laṭīf, quotes § 43 (see Fried, p. 47) in a form which follows neither the first nor the second Hebrew translation; Altmann surmised that he quoted directly from the Arabic original.

of which, called *Picatrix*, was highly valued during the Middle Ages, is a textbook of various branches of magic, which was compiled in the eleventh century in Spain (and falsely claimed to be by al-Majrīṭī). Its author had some philosophical interests and quotes various philosophical excerpts, either with or without the names of their authors. In several passages we find texts which correspond so well with passages of Israeli that we have to draw one of two conclusions: either the author used the same sources as Israeli or was directly indebted to Israeli. As there is nothing impossible, or even improbable, in the assumption that Israeli's *Book of Definitions* was available to a Muslim author in Spain in the eleventh century, we shall prefer the second alternative. (See above, p. 4, for the proof that the *Book of Definitions*, as well as the *Book of Substances*, circulated in Arabic characters; see above, p. xviii, for the fact that the *Book of Definitions* appears in the bibliographical lists given by Muslim authors; and compare the case of Moses ibn Ezra, a Spanish—though admittedly Jewish—author.) The borrowings consist in definitions of the soul and of nature; see the translation of the passages in question in the Comments on §§ 4 and 9.

It remains to say a few words concerning the structure of the *Book of Definitions*.

The first nine paragraphs (the division into numbered paragraphs has been introduced by me and does not exist in the manuscripts) are comparatively extensive *exposés* of their subjects. §§ 1–2 form a kind of introduction, dealing with the four types of inquiry and the various descriptions of philosophy; for the connexion which had originally existed between these two topics see the Comments. There follow (§§ 3–9) definitions, amplified by further explanations, of the various substances arranged according to their rank in the order of emanation: wisdom, intellect, the three souls, sphere = nature. (The paragraphs on earthly and heavenly body and on the vital spirit are in the nature of digressions.) Afterwards the style changes, and short and abrupt definitions, obviously taken out of their context, follow. §§ 10–19 and 31–33 concern various psychological notions; §§ 20–30 various logical ones. §§ 34–37 define some terms of physics; §§ 38–40 various kinds of love. §§ 41–47 explain the various kinds of movement (including *creatio ex nihilo*, cf. Comments); §§ 48–50 various concepts of time. §§ 51–53 deal with various curiously assorted ethical definitions; §§ 54–56 explain the distinction between different terms concerning action. This survey shows that the scope of the definitions contained in the book is far from being exhaustive, nor is the arrangement very systematic; the author cannot be absolved from the charge of haphazardness and abruptness.

It has been pointed out in the introduction that in the present treatise Israeli makes ample use of the writings of al-Kindī and that here and there the influence of Ibn Ḥasdāy's Neoplatonist can also be discerned. For the details of his indebtedness see the Comments on the various paragraphs.

For the sake of easier orientation the following table of contents is appended, divided into sections according to the explanations given above.

§ 35. Contact.
§ 36. Touch.
§ 37. Adherence.

§ 38. Love.
§ 39. Passion.
§ 40. Desire.

§ 41. 'Being innovated.'
§ 42. Creation.
§ 43. Coming-to-be.
§ 44. Passing-away.
§ 45. Growth.
§ 46. Decrease.

§ 47. Locomotion.

§ 48. Time.
§ 49. Eternity.
§ 50. Perpetuity.

§ 51. Decision.
§ 52. Sadness.
§ 53. Fear.

§ 54. Creature.
§ 55. Artifice.
§ 56. Operation.

Collections from the Sayings of the Philosophers concerning the Difference between the Descriptions and Definitions of Things, and why Philosophy has been described, but not defined—Collected and arranged by Isaac the Physician, Son of Solomon[1]

§ 1. Isaac says: Many of those who read the books of the ancients and see their differences in defining things come to the conclusion that this must be due to differences in their opinions; this is not, however, so. As they endeavoured to investigate the definitions of things, they found that there are four inquiries without which one cannot reach the knowledge of these definitions. (1) The first is existence: when one

A = the Arabic original; H = the Hebrew version of Nissim; H^2 = the second Hebrew version; L = the Latin version (L^A, &c. = the various manuscripts of this version; L^{ab} = the abbreviated Latin version).

Title: *Collections . . . Solomon* L *Book of Definitions* [. . .] *collected from the sayings of the phil*[*osophers* . . .] H^2 *The compilation of Isaac the physician, the Israelite, translated from the Arabian into the holy tongue by Nissim, son of Rabbi Solomon, may God give him rest* H.

§ 1. 10 *existence*: *anitas* L *halūth* H (original probably *haliyya*).

[1] 'Definition can be composed only from genera and substantial differentiae' below, § 2, ll. 2–3 = Aristotle, *Topics* i. 8. 103^b, 15: 'The definition consists of genus and differentiae.' Definition declares the 'nature and substantiality' of a thing (§ 1, l. 21), whereas 'description' (*rasm*) indicates the 'quality' or 'property' (cf. ibid., ll. 22–23, 39–40). (A definition giving the quality instead of the quiddity is rejected by Israeli, see § 24.) The 'property' may be divided into three kinds,

inquires whether so-and-so exists; (2) the second is quiddity: when one inquires what so-and-so is; (3) the third is quality: when one inquires how so-and-so is; (4) the fourth is 'quarity': when one inquires why so-and-so is.

This can be explained as follows. (1) Existence inquires about the being of a thing, viz. if it has existence or not. The answer to this question must always be either 'yes'—if one admits the existence of the thing—or 'no'—if one denies it.

(2) Quiddity inquires about the nature and the essence of a thing, viz. what it is, and thus the answer to it is given by the definition of the thing, which declares its nature and substantiality.

(3) Quality inquires about the property and the inseparable concomitants of a thing. . . . For this reason, before replying, one must turn to the inquirer and say that a thing has many properties and concomitants;

15–16 The original of *existence* in l. 15 was *haliyya,* in l. 16 *wujūd.* 23 '. . .': *notis forma quod eorum sit* L *ha-nikkārīm ba-'ăbhūr ha-hăwāyā bě-ēzeh mēhem hū*; I am unable to translate this.

---

see § 1, ll. 38–45, and *BEl.*, pp. 29–30, where the term 'property' is reserved for the first category only. A 'description' may be given by indicating the 'property' of the thing. Thus Israeli describes by their properties philosophy (§ 2), wisdom (§ 3), nature (§ 9). This usage is in accord with the ancient authorities. Aristotle had distinguished between the essence and the property of a thing. Definition was 'a formula designating the essence' (*Topics* i. 5. 101^{b}; *Posterior Analytics* ii. 10. 93^{b}; *Metaphysics* vii. 5. 1031^{a}), but 'the property of a thing ought not to show the essence' (*Topics* v. 3. 131^{b}, 38–132^{a}, 1). Aristotle did not use the term 'description' (ὑπογραφή), which was first introduced by the Stoics and known to the Islamic philosophers from Galen and from the Alexandrian commentators. (See S. van den Bergh, *Epitome der Metaphysik des Averroes*, Leiden, 1924, pp. 168–9; I. Madkour, *L'Organon d'Aristote dans le monde arabe*, Paris, 1934, p. 119; S. Munk, *Mélanges de philosophie juive et arabe*, Paris, 1859, p. 108; M. Steinschneider, *Al-Farabi*, St. Petersburg, 1869, p. 75; D. Kaufmann, *Geschichte der Attributenlehre*, Gotha, 1877, p. 314.) The difference between definition and description is nowhere actually explained in the text of Israeli, but is explicitly understood throughout; 'why philosophy has been described, but not defined' is explained at the beginning of § 2. Nevertheless, it is rather strange that in the title Israeli referred to a feature which plays only a secondary role; but he did the same in the *Book of the Spirit and the Soul* (cf. below, p. 108). (That the phrase 'the difference between definition and description' belongs to the original title is confirmed by the concerted testimony of the title in L and the colophon of H, see below, p. 78.) That the form 'descriptions and definitions of things' corresponds to the title given by al-Kindī to his work on definitions (*Treatise on the definitions and descriptions of things* (*Risāla fī ḥudūd al-ashyā' wa-rusūmihā*)) is surely not a coincidence. In the biographical tradition the treatise is quoted as 'Book of Definitions and Descriptions' (cf. above, p. xviii), which is obviously a shortened reference. Maimonides calls it by the same name (see above, p. xiii). Ibn Laṭīf refers to the work as *Sēfer gěbhūlē ha-děbhārīm*, 'Book of the definitions of things' (see above, p. 7).

say therefore which of them you have in mind. When the inquirer explains his meaning, one can answer with either 'yes' or 'no', as we have explained above. On account of this the answer concerning existence and quality must always be 'yes' or 'no'.

(4) 'Quarity' inquires about the final cause of a thing, which is necessary for the generation or the being of the thing, why it is such.

The following is an instance: (1) If someone inquires about man whether he exists, the answer must always be 'yes', because man has reality, and what has reality has being, and what has being has no doubt existence. (2) If one inquires what is man, the answer is given by the definition, viz. that man is a rational and mortal living being; 'living being' is man's genus and the matter forming the substratum for his form, while rationality and mortality are the differentiae and the complements of his speciality, as man alone is rational and mortal. (3) If one inquires of what kind is man, the answer will be as follows: Quality inquires about the property and the concomitants of a thing. Now man's properties are threefold: (*a*) those that belong to every man at every time, e.g. laughter; (*b*) those that belong to every man, but not at all times, e.g. grey hair at old age; (*c*) those that are found in some men, but not at all times, e.g. mildness, science, geometry, medicine, and similar things, which are man's properties, but do not belong to every man. Say therefore which of these properties you have in mind. When the inquirer clarifies his intention, one can answer him 'yes' or 'no'. (4) If one inquires why man is rational, we can answer: That he may discern with his intelligence and investigate with his deliberation and cogitation, in order to understand the truths of things and do what corresponds to truth in justice and rectitude, follow the good and keep away from the evil, so that he should obtain the reward of his Creator, may He be exalted.[1]

30 *why it is such*: read in L *quare fuit secundum hoc* (so L^{AB}; L^{L} om. *secundum*, L^{C} om. *quare . . . hoc*); in H read: *lāmmā hāyā ʿal* (MSS.: *wĕʿal*) *zeh*. 43–44 *but not at all times*: *at some times* H *not always* L^{ab} *but not in all of them* L (read: *at non in omni ⟨tempore⟩*?). 44 *mildness . . . medicine* L *mildness, medicine, geometry* H. 50–51 *do . . . rectitude* L *do what is convenient, viz. truth, justice, and rectitude* H. 53 Here begins the second fragment of H^2.

[1] Cf. the passage from the *Book of Fevers* (fol. 204, quoted by Guttmann, *Israeli*, p. 23). 'If one inquires why man is, we can answer: Man, being constituted of a natural body, is the tool of the rational soul for the sake of understanding thereby the truths of things and acting through it according to what corresponds to reason. If one asks why man is rational, we can answer as follows: in order to discern good from evil and truth from falsehood; reason being nothing but the separation of good from evil.'

COMMENTS

Israeli's discussion of the four types of inquiry depends on the formulation which al-Kindī had given to the four Aristotelian types. We possess the following passage by al-Kindī on the subject in his *On First Philosophy* (see al-Kindī, p. 101).[1]

. . . A cause is either matter, or form, or efficient cause, viz. from which movement starts, or final cause, viz. at which a thing aims.

The scientific inquiries are four, as we have determined in various of our philosophical treatises: (1) 'whether'; (2) 'what'; (3) 'which'; or (4) 'why'. (1) 'Whether' inquires exclusively about the existence.[2] (2) 'What' inquires about the genus of such essences as have a genus. (3) 'Which' inquires about their differentia; 'what' and 'which' together inquire about their species. (4) 'Why' inquires about their final cause, as it inquires about the absolute cause. It is clear that if we obtain the knowledge of their matter, we thereby obtain the knowledge of their genus, if we obtain the knowledge of their form, we thereby obtain the knowledge of their species; in the knowledge of the species there is comprised the knowledge of the differentia; thus, if we obtain the knowledge of their matter, form, and final cause, we thereby obtain the knowledge of their definition. . . .

The ultimate basis for this list is Aristotle's enumeration of the four types of inquiry in the *Posterior Analytics* ii. 1: (1) τὸ ὅτι; (2) τὸ διότι; (3) εἰ ἔστι; (4) τί ἐστιν; (1) whether a thing has a certain attribute; (2) why it has a certain attribute; (3) whether a thing exists; (4) what the thing is. The first two points refer to statements, the last two to substances; this distinction, which corresponds to Aristotle's intention, was even more sharply

[1] Another passage on the four types of inquiry occurs in al-Kindī's treatise on Ptolemy's *Almagest*; see F. Rosenthal, 'Al-Kindī and Ptolemy', *Studi orientalistici in onore di Giorgio Levi della Vida*, Rome, 1956, ii. 441: '. . . fol. 54^b, where al-Kindī refers to his four epistemological categories, as he also does in the *Kitāb al-falsafah al-ūlā*.'

[2] The Arabic term is *anniyya*. A synonym is *haliyya*, see farther on in the Comments, *passim*. The evidence of the Latin and Hebrew (*anitas*, *halūth*) seems to show that Israeli used *haliyya*. If so, the Latin term *anitas*, which occurs for the first time in this passage of Israeli as translated by Gerard of Cremona, and in some translations of Gundissalinus (see M.-Th. d'Alverny, in *Archives d'histoire doctrinale et littéraire du moyen âge*, 1952, p. 346), is probably coined (by Gerard?) to render *haliyya* and was also used (taken over by Gundissalinus?) to render the synonymous *anniyya*. (It is more likely that *anitas* is derived from *an est*, and is not an imitation of *anniyya*.)

emphasized by the commentators, whose formula is that the first two points refer to simple, the last two to compound, terms.

The immediate source of the list 'whether', 'what', 'which', and 'why' is, however, to be found in the Alexandrian introductions to philosophy, more precisely in the introductions by the two pupils of Olympiodorus—Elias and David: εἰ ἔστι, τί ἐστιν, ὁποῖόν τί ἐστι καὶ διὰ τί ἐστι (Elias, *Introduction to Philosophy*, *CAG* xviii/1. 3; David, *Introduction to Philosophy*, *CAG* xviii/2. 1). Elias and David enumerate the four types near the beginning of their introduction. As is well known, both of these authors depend on the lost introduction by Olympiodorus. Olympiodorus evidently introduced the four types of inquiry in order to conduct his preliminary inquiry concerning philosophy according to them, treating subsequently of the questions whether philosophy exists, what philosophy is, of which kind it is, and what is its aim. This lost account of Olympiodorus is reflected differently in the versions of Elias and David. Elias says (p. 3) that the first question is unnecessary in the case of philosophy, as its existence is self-evident and needs no discussion. The second question is elaborated at great length (pp. 3–25) by discussing the various answers given to the 'what' of philosophy, i.e. its various definitions. At this point, however, he forgets all about the rest, and the third and the fourth inquiries are not mentioned at all. This is no doubt due to Elias's negligence, as David discusses all the four questions (first question, pp. 2–9; second, pp. 9–76; third, pp. 76–78; fourth, pp. 78–79), so that we may safely conclude that Olympiodorus also treated in his lost lectures of all the four questions, and that David has more faithfully preserved Olympiodorus's disposition, while Elias has through carelessness mutilated it.[1]

[1] It will be instructive to quote here the passages concerning the four types of inquiry and the definitions of philosophy from an Arabic commentary on the *Isagoge*, depending on the Alexandrian tradition: the one by Ibn al-Ṭayyib, who flourished in the first half of the eleventh century and died in 1043. The whole of the introductory part has been translated by D. M. Dunlop, 'The existence and definition of philosophy, from an Arabic text ascribed to al-Fārābī', *Iraq*, 1951, pp. 76 ff. (I have shown that the attribution to al-Fārābī is erroneous and established the true authorship in a note: 'Ibn al-Ṭayyib's commentary on the Isagoge', *Bulletin of the School of Oriental and African Studies*, 1957, pp. 419–25.) § 1:

The exponents of the art of logic are accustomed, before they consider the

In his next paragraph Israeli applies the four inquiries to the 'description' of philosophy. Though the two subjects—the four

book of Porphyry known as the *Introduction*, to inquire about philosophy itself, for which the art of logic is an instrument. The reason for this procedure on their part is that in view of the length of the art of logic and being apprehensive that it will be found tedious, they prefer to inform us first of that for the sake of which we learn it, viz. of philosophy, so that when we have paid regard to its excellence we shall not find tedious the instrument which we learn on its account. Since every subject of inquiry is inquired in four ways: (*a*) Does it exist (*hal lahū wujūd*), or not? (*b*) What is it (*mā huwa*)? viz., in its genus or matter, (*c*) Of what kind is it (*ayyu shay'in huwa*)? viz., in its differentia or form, and (*d*) Why is it (*lima huwa*)? viz. the cause of the Creator's bringing it into being and, in general, the end for which it exists, and since our inquiry now is in regard to philosophy, it is necessary that we should inquire about these four questions in regard to it.

§§ 3–6 are devoted to the first inquiry, viz. whether philosophy exists. § 7, which opens the Second Lecture, reads as follows:

We have already said in the preceding lecture that every inquiry has to proceed in four ways, and we promised to inquire about philosophy, which we have proposed as our inquiry, in these four directions. In the preceding lecture we have inquired according to one of the four ways. We must now begin the rest of the four questions, viz. (*b*) What is it? (*c*) Of what kind is it? and (*d*) Why is it? Since consideration of what a thing is necessitates consideration of its genus, and in general its subject, and consideration of what kind of thing it is necessitates consideration of its differentia, and in general its form which constitutes it, and from the combination of these two the definition of the thing is made up, we must consider the definition of philosophy, for our consideration of its definition includes our consideration of these two. Before we consider the definition of philosophy we must consider definition itself.

§§ 8–12 contain a discussion concerning definition. § 13 gives some preliminary points of view for the enumeration of the definitions of philosophy contained in § 14, which reads as follows:

Let us now inquire into the definitions of philosophy, because it would be wrong that every art should be defined and divided and the thing which afforded the arts and afforded us the two methods of definition and division should be undefined and undivided. We say that all the commentators have agreed to define philosophy by six definitions, two from its subject, one from its name, two from its end and one from its relation to the other arts. (*a*) The first definition, which is from its subject, says that philosophy is knowledge of all existent things, so far as they exist. This definition of philosophy is from its subject, in a general sense. Understand that the theoretical end is involved in it. (*b*) The second definition says that philosophy is the knowledge of the divine and human things. This definition is from its subject, but in a particular sense. Understand that the theoretical end is involved in it. (*c*) The third definition is from its name, and says that philosophy is love of wisdom, since all the ancients thought it worthy of the name of wisdom, above the other sciences, because it teaches more than what it does not teach, while the remaining sciences and arts teach less than what they do not teach. These three definitions are due to Pythagoras. (*d*) As for the fourth definition, it is from the immediate end. Understand it of practical philosophy. It says that philosophy inquiries and the definition (in Israeli: 'description') of philosophy —remain intimately connected, as in the Alexandrian introductions, the application of the first theme to the second is different. Moreover, in Israeli a wider application is given to the theme of the four inquiries: he uses them to solve apparent contradictions in the statements of the ancients. The best instance is the classification of the various definitions of 'nature' in § 9. We have a definition by the essence, which obviously answers the question 'what'; 'definitions' (the word is vaguely used for 'descriptions') by property; one may hazard the guess that this corresponds to the question 'how', which inquires as to the quality of a thing, while the 'definition' (i.e. description) from the effect corresponds to the question 'why', or final cause. Philosophy and wisdom have no definitions (Israeli explains this in the case of philosophy and implies it in the case of wisdom); thus we have no answer to the question 'what' (given by the 'definition') but we have the answers to the questions 'how' and 'why' by the descriptions taken from property and effect respectively. Thus the different definitions and descriptions given by the ancients were not due to differences of opinion, but arose from the variety of questions which the definitions sought to

is the study of death, viz. love of death—not natural death, as Cleombrotus understood it, but the death of the will, that is a man's killing his desires and making the rational part of him victorious. (*e*) The fifth definition is from the remote end. Understand it of practical and theoretical philosophy. It says that philosophy is likeness to God, may He be exalted, according to man's capacity, through the knowledge of truth and the doing of good. These two definitions are due to Plato. (*f*) The sixth definition is from its relationship to the other arts. It is the definition given by Aristotle in the first book of the *Metaphysics*, viz. that it is the art of arts and the science of sciences, i.e. the art which all the arts need and the science which all the sciences need.

There follows the demonstration that the definitions of philosophy are six (§§ 15–16) and the explanation of each definition (*a*: §§ 17–18; *b*: § 19; *d*: § 20; *e*: § 21; *f*: § 22; *c*: § 23), and finally the division of philosophy (§§ 24–28). The whole ends with the words:

So let us break off the discussion of this doctrine, at the point where the introduction breaks off, which the Alexandrians prefaced to the consideration of Porphyry's *Isagoge*.

We see that Ibn al-Ṭayyib discusses the first question, 'whether philosophy exists', like David; but the last two questions are omitted. Thus it seems that the commentary on which Ibn al-Ṭayyib relies (no doubt through the intermediacy of his masters, more expecially Ibn al-Khammār, who was an important commentator) was a representative of the Olympiodorian school, independent of both Elias and David.

answer. The seemingly conflicting definitions of things are capable of reconciliation once the questions underlying them are recognized; in other words, it all depends from which angle one defines a thing.

The preceding suffices for the purpose of explaining Israeli's text, but I think it worth while to give some of the materials which I have collected concerning the four types of inquiry.

First, the transition from Aristotle's list in the *Posterior Analytics* to that given by the pupils of Olympiodorus remains to be explained. The somewhat tentative and heterogeneous list of Aristotle ('Aristotle is making his vocabulary as he goes, and has not succeeded in making it as clear-cut as might be wished' is Sir David Ross's comment on the passage, *Aristotle's Prior and Posterior Analytics*, p. 610) was systematized and put into a more logical order. Instead of the dichotomy of inquiries concerning statements and substances, the whole list was referred to substance; this being so, it was more logical to begin the list with 'whether a thing exists at all' (Aristotle's third question), which was followed naturally by 'what a thing is' (Aristotle's fourth question). Thus the whole order was reversed. We actually find this new order in the commentators,[1] starting with Themistius (*CAG* v/1. 42): 'If we inquire about a simple thing, we first inquire whether it is, then what it is; if about a compound proposition, we first inquire whether the subject has that which is predicated in the proposition; when we know this, we inquire why and how it has it.' This order became traditional among the later commentators who followed Themistius (Eustratius, *CAG* xxi/1. 8 and 9; Anonymous Commentator, *CAG* xiii/3. 547, who expressly states that εἰ ἔστι precedes by nature ὅτι ἔστι). The third question, quality, is also easily explained; Aristotle himself meant by the question ὅτι 'whether a thing has certain attributes', and this is made even more explicit by the commentators. This is more or less identical with the inquiry concerning quality, as is clear from the words of Aristotle concerning εἰ ἔστι, presumably in order to distinguish it from ὅτι ἔστι: ἁπλῶς

[1] Plotinus's list of the four inquiries already shows some of the characteristics of the list of the commentators (*Enn.* vi. 8. 19): ζήτησιν ἅπασαν χρὴ νομίζειν ἢ τοῦ τί ἐστιν εἶναι ἢ τοῦ οἷον ἢ τοῦ διὰ τί ἢ τοῦ εἶναι ('Every inquiry must be either about 'what', or 'which', or 'why', or the existence').

λέγω, ἀλλ' οὐκ εἰ λευκὸς ἢ μή. That 'why' should be identified with the final cause is not surprising either. Olympiodorus then used the series thus constituted as a guide to follow in his introductory inquiries concerning philosophy. Al-Kindī in his turn apparently used the series in the (lost) introduction to philosophy (here depending directly on the Alexandrians) as well as for general purposes (*On First Philosophy*).

In the latter passage al-Kindī equated the four types of inquiry with the four causes (material, formal, efficient, and final) explained in Aristotle's *Physics* (ii. 7) and *Metaphysics* (*passim*). In this, too, he was preceded by the commentators. It is true that the corresponding passage is found in such a late commentator as Eustratius, who lived two hundred years after al-Kindī; but there is no doubt that the idea goes back to some earlier commentator, from whom both Eustratius and al-Kindī derived it. The following is a translation of Eustratius's passage (p. 9): 'As it is shown in the *Physics* that there are four causes, it is fit that each type of inquiry should correspond to one of these causes: (1) The "whether" imitates the cause of movement, the cause of simple existence corresponding to the inquiry concerning simple existence. (2) The "what" corresponds to the formal cause, as definition is a form and *logos*. (3) The "whether there is an attribute" corresponds to the material cause, as it introduces a substratum which contains something else. (4) The "why" corresponds to the final cause, as it gives the reason of the composition.' (While according to al-Kindī 'what' corresponds to matter, 'which' to form, Eustratius relates 'what' to the formal and 'which' to the material cause.)

In the second place, I wish to quote some passages from early philosophical writers in Arabic which give the same four types of inquiry as appear in al-Kindī and Israeli.

'Alī ibn Rabban al-Ṭabarī, a contemporary of al-Kindī, in his introduction to his medical encyclopaedia, *Firdaws al-Ḥikma* (ed. M. Z. Siddiqi, p. 6), applies the four questions to medicine.[1] He begins the passage with the words: 'Aristotle said: He who seeks the knowledge of a thing, cannot do without the knowledge of four

[1] In the same way Israeli begins his treatise *On Fevers* with an application of the four types of inquiry to medicine.

things: (1) whether that thing exists (*a-mawjūd*) or not; if it exists, (2) what it is (*mā huwa*); (3) how it is (*kayfa huwa*); and (4) why it is (*lima huwa*).' Though Aristotle is named, the series shows that it is derived not directly from him but from the commentators, most likely from an introduction to philosophy (whence it was easily adapted to serve in an introduction to medicine); it is not uncommon to find in Arabic philosophical literature the name of Aristotle prefixed to a passage taken from a commentator or a paraphrast.

Next I translate in full two chapters from the collection of replies given by Miskawayh (mid-tenth century) to questions posed by Abū Ḥayyān al-Tawḥīdī, as they illuminate some aspects of the problem. The questions and replies were put in writing by Abū Ḥayyān al-Tawḥīdī in a book called *al-Hawāmil wa'l-Shawāmil*, Cairo, 1951. The two chapters bear the numbers 159 and 170, pp. 341–3 and 360–1 respectively.

159. *Question.* Why is the number of the types of inquiry concerning every being four, viz. 'whether' (*hal*), secondly 'what' (*mā*), thirdly 'which' (*ayy*), fourthly 'why' (*lima*).

Answer. Abū 'Alī Miskawayh, God's mercy on him, said: For the reason that these four things are the principles and first causes of all beings, and doubts only arise concerning these; when they are dealt with, no further doubt can arise.

The first principle for the being of something is the establishment of its essence (*dhāt*), I mean its ipseity (*huwiyya*), for which the inquiry is by 'whether' (*hal*). If someone doubts a thing's ipseity, one will inquire no farther.

If the doubt concerning the thing's existence (*wujūd*) is removed and essence and ipseity are established for it, one can inquire about the second principle of its being, viz. its species which constitutes it and by which it is what it is, i.e. the inquiry concerning 'what', the which is an inquiry about the species and the constitutive form.

If these two things are found out concerning a hidden thing—viz. the first existence (*wujūd*) and the ipseity about which one inquires by 'whether', and the second existence which is the specificality (*naw'iyya*), i.e. the constitutive form, about which one inquires by 'what'—one can inquire about that which makes it different from other things—i.e. the differentia; this is the third principle, because that by which a thing is distinguished from others is that about which one inquires by 'which', i.e. the differentia essential to it.

If these three principles are found out concerning a thing, no doubt can arise about it and the knowledge of it is complete, except that which concerns its perfection and for the sake of which it came into being; this is the last cause, called the final cause, and is the noblest of all causes. It was Aristotle who first drew attention to it and discovered it. The other three causes are subservient to, and cause for, this last cause, and exist, as it were, because of it and for its sake. About it one inquires by 'why'.

When one knows why a thing came into being and what its last aim is, i.e. the thing for the sake of which it came into being, inquiry stops and a complete knowledge of the thing is achieved, all the doubts concerning it cease, and nothing remains for the soul to desire concerning its knowledge, as all its principles and causes are comprehended and no scope for doubt remains. This is the reason why the inquiries are four, no less, no more.

The other chapter reads as follows.

170. *Question.* If we seek to know something, we either know it already or do not. If we do, there is no use in the search and our exertion. If we do not, it is impossible to seek something of which we have no knowledge; it would be like one who seeks a fugitive slave of his whom he does not know.

Answer. If we were making our search according to one aspect only, and this an unknown one, your question would be justified. But we have already explained before that each problem can be investigated according to four inquiries: (1) its existence (*anniyya*), which inquiry is made by 'is it' (*hal*); (2) by 'what' (*mā*); (3) by 'which' (*ayy*); (4) by 'why' (*lima*). These are the aspects of every inquiry; when one is known, the others still remain unknown and the knowledge of one does not make us dispense with the others. For instance, when you inquire about the body of the ninth sphere, whether it has existence (*wujūd*): when this inquiry is settled, the other aspect, viz. what it is, still remains, because although you are now acquainted with the aspect of 'is it', you are still ignorant of the aspect of 'what'. When you are acquainted with that aspect, the third, namely that of 'which', still remains; we have already explained these aspects. After them remains the last aspect, viz. 'why', which is the inquiry about the thing for the sake of which it exists in the manner shown by the essence (*mā'iyya*) and quality (*kayfiyya*). When this aspect is known, only the particulars, which are infinite, remain unknown; and these, being of little use, are not investigated: I mean the investigation of its measure; the number of the parts measuring it and their mutual relation; its position; and similar things. These last inquiries consist in the investigation of the quality and the other categories with their various species and individuals. Now when you know the highest genus, you do not seek its parts—as you had already reached the highest aspect. Thus it is clear that what we seek is the unknown aspect, not the known one, and that a certain thing can be known from one aspect and unknown from another; and thus the problem is solved, God willing.

The four types are enumerated in al-Khuwārizmī's (late tenth century) glossary of technical terms (*The Keys of Sciences*), in the paragraph on 'apodictic' (i.e. the *Posterior Analytics*) contained in the chapter on 'logic' (ed. van Vloten, p. 150). The combination of the four types with the four causes is worthy of special note.

Material cause is the knowledge of whether (*hal*) a thing is. Formal cause is the knowledge of what (*mā*) a thing is. Efficient cause is the knowledge of how (*kayfa*) a thing is. Final cause[1] is the knowledge of why (*lima*) a thing is.

The four types of inquiry became theologically important in the discussion on the unknowableness of God, more especially concerning the thesis that only the existence of God can be known. It has been pointed out by G. Vajda, 'La Philosophie et la théologie de Joseph Ibn Çaddiq', *Archives d'histoire doctrinale et littéraire du moyen âge*, 1949, pp. 160–2, that the idea is expressed by Philo (cf. H. A. Wolfson, *Philo*, ii. 110–26, 153 ff.) and more especially by Plotinus, *Enn.* v. 5. 6: *ὁ θεάσασθαι θέλων τὸ ἐπέκεινα τοῦ νοητοῦ τὸ νοητὸν πᾶν ἀφεὶς θεάσεται, ὅτι μὲν ἔστι διὰ τούτου μαθών, οἷον δὲ ἔστι τοῦτο ἀφείς*, 'Who wishes to contemplate what is beyond the intelligible, will contemplate it by leaving everything intelligible behind; he will thus learn that it exists, but will leave behind the question how it is'.

A developed form of the idea, applied to the four types, occurs in Arabic in the *Book of Indications and Considerations* (*al-Dalā'il*

[1] It may be noted that most of the manuscripts have *limā'iyya* (or corruptions of it); one manuscript has *al-ghā'iyya*, which is in itself a possible form, but may nevertheless be a corruption of *limā'iyya*.

wa'l-I'tibār) attributed to al-Jāḥiẓ and derived from Greek sources (Aleppo, 1928, p. 77):

The knowledge of a thing can be sought from four aspects: Firstly, one can inquire whether it exists (*a-mawjūd huwa*) or not; secondly, one can learn what it is (*mā huwa*) in its essence and substance; thirdly, one can inquire how it is (*kayfa huwa*) and what is its description; fourthly, wherefore it is (*limā-dhā*) and for what cause. About the Creator, however, we can only know that He exists—but we can have no perfect and real knowledge of what He is and how He is, while 'why' is altogether eliminated in the description of the Creator, as He is the cause of everything and nothing is His cause. Moreover, if one knows that He is, this does not necessitate the knowledge of what and how He is; likewise, if one knows that the soul exists, this does not necessitate the knowledge of what and how it is; similarly in the case of the refined spiritual things.[1]

A related but slightly different theory—that one can know the existence and the final cause, but not the quiddity and quality of spiritual substances—is found in an Ismā'īlī text in Persian: the commentary by Muḥammad ibn Surkh of Nīshāpūr (tenth or eleventh century) on a philosophical poem by a certain Abu'l-Haytham al-Jurjānī (ed. H. Corbin and M. Mo'in, Teheran–Paris, 1955). The theory is applied (p. 5) firstly to the difference between specific form (which is 'due to the wisdom of the Creator') and the individual shape (which is 'due to nature').

The philosophers say: There are four things which make up knowledge: 'whether' (*hal*), 'what' (*mā*), 'how' (*kayfa*), and 'why' (*lima*). Everything which is corporeal can be known from all these four aspects, while everything which is spiritual can be known only from two aspects, namely the existence (*haliyyat*) and quarity (*limiyyat*).

The author then shows that only these two last questions can be answered in the case of the specific form (which is spiritual), but all four in the case of individual shape (which is corporeal). The theory is repeated in almost the same words (p. 51) in another con-

[1] Cf. the affirmation that of God one knows only the 'quoddity' (*anniyya*) not the 'where' and 'how' in Abū Ḥayyān al-Tawḥīdī, *al-Muqābasāt*, chs. xci (pp. 317–18) and lxiii (p. 259), translated by G. Vajda, 'La Philosophie &c.' [see p. 21], p. 161. The Ikhwān (iv. 48–49) admit two questions: 'whether He is' (*hal huwa*), and 'who He is' (*man huwa*), but not the rest of the nine questions referring to the categories.

text: in the course of the author's polemics against al-Rāzī (end of ninth–beginning of tenth century), who said in his *Book of Properties* that one can know the existence and the quality of the (supernatural) properties of various substances, but not their causes.

In Jewish Neoplatonism this application of the four questions plays an important part. Ibn Gabirol reproduces the questions and connects them with the Neoplatonic quaternity of God, intellect, soul, and nature. The order of the questions corresponds to the hierarchical order of the ontological scheme. The most exalted (*dignissima*) question is the one asking 'whether it is' (*an est*), and is the only one applicable to God. The second question 'what it is' (*quid est*) may be applied to the intellect. The third question 'how it is' (*quale est*) may be applied to the soul. The fourth 'why it is' (*quare est*) may be applied to nature. In other words, all the four questions may be asked concerning nature, only three concerning the soul, only two concerning the intellect, and only one concerning God. (*Fons Vitae*, v. 24, ed. Baeumker, pp. 301–2; the Hebrew epitome, in Munk, *Mélanges de philosophie juive et arabe*, pp. 109–15.) Other Jewish Neoplatonists are content to explain that in regard to God the only question which may be legitimately asked is the one asking 'whether' He is, not what, how, and why He is. (See Baḥyā, *Duties of the Heart*, i. 4, ed. Yahuda, p. 41; Joseph ibn Ṣaddīq, *Microcosm*, ed. Horovitz, p. 48, where *immūth* stands for *haliyya*;[1] cf. also Judah Halevi, *Kuzari*, iv. 25, ed. Hirschfeld, p. 280, and Abraham ibn Dā'ūd, *The Lofty Belief*, ed. Weil, pp. 46 and 52).[2]

§ **2.** When the philosophers understood this and it became clear to them that definition can be composed only from genera and substantial differentiae,[3] and found for philosophy no genus from which its definition could be composed, they made a subtle investigation according to their superior deliberation and cogitation and described it by three

§ 2. 2 *substantial* L^BCLab H H² *special* L^A.

[1] I think that both Israeli and Ibn Ṣaddīq used the term *haliyya* (for Israeli see p. 13, n. 2) rather than *anniyya* (as assumed for Ibn Ṣaddīq by Vajda, loc. cit. [see p. 22, n. 1]).

[2] Cf. D. Kaufmann, *Die Theologie des Bachja ibn Pakuda*, p. 35; id., *Geschichte der Attributenlehre*, p. 313; id., *Studien über Ibn Gabirol*, p. 60; G. Vajda, as quoted above, p. 21.

[3] See p. 10, n. 1.

descriptions: (i) one derived from its name, (ii) another from its property, (iii) and a third from its traces and actions.

(i) The description taken from its name is as follows: Philosophy is the love of wisdom. This is deduced from the name of 'philosopher': philosopher is composed of *phila* and *sophia*, and in Greek *phila* means lover and *sophia* wisdom; thus it is clear that 'philosopher' means 'the lover of wisdom', and if 'philosopher' means the 'lover of wisdom', 'philosophy' must mean 'love of wisdom'.

(ii) The description of philosophy taken from its property is as follows: Philosophy is the assimilation to the works of the Creator, may He be exalted, according to human capacity. By the words 'assimilation to the works of the Creator' is meant the understanding of the truth of things, viz. acquiring true knowledge of them and doing what corresponds to the truth; by the words 'understanding the truth of things' is meant understanding them from their four natural causes, which are the (1) material, (2) formal, (3) efficient, and (4) final causes.

(1) The material cause can be either spiritual or corporeal. A case of a spiritual material cause is that of the genera which are divided into their species and are the substratum for their forms which complete their speciality, as for instance 'living being', which is the genus of man and horse and other species, and is the substratum for their forms which constitute their essence. A case of a corporeal material cause is silver, which is the matter of the *dirham* and the ring and the substratum for their forms, or gold, which is the matter of the *dīnār* and the bracelet and the substratum for their forms.

(2) The formal cause can also be either spiritual or corporeal. A case of a spiritual formal cause is that of the substantial forms which are predicated of the genus and constitute the essence of the species. For

6–7 quoted by Ibn Ezra. 7 *from its traces and actions* H^2 (*mē-ōthōthehā ū-phĕʿūlōthehā*) *from its traces and science* (*min āthārihā wa-ʿilmihā*) Ibn Ezra; *from its effect*, a variant quoted in L^{AL} (*in alio, ex operacione sua*), and L^{ab} (*ex effectu eius*); *from its science* LH; the correct reading is no doubt *min āthārihā wa-fiʿlihā* (or *ʿamalihā*?), which is also corroborated by § 3, l. 4, while *min ʿilmihā* is an old and deeply rooted scribal error. 9–13 *this is deduced . . . love of wisdom* L H^2 *This is a Greek name and is composed of the Greek language, as philo is love and sophia is wisdom and as philosophy means love of wisdom, philosopher is lover of wisdom; thus the explanation is clear* H. 15 *to the Creator* H *to the works of the Creator* L. 15–20 *Philosophy . . . meant* L H^2 *Philosophy is the assimilation to the Creator, may He be exalted, according to human capacity. By the words 'assimilation to the Creator' is meant assimilation to the works of the Creator, and by these words in turn is meant* H. 24 *which complete* L *and complete* H. 28. *dirham* H^2 *denarii* L *coin* H. 29 *dīnār* H H^2 *drachmae* L. 32–33 *forms . . . are . . . constitute* H *form . . . is . . . constitutes* L.

instance rationality, which is predicated of the living being and thus constitutes the essence of man, and the faculty of neighing, which is predicated of the living being and thus constitutes the essence of the horse. A case of the corporeal formal cause is the form of the brick, the sandal, the bell, and suchlike.

(3) The efficient cause can also be either spiritual or corporeal. A case of the spiritual efficient cause is the power of the sphere which was appointed by the Creator, may He be exalted, in nature, and ordained in it over the effects which take place in the corporeal microcosm, viz. coming-to-be and passing-away, growth and decrease, newness and oldness, health and illness, and other natural actions. A case of a corporeal efficient cause is the craft of the goldsmith in making a ring, the form of a picture made on the wall, and the work of the builder of a house.

(4) The final cause can also be either spiritual or corporeal. A case of a corporeal final cause is the form of a house and its completion which is necessary in order to make it suitable for habitation and protection, and the form of a ring in order that it should have a seal and be suitable for sealing. A case of a spiritual final cause is the union of soul and body to the end that the truths of the subject of science may become clear to man; that he may distinguish between good and evil, between what is laudable and what is not; that he may do what corresponds to truth, in justice and rectitude; that he may sanctify, praise, and exalt the Creator, and recognize His dominion; that he may avoid beastly and unclean actions in order thereby to obtain the reward of his Creator, blessed be He, which is the union with the upper soul, and the illumination by the light of intellect and by the beauty and splendour of wisdom. When attaining this rank, he becomes spiritual, and will be joined

34 *predicated of* H *exists in* L. 34–36 *thus constitutes . . . predicated* L (which has, however, again: *exists in*) om. H (homoioteleuton). 37–38 *A . . . suchlike* om. H^2. 37–38 *the brick . . . suchlike* L^B om. L^{ACL} *the form of the statue* L^{ab} *the body of man and bodies in general* H. 41 *the Creator, may He be exalted* L *God* H. 40 ff. *power*, &c.; the original can be reconstructed according to parallel passages *BDef.*, §§ 9, 44; *BSubst.* iii. 2^v; the translation in L and H is in places rather awkward: *al-quwwatu 'l-falakiyyatu 'allatī rattabaha 'l-bāri ʿazza wa-jalla fi'l-tabīʿati wa-qaddarahā bihā* (*ipsam ea commensuravit* L *et natura modificat ea* L^{ab} *ū-mĕdhādhō bō* H) *ʿalā ta'thīri 'l-kā'ināti* (*mitō'ar kol ma she-yēsh*? H) *fi'l-ʿālami 'l-ṣaghīri min kawnin*, &c. (*generacionis*, &c. L). 43 *newness and oldness* L om. H H^2. 45–46 *the form of a picture made on the wall* H and a variant in L^A (*in alio, in pariete*) *the f. of a p. made in copper* L (*in aere*) H^2. 49 *in order to make it . . . protection* L *for the inhabitants of the house to stay in it without fear* H [so also H^2? The rest illegible]. 54 Here ends the second fragment of H^2. 54–55 *do what . . . rectitude* L, H as above, § 1, l. 55.

in union to the light which is created, without mediator, by the power of God, and will become one that exalts and praises the Creator for ever and in all eternity. This then will be his paradise and the goodness of his reward, and the bliss of his rest, his perfect rank and unsullied beauty. For this reason Plato said that philosophy is a zeal, a striving, an effort, and concern for death. Says Isaac: This is a description of great profundity and elevated meaning. For in saying 'concern for death' the sage meant it to be understood in the sense of the killing of beastly desires and lusts, for in their mortification and avoidance is the highest rank, the supernal splendour and the entry into the realm of truth. And by vivifying beastly desires and lusts and by strengthening them, men of intellect are drawn away from that which is due to God in the way of obedience, purity, and attention to prayer at the prescribed hours. The saying of the philosopher means this, and intellect testifies to its truth. He said: God has intellectual precepts which He reveals to the elect among His creatures, meaning thereby the prophets and messengers and the true teachers who guide His creatures towards the truth, and who prescribe justice and rectitude and the acceptance of things permissible; the pursuit of goodness, loving-kindness, and mildness, the shunning of evil, injustice, and injury; and the refusal of things unlawful. He who does not attach himself to the intellectual precepts which God has revealed to the elect among his creatures, his priests, and teachers, and perseveres in his own injustice, sinfulness, coarseness, and in the evil of his ways, will be rendered unclean by his impurities, and they

64 *the bliss of his rest* H, not in L. 66 *concern for death*: *sollicitudo mortis* L *help* (*'ezrath*) *of death* H; the original can be reconstructed as: *mu'ānāt al-mawt* (root *'ny*; mistaken by H as a derivative of the root *'wn*). 66–67 *This is a description of great profundity and elevated meaning* L (*est longae profunditatis et sublimis intelligenciae*) *For this great sage, who is far from injustice and elevated in his meaning* H (*'far from injustice'* mistranslation as below, ll. 93–94, see note; original to be reconstructed: *ba'īd al-ghawr sharīf al-ma'nā*). 70 *realm of truth* H (*bēth hā-ĕmeth* L[AB] (*curiam veritatis*) *curam v.* L[CLab]; the original no doubt had *dār al-ḥaqq*. 72 *are drawn away* L *are given into the hands of those who draw them away* H (originally probably *mā yarudduhum*, wrongly read by H *man y.*). *from that which is due to God*: *ab eo quod oportet de veritatibus Dei* L *from the duty of the laws* (*ḥuqqē*) *of God* H (original probably *mimmā yajibu min huqūqi 'llāh*, *ḥuqūq* being misunderstood, in different ways, by both L and H; cf. also § 6, l. 48). 74–75 *The saying . . . He said* L *This shows another thing said by the philosopher, and intellect testifies to its truth, when he says* H. 75–76 *which He reveals to the elect among His creatures* H *quae ostendunt qui ex creatura sua boni sunt* L, mistranslation (the phrase is correctly translated by L below, ll. 81–82). 76 *prophets and messengers* L *the p. sent by Him* H. 79 *loving-kindness and mildness* H *optimi et honesti* (mildness, *'ănāwā*, cf. § 1, l. 44, where L has *paciencia*). 81 *intellectual* H *rational* L (cf. 75).

will weigh him down and prevent him from ascending to the world of truth. He will not attain the light of intellect and the beauty of wisdom, but remain contained under the sphere, sorrowful, in pain without measure, revolving with the revolution of the sphere in the great fire and the torturing flame. This will be his hell and the fire of his torture which God has prepared for the wicked and sinners who rebel against the precepts of the intellect.

(iii) The description of philosophy from its effect is as follows: Philosophy is man's knowledge of himself. This also is a description of great profundity and elevated intelligence, for the following reason. Man, if he acquires a true knowledge of himself, viz. of his own spirituality and corporeality, comprises the knowledge of everything, viz. of the spiritual and corporeal substance, as in man are joined substance and accident. Substance is twofold, spiritual and corporeal; spiritual, as for instance soul and intellect; corporeal, as for instance the long and broad and deep body. Accident is also twofold, spiritual and corporeal; spiritual, as for instance mildness, knowledge, and similar spiritual accidents which are predicated of the soul; corporeal, as for instance blackness, whiteness, yellowness, redness, thickness, variety, and the other corporeal accidents which are predicated of the body. This being so, it is clear that man, if he knows himself in both his spirituality and corporeality, comprises the knowledge of all, and knows both the spiritual and the corporeal substance, and also knows the first substance which is created from the power of the Creator without mediator, which is appropriated to serve as substratum for diversity; as well as the first generic accident, which is divided into quantity, quality, and relation, together with the remaining six compound accidents which derive from the composition of substance with the three accidents. If man comprises all these, he comprises the knowledge of everything and is worthy to be called a philosopher.

COMMENTS

Israeli's paragraph on the descriptions of philosophy is closely related to al-Kindī's on the definitions of philosophy in his treatise

92 *science* H L *effect* L[ab], see note to l. 7. 92–93, 94–107 quoted by Ibn Ezra. 93 *a description* H om. L. 93–94 *of great profundity and elevated intelligence* L (*est longae profunditatis et sublimis intelligentiae*) *hā-rāḥōq mē-hā-ʿāwel hā-ʿōle bĕ-daʿtō* H; the original is to be reconstructed as: *baʿīd al-ghawr sharīf al-ʿaql* (cf. al-Kindī, see Comments), *al-ghawr*, 'profundity', was mistaken by H as *al-jaur*, 'injustice'; cf. also note to ll. 66–67. 102 *predicated of* H *existing in* L (as l. 34). *of the sou l* L H *and the intellect* adds Ibn Ezra. 103 *thickness*: *variety* L *greenness* H. 106 *and knows*: in L read *et scit* (L[ACL] = H; *scilicet* L[B]).

On the Definitions and Descriptions of Things (see al-Kindī, pp. 172–3).[1]

Philosophy. The ancients defined it in various ways.

(1) Either from the derivation of its name, which is 'love of wisdom' because 'philosopher' is composed of *fila*, i.e. 'lover' and *sofa*, i.e., 'wisdom'.

(2) They also defined it from its effect, saying: Philosophy is assimilation to the actions of God according to the power of man, meaning by this that man should have perfect virtue.

(3) They also defined it from its effect, saying: Being mindful of death. Death in their view is twofold: natural, i.e. the soul's ceasing to make use of the body—and, secondly, the killing of desires; it is the second which they meant here, because the killing of desires is the way to virtue. For this reason, many of the most eminent philosophers said: Pleasure is evil. As the soul has two uses, the one sensual, the other intellectual, it follows that what people call pleasure happens by sense-perception, because if one busies oneself with sensual pleasures, one necessarily ceases to employ one's intellect.

(4) They also defined it from its pre-eminence, saying: Art of arts and science of sciences.

(5) They also defined it saying: Philosophy is man's knowing himself. This is a saying of noble scope and great profundity. I give an example. Things are corporeal or non-corporeal; the non-corporeal things are either substances or accidents; man consists of body, soul, and accidents; soul is a substance, not a body; therefore, if man knows himself, he knows body with its accidents, the first accident, and the substance which is not a body; as he knows all these, he knows everything. For this reason the philosophers called man a microcosm.

(6) Its definition by ⟨its subject⟩ (?) is: Philosophy is the knowledge of the eternal, universal things, of their essence, their quiddity, and their causes, according to man's capacity.

Al-Kindī's passage derives from the Alexandrian commentators of Aristotle, among whom it became a convention to include in the introduction to their commentaries on the *Isagoge* an enumeration of the various definitions of philosophy. The first commentary to

[1] Abū Sulaymān Rabī' ibn Yaḥyā quotes in his paraphrase of the *Arithmetic* of Nicomachus of Gerasa (preserved in a Hebrew version) definitions of philosophy by al-Kindī: one taken from its name (= (1) below), another from its effect (= (2) below); see Steinschneider, *HebrÜb.*, p. 518; id., in *Monatsschrift für Geschichte und Wissenschaft des Judentums*, 1893–4, pp. 68 ff.

contain this material is that by Ammonius, who was followed by Elias and David (both of whom derived their material from their teacher Olympiodorus) and the Syriac commentators. (See Ammonius, *In Porphyrii Isagogen*, *CAG* iv/3. 1 ff.; Elias, *Prolegomena*, *CAG* xviii/1. 7 ff.; David, *Prolegomena*, *CAG* xviii/2. 20 ff.; A. Baumstark, *Syrisch-arabische Biographien des Aristoteles*; *Syrische Commentare zur ΕΙΣΑΓΩΓΗ des Porphyrios*, Leipzig, 1900, pp. 197–8, 219–22; cf. also, for a short résumé and for the provenience of the definitions, K. Praechter, *Die Philosophie des Altertums*, § 1.[1]) In the list of the Alexandrians six rather heterogeneous definitions are put together: (1) *γνῶσις τῶν ὄντων ᾗ ὄντα ἐστί*—(2) *γνῶσις θείων τε καὶ ἀνθρωπίνων πραγμάτων*—(3) *μελέτη θανάτου*—(4) *ὁμοίωσις θεῷ κατὰ τὸ δυνατὸν ἀνθρώπῳ*—(5) *τέχνη τεχνῶν καὶ ἐπιστήμη ἐπιστημῶν*—(6) *φιλία σοφίας*. The first two ('the knowledge of beings' and 'the knowledge of divine and human affairs') are said to be taken from the subject of philosophy and are attributed (quite wrongly) to Pythagoras. The next two ('being mindful of death' and 'assimilation to God as far as is possible for man') are said to be taken from the aim of philosophy and are (correctly) attributed to Plato. The fifth ('art of arts and science of sciences') is said to be taken from the pre-eminence of philosophy and is (correctly) attributed to Aristotle. The last ('love of wisdom') is said to be taken from the etymology of philosophy and is again attributed to Pythagoras. The relation of al-Kindī's first four definitions to the Alexandrian series is obvious: Al-Kindī's first definition is the Alexandrian's sixth, al-Kindī's second and third are the Alexandrian's fourth and third. Al-Kindī's sixth definition may be somehow connected with the first (and second) of the Alexandrians. This correspondence also gives the clue for the meaning of al-Kindī's expression 'from its effect' used in connexion with (2) and (3): it must be taken in the sense of the Alexandrians' 'from its aim'. The first and the second definitions of the Alexandrians do not occur in al-Kindī. On the other hand, his fifth one is new; it is the famous 'Know thyself', which was not adopted by the Alexandrians whose commentaries are extant. Obviously al-Kindī had access to some lost Alexandrian

[1] See also the introduction in the commentary of Ibn al-Ṭayyib, analysed above, p. 14, n. 1, which depends on a commentary of the Olympiodorian type.

commentary, which, though akin to those of the other Alexandrians, introduced some features of its own and also included 'knowing oneself' in the list of definitions.

It remains to be noted that some of the amplifications of the definitions can also be shown to derive from the Alexandrian commentators. The original definition 'assimilation to God' is explained as 'assimilation to the works of God' and the comment is added: 'that man should have perfect virtue'. Behind this brief addition we can discern the interpretation given to the definition by the commentators, which can be read at great length in the passages quoted above. There is no need of long quotations. (For the Neoplatonic background of the idea of 'imitation of God' see Part II, ch. VII, below, pp. 197 ff.) The first sentence of the explanation given for 'being mindful of death' is a quotation from the commentaries: 'Death is twofold: natural, viz. the separation of the soul from the body . . . and voluntary, viz. not allowing the soul to follow the pleasures.' This notion of the 'twofold death' goes back to Porphyry, *Sententiae*, ed. Mommert, ix: 'Death is twofold, one known by all when body is loosed from soul, and the other that of the philosophers where the soul is loosed from the body.'[1] (Cf. also Plotinus, *Enn.* vi. 9. 9.) As the definition 'knowing oneself' does not appear in the extant commentaries, we can only guess that in the lost commentary which served as al-Kindī's source it was accompanied by comments similar to those in al-Kindī's text.[2]

[1] In addition to the references quoted in Part II, ch. VII, below, pp. 201–2, there is an important passage in Moses ibn Ezra's *al-Ḥadīqa* (for which cf. above, p. 7), which contains a quotation from the great translator Ḥunayn ibn Isḥāq (p. 113): 'The philosopher says: "Philosophy is a concern and preoccupation with, and being mindful of, death". Ḥunayn ibn Isḥāq says: He means the voluntary death, which is the killing of desires.' (*Qāla 'l-faylasūf: al-falsafatu 'htimāmun wa'ghtimāmun wa-'ināyatun bi'l-mawt. Qāla Ḥunayn b. Isḥāq: ya'ni 'l-mawta 'l-irādiyya 'lladhī huwa imātatu 'l-shahawāt.*)

[2] Joseph ibn Ṣaddīq derived the definition of philosophy as 'knowing oneself' from Israeli, as is shown by the motivation: man, comprising in himself the spiritual and the corporeal world, knows, by knowing himself, the whole universe (*Microcosm*, pp. 1–2; cf. also below, p. 208). G. Vajda ('La Philosophie &c.' [see p. 21], p. 96) quotes Israeli's definition in order to illustrate Ibn Ṣaddīq's, but derives it (see p. 97) from the Ikhwān. In view of Ibn Ṣaddīq's dependence on Israeli in other cases also (see above, p. xiii), it is very likely that here also Israeli is his source. The idea that the first substance is created from the power of the Creator without mediator, which appears in our passage, but is also repeatedly stressed by Israeli (cf. below, pp. 174–5), recurs in Ibn Ṣaddīq in the

There are, however, far-reaching differences between al-Kindī's text and that of Israeli. Firstly, Israeli does not admit that philosophy can be defined and therefore calls all the definitions given by al-Kindī 'descriptions'. Secondly, he evidently aims at distributing the descriptions according to the different types of inquiry, although this is only implicit in the juxtaposition of §§ 1 and 2. (The description 'taken from the name' may correspond to 'what'; the one 'taken from the property' corresponds to 'which'; and the one 'taken from the effect' to 'why'; cf. above, p. 16.) In the absence of evidence it is idle to speculate whether these changes were introduced by Israeli, or, more likely, go back to some lost text of al-Kindī in which he treated the definitions of philosophy in a different manner from the one we find in his *On Definitions*.[1] The possible Alexandrian antecedents of this variant are of course even more problematical, though it is perhaps not a coincidence that the theme of the four types of inquiry precedes that of the definitions in Israeli as well as in the Alexandrian tradition (cf. above, p. 14)—even though the application of the first to the second is so different.

For Israeli's elaboration of the rather bare definitions given by al-Kindī (an elaboration giving them a more Neoplatonic flavour) and for further discussion of the Neoplatonic background of the themes of 'assimilation to God' and 'knowing oneself' see Part II, ch. VII.

§ **3.** Having finished the three descriptions of philosophy, let us continue with what we have to say about the quiddity of WISDOM.

We say: Wisdom can be described by two descriptions, one taken

§ 3. 2 *continue* L *begin* H. 3 In L omit *Descripcio sapienciae* (with L^{ABL} = H).

---

form that the matter of intellect is pure light which emanates without mediator from the power (*gĕbhūrā*) of the Creator (pp. 37–38). Thus *gĕbhūrā* evidently reflects Israeli's term *qudra* (rather than *rubūbiyya*, as assumed by Vajda, p. 121).

[1] Al-Kindī probably dealt with the themes of the four types of inquiry and the definition of philosophy in his *Detailed treatise on the Introduction to Logic* (*Fi'l-madkhal al-manṭiqī bi'stifā'i 'l-qawl*), no doubt a paraphrase of Porphyry's *Isagoge*, which probably contained an introduction to philosophy in the Alexandrian manner; but we have no means of guessing how he dealt with the subject. (We may assume that his *Treatise on the Five Expressions* (*al-aṣwāt al-khamsa* = πέντε φωναί) was confined to an exposition of the subject-matter of the *Isagoge*, without an introduction.)

from its property, the other from its effect. The description taken from its property is as follows: Wisdom is the true knowledge of the first, enduring, and everlasting things. By 'first and everlasting things' is meant the understanding of things which are eternal by their nature, such as the species, which are the end and the complement of generation, the genera, which are superior to them, the genera of the genera—until one reaches the truly first genus which is created from the power of the Creator without mediator. While accidents are generated infinitely, the genera give for the species and the individuals their names and definitions, so that each individual becomes what it is. An individual is called a substance if it exists by itself and is the substratum of difference; it is called a body, if it is long, broad, and deep; it is called growing, if the extremities of its diameter recede into the distance after having been near; it is called alive, if it is susceptible of movement, sense-perception, and locomotion; it is called man, when it is alive, rational, and mortal. Thus it is clear that the individuals receive the names and definitions of their species and the names and definitions of their genus and genus of genera; and by receiving them, each of them becomes what it is—i.e. 'true'; because the definition of 'true' is: 'what there is', while the definition of 'false' is: 'what there is not', or 'the description of a thing in a manner in which it is not'.

The description of wisdom taken from its effect is as follows: Wisdom is that which completes the intellectual faculty so as to bring to light what is at the two extremities of a controversy, viz. truth and falsehood. The condition of controversy is that its extremities should be divided by truth and falsehood in three matters: necessity, possibility, and impossibility; as the condition of controversy is that the statement of one of the disputants should contradict and refute that of the other, in fulfilling the eight conditions of controversy.

The following are the eight conditions of controversy. (1) Firstly, that the name posited by the proponent should be the same as that refuted by the opponent. (2) Secondly, that the attribute posited by the proponent should be the same as that refuted by the opponent. (3)

6 *enduring* L om. H. 11–12 *While . . . give* L *which gives* H. 12 *the species* L om. H. 14 ff. *if* (repeatedly): *because* L (H can mean both)—I translate *if* on the assumption that L mistranslated an original *lammā* as *because*. 20–21 *and the names . . . genera*: this seems to be the intention of L[ABCab] (*generum*; *genera* L[L]; *generum generum*; *genera generum* L[CL]) and perhaps also of H (*ū-mĕqabbĕlīm lĕ-sūgēhem*). 23 *or . . . thing* L *because he described it* H. 26 *to bring to light* (*lĕ-hōṣī'*) H *secundum exitum* L, mistranslation of original *'alā ikhrāj*. 28–29 *The condition . . . falsehood* om. H (homoioteleuton).

Thirdly, that the subject and attribute predicated in both propositions should not be ambiguous. (4) Fourthly, that the time posited by both disputants should be identical. (5) Fifthly, that the part posited by the proponent should be the same as that refuted by the opponent. (6) Sixthly, that the relation of both should be to the same thing. (7) Seventhly, that they should agree whether their statements refer to something potential or actual. (8) Eighthly, that both should agree upon these conditions and the difference be only in the particle of negation, i.e. 'no'.

To explain the preceding (we say): (1) If the proponent states: ʿAbd Allāh is a scribe, and the opponent says: Jaʿfar is not a scribe, then both are proponents, not disputants. (2) If the proponent states: ʿAbd Allāh is a goldsmith, and the opponent says: ʿAbd Allāh is not a carpenter, then both are proponents, not disputants. (3) The same is true of common names, because if the proponent states: the dog has eaten the lamb, meaning the dog which barks, and the opponent says: the dog has not eaten the lamb, meaning (the constellation of) Canis Major, otherwise the Southern Sirius, or a dog made of copper, then both are proponents, not disputants. If the proponent states: ʿAbd Allāh is asleep, meaning natural sleep, and the opponent says: ʿAbd Allāh is not asleep, meaning accidental sleep, such as obliviousness, carelessness, and little intelligence and prudence, then both are proponents, not disputants. (4) Similarly, in the case of time, if the proponent states: ʿAbd Allāh went on pilgrimage, meaning this year, and the opponent says: ʿAbd Allāh did not go on pilgrimage, meaning last year, they are not disputants. (5) If the proponent states: the blind man does not see, having in mind

40 Here begins the third fragment of H^2. 41 *both*: *the proponent and the opponent* adds H. 45, &c. *ʿAbd Allāh*: *servus dei* L *Ezra* H *Reuben* H^2. *Jaʿfar*: *Iafar* L *Moses* H *Simon* H^2. 48 *is not* L *is* H. 49–50 *The same ... because* L H^2 om. H. 52–53 *Canis Major, otherwise the Southern Sirius*: *canem audacem, scilicet silvestrem dextrum* L, awkward etymological translation of the original *al-kalb al-ʿabūr wa-huwa 'l-shiʿrā al-yamāniya. Canis audax*=*al-kalb al-ʿabūr*, cf. the translation into Hebrew of *al-shiʿrā al-ʿabūr* (this, rather than *al-kalb al-ʿabūr*, is the usual form) as 'the courageous dog' (Steinschneider, *Hebr Üb.*, p. 347). *Shiʿrā* was probably taken as a derivation of *shaʿar*, 'vegetation', *yamāniya*, 'southern', as 'right'. H has *a constellation called dog*, H^2 *the dog which is a constellation. copper*: *or stone* adds H. 53–54 (also 57, 60, 63) *then ... disputants* H *they do not contradict* L. *disputants*: *The preceding case was one of ambiguous words, the following is one of ambiguous attributes* adds H. 54 *ʿAbd Allāh*: *servus dei* L *Jacob* H *Reuben* H^2. 56 *carelessness*: *insomnietatem* L *hithrashlūth* H^2 om. H. *intelligence* L *practice* (*hergēl*) H *ḥărīṣūth* H^2. 58 *ʿAbd Allāh*: *Abdala* L *Ezra* H *Reuben* H^2. 58–59 *went on pilgrimage* L H^2 *went to school* H. 58 (beginning of (4)) *Similarly, in the case of time* L H^2 om. H. 61 (beginning of (5)) *Similarly, in the case of the part* adds L. 61–66 L inverts (5) and (6).

eyesight, and the opponent says: he does see, having in mind the heart's sight, then both are proponents, not disputants. (6) If the proponent states: honey cures illnesses, meaning the illnesses caused by the phlegm, and the opponent says: honey does not cure illnesses, meaning the illnesses caused by the bile, then both are proponents, not disputants. (7) If the proponent says: ʿAbd Allāh is a scribe, meaning potentially, and the opponent says: ʿAbd Allāh is not a scribe, meaning actually, then both are proponents, not disputants. (8) Finally, both should agree to the same thing in respect of all the preceding points, and say 'yes', if admitting something, and 'no', if not.

Thus it is clear from what we have said that wisdom is that which completes the intellectual faculty, so that it brings to light what is at the two extremities of the controversy, viz. truth and falsehood.

Having come to the end of our explanation concerning the quiddity of philosophy and wisdom, we proceed to explain the quiddity of the intellect, which is the substratum to them both, as one cannot be a philosopher or a sage if one does not possess intellect.

COMMENTS

'Perfect wisdom, pure science, and unmixed knowledge which, we find, is the property of the intellect, as it is impossible that intellect should exist without wisdom, or that wisdom should be created except in the intellect, the existence of the one implying that of the other, the abolition of the one that of the other'—such is the description of wisdom given in *BSubst.* iv. 5^r. Some problems connected with 'wisdom' are treated in the subsequent passage of that work (6^r), in the course of which the first definition of the present passage recurs: 'Wisdom is the true knowledge of the eternal, everlasting things and acting according to knowledge.' Wisdom is the attribute of the intellect, both of the universal and the particular. (For a discussion of Israeli's somewhat inconsistent analysis of 'universal' wisdom and its relation to universal intellect see Part II, ch. II, pp. 160–2.)

The first definition is obviously connected with the sixth definition of philosophy in the passage from al-Kindī quoted in the Comments on the preceding paragraph. The definition seems to be

64 *caused by the phlegm* H *flaticas* L. 66 (beginning of (7)) *Similarly, in the case of potentiality and actuality* adds L. 69–71 om. L H^2.

derived from the *Introduction to Arithmetic* by Nicomachus of Gerasa, where it is attributed to Pythagoras (ed. Hoche, pp. 1–2): 'Wisdom is the knowledge of existing things. . . . Existing things are those which remain the same forever.' (Cf. the definition of wisdom in the pseudo-Platonic *Definitions*, p. 414B, 'the knowledge of the everlasting things', and the passage from Iamblichus quoted below, p. 188.) Al-Kindī was intimately acquainted with Nicomachus's book, as is attested by Rabīʿ ibn Yaḥyā, and probably took the definition directly from it. In Rabīʿ ibn Yaḥyā's edition of Nicomachus's treatise, based on the teaching of al-Kindī, the definition is given in a form very near to that which appears in Israeli: 'Wisdom is the true knowledge of the everlasting things' (see Steinschneider, *Monatsschrift* [as quoted above, p. 28, n. 1], p. 70).

The second definition deals with 'wisdom' in action, i.e. with its practical aspect: deciding the truth or falsehood of contradictory statements. It is altogether difficult to see why this is attributed to the domain of wisdom rather than to that of intellect. The example consists of the enumeration of eight rather elementary rules of conducting an argument.

For the relation of 'wisdom' and philosophy see Part II, chs. VI (p. 188) and VII (p. 196).

§ 4. ON THE QUIDDITY OF THE INTELLECT. The philosopher said: The intellect is the specificality of things. He means by this that the specificality of the enduring and everlasting things is present with it forever. Whenever it wishes to know one of them, it has recourse to itself and finds it prepared there and knows it from itself without cogitation or deliberation. This is clear from what happens in well-known things: we find that the expert craftsman, if he wants to make something, has recourse to himself and finds that thing prepared there and knows it from it. To be sure, there is a clear difference between the two kinds of knowledge. The intellect knows what it knows without cogitation

§ 4. 1–6 quoted (in a slightly shortened form) by Ibn Ezra. 7 *craftsman* L H^2 (*goldsmith* L^A) *goldsmith* H (*ṣāniʿ* and *ṣāʾigh* are almost identical in Arabic writing—but so are *artifex* and *aurifex*). 9–10 *two kinds of knowledge* H H^2 *the masters* L (original *al-ʿilmayn* misread by L as *al-muʿallimīn*)—*quamvis in hoc differant artifex et intelligencia: intelligencia* [read so] L^{ab}.

and deliberation, because it always finds its own essence without change or hesitation, nor does growth or decrease or any disposition affect it. On the other hand, because the expert and knowledgeable craftsman is affected by hesitation, oblivion, and doubt in difficult matters, the essence of his soul is divided and he is in need of cogitation, deliberation, investigation, and division before he can reach the object of his wish and desire.

If someone raises an objection concerning the individuals and says: Why do you not say also about the individuals that they are found within the intellect, so that if it wants to know any of them it can have recourse to its own essence and know them from it?—we answer as follows: You have made a vain objection and reasoned absurdly in comparing the enduring and everlasting species, which are not affected by locomotion, change, growth and decrease, coming-to-be and passing-away, with individuals which decrease, perish, and dissolve little by little, as they are constantly affected by growth and decrease, coming-to-be and passing-away. It is clear that things affected by growth and decrease, coming-to-be and passing-away, are not comprised by number, contained by cogitation, or comprehended by science. Of such things the intellect can only take what is present, but what has passed or is in the future is not comprehended by science; what is not comprehended by science is neither known nor intelligible.

For this reason the philosopher divided the intellect into three kinds. (1) Firstly, the intellect which is always in actuality: this is the intellect about which we were saying above that the specificality of things was present with it forever. (2) Secondly, the intellect which is in the soul potentially, before it passes into actuality. When it acquires knowledge, that which had been in potentiality passes into actuality—like the intellect of a child which is in him potentially until he grows up, studies, and acquires knowledge, so that what had been in him potentially passes into actuality and he becomes a possessor of knowledge. (3) Thirdly, what is described as the 'second intellect'. It is assimilated to sense when the

11–12 *because . . . hesitation* L *because it is always found with its essence without change or hesitation* H *because its essence is always united* (*yajidu* misunderstood as *yattaḥidu*) *without change or multiplication* H^2. 12 *any disposition*: in L read *aliqua disposicionum* (with L^{BCL}, *a. disposicio* L^{A}). 13 *On the other hand*: in L put a full stop after *disposicionum* and read *Artificis autem* (sic L^{C} *aut* L^{ABL}). Here ends the third fragment of H^2. 14 *hesitation* L om. H. 15 *matters*: in L write after *rerum* a comma (instead of a semicolon). 26–27 *coming-to-be and passing-away* L om. H. 31 *science* L *the intellect* H. *by science* L om. H. 42 *sense* L *the genus* H (misreading of *al-ḥiss* as *al-jins*, these words being very similar in Arabic script).

soul seeks the comprehension of things from sense. The sensitive faculty, when perceiving things by sensation, imprints their forms in the fantasy which is in the front part of the brain. Fantasy carries them to the rational soul, and when the soul knows them it becomes one with them—in a spiritual, not in a corporeal, sense. Subsequently, the soul conveys them to the intellect, and when the intellect takes cognizance of them they and it become one thing—again in a spiritual, not in a corporeal, sense. On account of this the philosopher described this kind of intellect as 'the second intellect', because it begins with sense and gradually ascends, step by step, until it reaches the intellect which passes in the soul from potentiality into actuality.

COMMENTS

'The intellect is the specificality (*nawʿiyya*) of things'—this definition[1] recurs in the *Book of Substances*, and the more detailed passages found there enlighten us about the meaning of this statement. Firstly, it becomes clear that the statement refers to the universal intellect; secondly, 'specificality' is used as a synonym of 'form'. Israeli explains in *BSubst.* iii. 3[r] that the ray and shade of the intellect are the specificality and form of the rational soul; that the ray and shade of the rational soul are the specificality of the animal soul, and so on and so forth. 'This being so, the intellect is the specificality of all substances and the form that establishes their essence, as the ray and light, which emanate from its shade, are the fountain of their substantiality and the root of their form and specificality.'

The definition is derived from al-Kindī, who says in *On the Intellect* (p. 356): '. . . the first intellect, which is the specificality of things which are [or: is] always in actuality'. An important parallel to this passage is the following definition, which is missing in the Istanbul manuscript (and therefore also in the edition) of *On Definitions*, but is found in the British Museum

47–50 *Subsequently . . . sense* om. $\mathrm{L^L}$ and H (homoioteleuton). 51 and 52 *it* L; in H it is not certain whether the masculine refers to the 'philosopher' or to 'this kind of intellect'.

[1] The English term 'specificality' may sound quaint—but so does the Arabic *nawʿiyya*. As *nawʿī* = 'specific', the abstract *nawʿiyya* must be 'specificality'. There is some authority for the use of the word in English in the sense of 'the quality of being specific': see the *Oxford English Dictionary*, s.v.

extracts from that treatise (Cat. no. 426, fol. 178); its congruence with the other al-Kindī passages and with Israeli confirms its authenticity. It reads: 'Universal Intellect: it is the specificality of things. There is a universal and a particular one.' Al-Kindī equates 'specificality of things' with the intelligible forms in the following passage (*On the Intellect*, p. 354): 'There are two kinds of form: firstly, the material form, which falls under sense-perception; secondly, the immaterial form, which falls under the intellect and which is the specificality of things and that which is above it [i.e. obviously the genus, which is a universal higher than the species].'

The scheme of the three kinds of intellect also evidently goes back to al-Kindī, though there are some puzzling discrepancies between Israeli and al-Kindī's treatment of the subject in his short treatise *On the Intellect*. I confront the enumerations given by the two authors.

Al-Kindī	*Israeli*
1. The intellect which is always in actuality.	1. The intellect which is always in actuality.
2. The intellect which is in potentiality.	2. The intellect which is in the soul potentially.
3. The intellect which has passed in the soul from potentiality into actuality.	3. The 'second intellect' which passes in the soul from potentiality into actuality.
4. The intellect called 'apparent'.	..

Al-Kindī's fourth kind does not appear in Israeli, whilst Israeli's term 'second intellect' (for no. 3) is absent in al-Kindī's *On the Intellect*.

It must also be pointed out that whilst the scheme of the intellect is more or less identical in the two passages (the absence of al-Kindī's fourth intellect does not make a serious difference), the two passages do not coincide in their treatment of the process of intellection. Al-Kindī explains how the objects of intellection present in the 'intellect in actuality' are communicated to the 'intellect in potentiality', and does not deal at all with the process of apprehension passing through the senses. Israeli, on the other hand, instead of bringing the enumeration of the different intellects to its natural conclusion by explaining the way in which the universal intellect imparts its objects to the potential intellect, speaks of the ascent of the objects of sensation. It does not seem that this is due to a difference in doctrine, because the first half of the paragraph, dealing with the presence of the universals in the universal intellect, seems to imply the doctrine; it seems likely that it was again Israeli's clumsiness, of which we had an example in the incoherence of §§ 1 and 2, which caused him to obscure the connexion between the proposition that the objects of intellection are present in the universal intellect and the process of human intellection.

According to Israeli's explicit statement, both the definition of the intellect as the specificality of things and its threefold division are derived from the 'philosopher', i.e. Aristotle—whereas we have seen that in reality they are taken from al-Kindī. (The temptation to refer the word 'philosopher' to al-Kindī must be withstood.) The explanation is, however, obvious. Al-Kindī expressly states at the beginning of his *On the Intellect* that he is going to expound the doctrine of the ancient philosophers, especially of Plato and Aristotle, on the subject; thus Israeli was justified in thinking that in referring to al-Kindī he was referring to Aristotle. (Such a reference to Aristotle, when passages from his commentators are used, also occurs elsewhere in Arabic philosophical literature.) Whenever Aristotle is quoted by Israeli, we are, therefore, dealing either with a genuine quotation from Aristotle or with one from an author who professes to reproduce Aristotle's doctrine or else from some pseudo-Aristotelian writing.

§ **5.** ON THE SOUL. The philosopher said: The soul is a substance which perfects the physical body that possesses life potentially. Plato said: The soul is a substance which is united with the heavenly body, and through this union it is joined to the bodies and acts in them.

§ 5. 1 In L place *sermo de anima* before *Inquit philosophus*. 2 *that possesses life*: *quod habet vitam* L *el ha-ḥayyīm* H (?; the same in l. 17). 3–4 Cf. for the Arabic wording the quotation in *Ghāyat al-Ḥakīm*: . . . *muttaḥidun bihī wa-bi-dhālika 'l-ittiḥādi tuwāṣilu 'l-ajrāma wa-taf'alu fīhā*; for *united* (*muttaḥid* Arabic, *unita* L) H has *mithḥaddēsh* ('arising in'), misreading *muttaḥid* as *mutajaddid* or *mutaḥaddith*, while various other forms of *ittaḥad* were misunderstood as forms of *ittaḥadh*, see next note and notes to ll. 9 and 28. 4 *union*: *ittiḥād* Arabic *unicione* L *ăḥīzā* H, misunderstanding *ittiḥād* as *ittiḥādh* ('holding fast'), see preceding note.

Isaac says: Someone may think that there is a difference between these two statements, but we shall make it clear that this would be an error. Plato, in his description of the soul, had in mind the soul at the beginning of its movement and action. He says that the soul at the beginning of its movement is united with the body of the sphere, joins the bodies, and acts in them. This is so because the rank of the sphere is intermediate between the rank of the soul and that of the bodies; through this intermediate position the junction of the soul with the bodies is achieved, because through the movement of the sphere the four kinds of matter, which are the elements of the bodies, come into being. The philosopher, on the other hand, had in mind the soul at the completion of its movements and perfection of its acts. He said: 'The soul is a substance which perfects the physical body that possesses life potentially', informing us that the bodies before the soul's junction with them possessed life potentially, while, when the soul was joined with them, it completed and perfected them and made them alive actually. Isaac says: When we say 'the bodies were at the beginning alive potentially, and afterwards they passed into actuality', we imply no temporal difference, separation, or distance, as things remain in the state in which the Creator had ordered them to be; it is only that corporeal expression cannot reproduce spiritual concepts except by separation and conjunction, so that the mind, which is in the corporeal bodies, should be willing to receive them. Someone may object and think that Plato meant by the words 'the soul is united with the heavenly bodies and through this union joins the bodies and acts in them' that it puts on the body, enters, and leaves it; but I shall make clear his error. It is impossible that Plato, occupying as he does such a high rank in philosophy, should not have realized that such a view would be mistaken; he, however, spoke in a corporeal manner, though his meaning was spiritual. The junction of the soul with the bodies only means that the soul infuses into them some of its light and brilliance in order to make them alive, mobile, and sensible; in the same way as the sun infuses some of its light and brilliance into the world, in order to make it bright and brilliant, so that sight becomes possible. It is true that there is a difference between the brilliance and light

9 *is united* L *nithaḥezeth*, cf. preceding notes. 14 *of the bodies*: in L read *corporum* (with L^{ABLab} = H, *corporea* L^{C}). 20 *and perfected them* L *hatĕmīmūth* H (?). *and made them* L *wĕ-ṣiyyĕrā ōthām* H (mistranslation of original *wa-ṣayyarahā*). 28 *is united* L *mithaḥezeth* H, cf. note to l. 3. *union* L *ăḥīzā* H, cf. note to l. 3. 35 and 37 *in order to make them* (*it*) L *kĕdhē she-tĕṣayyĕrēm* (*-rō*) H, mistranslation of *li-tuṣayyirahā*, cf. note to l. 20. 38 *and light* L om. H,

of the sun and those of the soul, because the brilliance of the sun is corporeal and can be apprehended by sight in its substrate, which is the air; while the brilliance of the soul is spiritual and can only be apprehended by intellect through wisdom, not sense-perception. Thus it has become clear that the junction of the soul with the body is not its entering the body and leaving it.

This being so, it remains to be known that the soul has three ranks. (1) The first is the rank of the rational soul; (2) the second, the rank of the animal soul; (3) the third, the rank of the vegetative soul. (1) The most noble in degree and most excellent in rank among the souls is the rational soul, for it came into being in the horizon and from the shadow of the intellect; it is for this reason that man became rational, discerning, susceptible of science and wisdom, distinguishing between good and evil, between praiseworthy and unpraiseworthy things, approaching virtues and shunning vices. Thus he is apt to be rewarded or punished, because he knows the difference between the acts for which he is rewarded or punished. (2) The animal soul is inferior to the rational soul in clarity and the excellence of its rank, for it comes into being from the shadow of the rational soul, on account of which it is removed from the light of the intellect and acquires shadow; it becomes shadowy, and inquiry and discernment leave it; it is, properly speaking, estimating or, metaphorically speaking, imagining; for it reveals things from outward appearance, not in reality. Its characteristics are sense-perception, movement, and locomotion. For this reason animals are daring and of great courage in seeking victory and power, but are without inquiry, discernment, or knowledge. Thus, for instance, the lion seeks to overcome the other animals, without inquiry or division, or knowledge of what it is doing. A proof of the fact that animals have estimation, but no faculty of discernment, is the behaviour of the ass, which, if it is very thirsty and comes near water and sees its own form or another form in it, is frightened and flees, regardless of the fact that water gives it its life and constitution. If, on the other hand, it sees a lion, it goes towards it, though it will be killed by it. For this reason animals do not receive reward or punishment, since they have no faculty of discernment and do

51 *science and wisdom* L *ḥokhmā* H (which is used by H indiscriminately for 'wisdom' and 'science'). 51–52 *distinguishing . . . evil* H om. L. 55–56 *The animal . . . rank* L *Under the rank of the rational soul is that of the animal soul* H. 57 *the shadow of* H om. L. 58 *acquires* L *ne'ěḥzā* H. 60 *metaphorically*: *transposicionem* L^B *transsumpcionem* L^AL *transicionem* L^C *metaphorically which is trnṣwṣy'wn in Romance* (read *trnṣyṣy'wn=transicion*) H. 63 *and power* L om. H. 63–64 *but . . . knowledge* H om. L. 72 *have . . . and* L om. H.

not know for what action they should be rewarded, or, on the other hand, punished. The reason is that they are deprived of the faculty of inquiry and discernment and of perceiving the truth of things, and have as property estimation and meditation. (3) The vegetative or desiring soul is inferior to the other souls in excellence and rank, for it comes into being from the shadow of the animal soul, on account of which it is the farthest removed from the light of the intellect, and its shadow is very much increased and it becomes dense. It is bereft of sense-perception and movement, and keeps to its place upon the earth, and is confined to desire, procreation, nutrition, increase and decrease, the appearance of flowers and vegetables, odours, and tastes, according to the various places.

COMMENTS

In the paragraph on the soul Israeli[1] combines two different sources. In the first half, where he attempts a conciliation of the Aristotelian definition of the soul with another ascribed to Plato, he follows al-Kindī, while the second half, in which he describes the successive emanation of the rational, animal, and vegetative souls, conceived as hypostases, is derived from Ibn Ḥasdāy's Neoplatonist.

Al-Kindī's conciliation of the Aristotelian and 'Platonic' definitions of the soul has come down to us in a short text preserved in the precious Istanbul manuscript of his works under the title 'An abbreviated, short statement by al-Kindī on the soul' (al-Kindī, pp. 281–2). The following is a full translation of the al-Kindī text.

75 *and . . . things* L om. H. 75–76 *have as property* L *enter* (*into the category of* H (and variant quoted in L^{AC} (*in alio, quia intrant in aestimacione*). 76–77 *The vegetative . . . rank* L *Under the rank of the animal soul is that of the vegetative soul* H. 79–80 *it is . . . dense* H; the reading of the different manuscripts of L does not appear quite clearly in the edition; at any rate, two variant readings are conflated, as seen from the note *in alio* given by L^{AC}. *Et propter hoc obtenebratur* (add. *in alio* L^{AC}) (*facta est remocior a splendore intelligenciae propter multitudinem umbrae et tenebrarum suarum*; om. L^{BCL}) *et elongatur* (om. L) *splendor eius a splendore mundo et puro*, &c. 83–84 *according to the various places* L om. H.

[1] The definition given here in the name of Aristotle recurs in *BEl.*, pp. 12–13, cf. *Book of Fevers*, fol. 204 (quoted by Guttmann, *Israeli*, p. 38): 'The soul is one in its essence, viz. an uncorporeal substance which perfects the natural and organic body which is alive potentially.' Guttmann has pointed out that 'organic' occurs only in the passage from the *Book of Fevers*, and that in Aristotle also it figures in one of the two versions of the definition of the soul (*De anima*, ii. 1. 412^{a}, 27) but is absent in the other (ibid. 412^{b}, 4).

An abbreviated, short statement by al-Kindī on the soul

Al-Kindī says: Aristotle says about the soul that it is a simple substance, the actions of which appear from the bodies.

Plato says: It is united with the heavenly body and by this union it is joined to the bodies and acts in them. He makes a distinction between 'body' (*jirm*) and 'heavenly body' (*jism*), saying: the 'body' belongs to the sensible substances and is the substrate for the accidents which are in the world of coming-to-be; a heavenly body, on the other hand, is, for instance, the sphere.

One might think that there is a difference between these two statements ⟨but this is not so⟩. Both assert, in more than one passage, that the soul is a substance which has no length, breadth, or depth; both assert that one can speak of the body joining the heavenly bodies only in the sense that it makes its actions appear in the heavenly body and through the heavenly body, not in the sense that they are joined in the same way as heavenly bodies and bodies are. Both assert in ⟨more than one⟩ passage that the actions of the soul appear in the bodies which are coming-to-be only by the intermediacy of the sphere.

Plato does not mean by his definition, 'united with the heavenly body through which its actions appear in the bodies', that it is united with the heavenly body, but only means to say that it acts in the bodies by the intermediacy of the heavenly body which is the sphere; not that it puts on a heavenly body by which it enters into a body and by which it leaves it.[1] Such a view is manifestly erroneous, and this would have been realized by one of even much lower standing than Plato. This for the following reason. If it is a heavenly body, it must occupy a place either inside the world of coming-to-be, or outside it. If it is outside it, there is no reason why it should come hither and be united with the bodies. If it is inside the world of coming-to be, it must be, like all that is inside the world of coming-to-be, a body, either earth, or water, or air, or fire, or something composed of these; a thing of this description is a body, and the heavenly body would thus be a body, and the word 'heavenly body' would have no meaning.

The end, praise be to God.

It is clear that there is a close relation between this text and Israeli's paragraph, while there are at the same time considerable differences also.

[1] The text as printed in the edition is unintelligible. Read with the manuscript: *lā annahā lābisatun jisman tadkhulu bihī fī jirmin wa-takhruju bihī min jirm.*

The 'Platonic' definition quoted by both authors is identical; it describes the descent of the universal soul into the world of the sphere (for which see § 6) and through it into the sublunar world, where it acts (in the guise of individual souls) through the human bodies. The distinction established by al-Kindī between the terms *jism*, 'heavenly body', and *jirm*, '(material) body', is also observed by Israeli, and though he does not draw attention to it in this passage, he does so in a special paragraph devoted to the subject (see below, § 7). In the interpretation of Plato's definition, too, Israeli, as his wording shows, is clearly inspired by al-Kindī. There is, however, this difference: al-Kindī seems to polemize against the common Neoplatonic doctrine according to which the soul in its descent assumes a 'heavenly body' (ὄχημα), Israeli against a literal interpretation of the junction of the soul with the body. As the doctrine of the ὄχημα played practically no part in Islamic philosophy, Israeli either considered a refutation superfluous or even missed the reference to that doctrine in al-Kindī altogether.

On the other hand, the two authors quote quite different definitions in the name of Aristotle: Israeli quotes the well-known authentic definition by Aristotle in the *De anima*,[1] while al-Kindī gives a spurious definition which is in fact very near to the 'Platonic' definition quoted subsequently. It is impossible to decide whether Israeli's argument derives from a lost text of al-Kindī or whether he himself constructed the argument to reconcile the authentic definition of Aristotle with the 'Platonic' text, known to him from al-Kindī.

The second half of the paragraph (ll. 45 ff.) expounds Israeli's doctrine of the three hypostases of the soul, a doctrine also treated by him in *BSubst.* iii, *BSpirit*, § 11, and *Mant.*, § 1, and derived from his Neoplatonic pseudo-Aristotelian source: see Comments on *BSubst.* where the passage from Ibn Ḥasdāy's Neoplatonist is reproduced. For the doctrine in general cf. also Part II, ch. III; for the statement that the animal soul has estimation ('for it reveals things from outward appearances') cf. below, § 33. (The qualification that one can ascribe imagination to the animal soul only

[1] The Aristotelian definition is, however, given a more Platonic turn by the rendering of 'entelechy' as 'a substance which perfects'. Joseph ibn Ṣaddīq, perhaps under the influence of Israeli, uses the same expression (*Microcosm*, p. 37; cf. G. Vajda, 'La Philosophie &c.' [see p. 21], p. 119).

metaphorically, resolves the apparent contradiction between § 33 and the passages on the animal soul in the other books, according to which the animal soul possesses estimation and imagination.)

Finally, it ought to be noted that the 'Platonic' definition of the soul is quoted in the *Ghāyat al-Ḥakīm*, probably from Israeli (cf. above, p. 8); see p. 294:

Plato says: The soul is an intellectual substance, which moves by itself according to a harmonious number.[1]

In another passage he says: The soul is an immaterial substance which moves the body[2] and is united with it; by this union it joins the bodies and acts in them.

§ **6.** Having reached our aim in the discussion of the quiddity of the higher spiritual beings to the very limit of their rank, we continue by mentioning that which is next in spirituality and sublimity, viz. THE SPHERE. The sphere is more sublime and higher in rank than the corporeal substance and follows immediately the rank of the soul; because it is not really body in so far as its matter is concerned, as it is in the horizon of the vegetative soul and came-to-be out of its shadow, without mediator between them. On account of this, its issue is from existence to existence. In saying 'to existence', I mean a lasting existence, which is not affected by growth and decrease, movement, coming-to-be and passing-away. In saying 'from existence', I mean the vegetative soul; as it and the rest of the higher spiritual substances are exempt from change and alteration of the order which is ordained for them by their Creator. Therefore, the issue of that which is derived from them causes no growth or decrease in them. Everything which is subject to change, alteration, permutation, growth, and decrease, is diminished

§ 6. 1–6, 11 (*In saying*) . . . 15 (*them*) is altogether missing in H, while 7–11 is paraphrased *The sphere comes-to-be from existence into existence, as its issue is from the horizon of the vegetative soul and the shadow of the souls, without it being increased or decreased by that which comes-to-be out of it.*

---

[1] This is derived from pseudo-Plutarch, *Placita Philosophorum* iv. 2 (H. Diels, *Doxographi Graeci*, p. 386), in the translation of Qusṭā ibn Lūqā: see ed. 'A. Badawī, Cairo, 1954, p. 157, and P. Kraus, *Jābir ibn Ḥayyān*, ii, Cairo, 1942, p. 332.

[2] *Al-badan*, i.e. 'the human body'—this is an erroneous substitution for the original *jism*, 'celestial body', and shows that, owing to the peculiar use of this term (cf. p. 48), the author of the *Ghāya* did not correctly understand the definition.

by the issue of that which is derived from it; bodies which are affected by the various contrary natures, such as the four corporeal elements, fire, air, earth, and water, are changed or decreased by the issue of what derives from them, such as the bodies of the animals and plants, and are corrupted and changed into them, as they come-to-be out of these elements by the celestial power which is ordained in nature by the Creator, may He be exalted, and appointed in it over the action of coming-to-be and passing-away, in order that the world of coming-to-be and passing-away should be completed. The lights, however, of the higher substances, viz. the three souls, are not increased or decreased by the issue of what is derived from them, as these come from the shadow of their light, not from their light itself in its essence and substantiality. It is clear that in every brilliant thing the light in its essence and substantiality is brighter and has a greater splendour than the light of its shadow—thus it is also clear that the brilliance of the vegetative soul is greater and stronger than that of the sphere which is derived from its shadow. For this reason the sphere is solid and casts a shadow, has a cover, is coarse and bulky, and is apprehended by the sense of sight only—not, however, by the other senses, because in spite of its being bulky it is, in its shape, spirituality and sublimity, still near to the order of the higher souls. On account of this it moves with a perfect movement, i.e. the circular movement, which is more complete and perfect, and farther removed from attrition and change than the others; it has therefore no growth or decrease, issue or intake, beginning or end. This is on account of its spirituality and eternity, permanence and perpetuality; for its coming-to-be is not out of various diverse things, so that it should be possible for it to change and to return into what it had come-to-be; it is fixed, consistent, perpetual, and eternal. Therefore the intellect poured over it some of its brilliance and some of the light of wisdom and elevated it, so that it became intellectual, rational, not lacking scrutiny, the faculty of discernment, cogitation and delibera-

17 *by the issue . . . from it* L om. H. 18–19 *fire . . . water* L om. H. 23 *in it* H, *cum ea* L (mistransl. orig. *bihā*). 23–24 *action . . . away*: a variant in L[AC]: *the creation of things which come-to-be and pass-away.* 27–28 *from the shadow . . . and substantiality* L *from them in their light, not their light in them* H. 28–31 *It is clear . . . shadow* om. H (homoioteleuton). 33–34 *casts . . . cover* om. H. 35–37 *not however . . . souls* om. H. 38–41 *the . . . end* L *the complete and perfect circular movement, which is not affected by growth or increase 'from where' and 'whereto'* H. 41–44 *This . . . come-to-be* L *As the sphere is not composed of things which increase, and change and permute into that out of which they came-to-be* H. 47–48 *not lacking . . . deliberation* L om. H. *lacking*: *indigens* (rather than 'needing no'; though L[ab] paraphrases *non egeat*).

tion, the knowledge of its Creator, and how it is due to Him to praise, sanctify, and glorify Him for ever without ceasing. On account of this the Creator, may He be exalted, elevated and raised it and gave it an order from which it should not be removed, and which should not end, or be interrupted, and He appointed it to distinguish the four seasons, the years, months, days, and hours, and gave it charge of the contingencies of this world, such as influencing the appearance of religions, the limits of the reigns of kings, their share in good and ill fortune, until the religion in question comes to an end, according to what is ordained by the knowledge of the Creator, may He be exalted.

COMMENTS

In the chain of emanation the sphere follows the soul, more precisely the vegetative soul; this is in accordance with the doctrine of Ibn Ḥasdāy's Neoplatonist—see his exposition of emanation, below, p. 99. Israeli, however, identifies the sphere with 'nature' (see below, § 9). We have here a harmonization of the Plotinian ideas about nature, as a hypostasis next in rank to the universal soul, and the Aristotelian doctrine about the sphere. Israeli also follows Aristotle in considering the sphere as a 'fifth essence'. (As is well known, Plotinus rejected the notion of 'fifth essence'.) This is implied in the distinction established in § 7 between the heavenly and the sublunar bodies, though the Aristotelian term of the 'fifth essence' does not occur there; it is used, however, in the passage about nature in *BSubst.* iii. 3^r (cf. Comments to § 9). (A curious, non-Aristotelian, feature of the doctrine is the statement that the sphere can be apprehended by sight.) For further comments see Part II, ch. III.

§ 7. Having reached our aim in the discussion of the order of the souls and their junction with what is appropriate for their actions in the bodies and their passions and the reception of their impressions and the

48 *the knowledge of* L *knowing* H. *due to Him*: *necessarium sit de veritate* L *wĕ-hā-rā'ūy 'ālāw min ḥuqqāw* H (both different mistranslations of original *mā yajibu min ḥaqqihī*; cf. § 2, l. 72). 52–57 *the years . . . exalted* L *and made it rule over the actions of the things which come-to-be and pass-away in the world of coming-to-be and passing away so that the higher souls should find bodies to join and over which to pour their light and show their actions which were in the foreknowledge of the Creator* H.

property of the sphere, i.e. the light and spirituality poured over it by the intellect, we must explain the DIFFERENCE BETWEEN THE SUBSTANCE OF THE BODY (*jirm*) AND THAT OF THE HEAVENLY BODY (*jism*). We say that the substance of the body comes-to-be from various elements, which are qualified by opposite qualities, on account of which they are affected by accidents and subject to coming-to-be and passing-away. In contrast, the substance of the sphere does not come-to-be from anything nor change into anything, nor is it qualified by any quality. If it were qualified, it would be necessarily either warm, cold, humid, or dry; if it were warm, it would rise upwards infinitely; if cold, sink downwards and rest in the centre; if humid, swim and float to the four sides; if dry, turn solid and compact, and lose movement altogether. Thus it is clear that it is not qualified by any quality and is therefore not affected by the accidents or subject to coming-to-be and passing-away.

COMMENTS

The distinction between body and heavenly body is merely the Aristotelian one between the four elements of the sublunar world and the fifth substance of the sphere. (Cf. the Comments on the preceding paragraph.) The terminology, however, i.e. the distinction between *jirm*, 'body', and *jism*, 'heavenly body', is derived from al-Kindī: see above, p. 43.[1] (As is well known, the later general usage is the opposite one: *jirm* stands for the heavenly, *jism* for the sublunar, body. In al-Kindī we find both terminologies.)

§ 8. ON THE VITAL SPIRIT. The ancients agree that the spirit is a subtle body which pervades, from the heart and through the arteries, the whole body and gives it life, respiration in the lung and pulse in the arteries. It ascends to the brain and from there it pervades, through the nerves, the whole body and gives it sense-perception and movement.

If someone asks about the difference between the soul and the spirit,

§ 7. 4 *the light*: here begins A. 7 *various* A L om. H. 8 *by opposite* A L om. H.

§ 8. 1 *On*: in L omit *alia* (with $L^A = A$, as against L^C; L^{BL} omit the whole title); H has *On the spiritual faculty and the difference between the spirit and the soul, and they said* (or: *his saying*) *that the soul is a spiritual substance*.

[1] For *jirm* = sublunar body cf. also al-Kindī, p. 165 ('*al-jirm*: that which has three dimensions'); p. 294 ('man, which is living and growing body (*jirm*)').

we answer that the difference is twofold. (1) Firstly, the spirit is a corporeal substance contained, confined, and surrounded by the body, while the soul is an incorporeal spiritual substance which surrounds and contains the body from without. (2) Secondly, the spirit is dissolved and destroyed together with the body, while the soul persists and remains after its separation from the body, though its action does not penetrate the body after the absence of the spirit which has given it life, sense-perception, and movement; when the body is deprived of the spirit and is dead, the soul does not penetrate it.

If someone asks about the difference between 'vein' and 'artery', we answer as follows. A vein is composed of one tube and one channel in which the blood flows from the liver to all parts of the body, which derive from the blood their food, power, and constitution. An artery, on the other hand, is composed of two tubes and two channels, in one of which flows the spirit to the whole of the body, giving it life and generating breath in the lung and pulse in the arteries in order to expel through them the warm vapours from the heart and draw in subtle air; while in the other flows the pure blood which has been cleansed from impurities in order that the vital spirit should be nourished by it, in the same manner as fire is outwardly nourished by oil. The cause which makes it impossible that the spirit and the blood should flow in the same channel and the same course is as follows. The spirit, on account of its subtlety, flows in the body suddenly and without a temporal interval; while the blood, on account of its thickness and the gravity of its movement, flows slowly, like water which flows in the pores and channels of the earth, blood being still thicker and slower than water. If, therefore, blood and spirit were to flow in the same channel and the same course, the blood would hinder the spirit and restrain it from flowing suddenly in the body, and this would result in the corruption of the natural order.

COMMENTS

The physiological theories concerning the vital spirit, blood, arteries, and veins are the conventional ones derived from Galen. They were naturally perfectly familiar to a physician such as Israeli, and there is no need to ask for specific sources. The account of the difference between spirit and soul (which is explained briefly also in *BSpirit*, § 1), on the other hand, though in a way a natural

7 Here begins the fourth fragment of H^2. 9–10 *while . . . body* om. H^2 (homoioteleuton). 14 *of the spirit* A *of life, sense-perception, and movement* LHH^2.

corollary of the current doctrines, has very definite parallels in Qusṭā ibn Lūqā's treatise *On the Difference between the Spirit and the Soul*;[1] the beginning of the third part of which reads as follows.

On the difference between the spirit and the soul

Having discussed the quiddity of spirit and soul, we shall now explain the difference between them. (1) The first difference is that the spirit is a body, while the soul is not a body. (2) The spirit, moreover, is contained in the body, while the soul is not contained in the body. (3) Furthermore, the spirit, when separated from the body, perishes; while the soul, though its actions disappear from the body, does not itself perish in its essence.

Israeli's first 'difference' is a combination of Qusṭā's first and second 'differences'; his second 'difference' corresponds to Qusṭā's third. It cannot be decided with certainty whether Israeli depends directly on Qusṭā or whether both go back to a common source.

The notion that the soul 'contains' the body, instead of being contained by it, goes back to Plotinus, *Enn.* iv. 3. 20: 'The soul is not a body, and it contains, rather than is contained' (and see the whole chapter). The idea recurs, in various forms, in Islamic and Jewish Neoplatonism (cf. G. Vajda, 'La Philosophie &c.' [cf. above, p. 21], pp. 123–4); but as the idea in Qusṭā and Israeli is expressed in very general terms only, there is no need for more detailed comment.

§ 9. ON NATURE. 'Nature' is an equivocal term. It stands for (1) constitution (*khalq*), and (2) everything which possesses a nature peculiar to itself. It also stands for (3) the humours, i.e. the four mixtures, viz. blood, the two biles, and the phlegm, and (4) the four elements, viz. fire, air, water, and earth. Also for (5) the sphere and the spherical power

§ 9. 1–5 (up to *sphere*), 9–13 (up to *bodies*), 15 (from *Plato*)–23 quoted by Ibn Ezra. 1–2 *constitution*: *living being* (*ḥayy*), *Ghāya* (see Comments). 3–4 *It also stands for the 'mothers', i.e. the elements* (*'anāṣir*) *and the 'daughters', i.e. the mixtures* (*akhlāṭ*) Ibn Ezra *for the four humours* H². 4–5 *and* (4) . . . *earth* om. A.

[1] For the book, which was very popular among Muslims, Jews, and Christians, see Brockelmann [see above, p. xii, n. 2], i. 222, suppl. i. 365; G. Graf, *Geschichte der christlichen arabischen Literatur*, ii, Rome, 1947, 31; ed. L. Cheikho, in *al-Mashriq*, 1911, pp. 94–104 = *Maqālāt Falsafiyya Qadīma*, Beirut, 1911, pp. 117–28; ed. G. Gabrieli, in *Rendiconti della R. Accademia dei Lincei*, 1910, pp. 652 ff. A very early manuscript (from the year 960–1) is published in facsimile in *İbn Sina Risâleleri*, ed. H. Z. Ülken, Istanbul, 1953, ii. 95–108. (The accompanying printed version—pp. 83–94—is very faulty.)

which is appointed by the Creator, may He be exalted, in nature for the sake of influencing coming-to-be and passing-away, increase and decrease, movement and rest; for this reason the ancient philosopher defined it from its property (*a*) and said that 'nature' was movement out of rest and rest out of movement. The philosopher defined it from its essence (*b*) by saying: 'Nature' is a power belonging to the heavenly body (*quwwa jismiyya*) which is in human bodies through the mediation of the sphere between the soul and the bodies. By a 'power belonging to the heavenly body' he meant a spherical power, as he used the expression *jism*, and not *jirm*. Plato defined it from its effect (*c*), saying: 'Nature' is a substance, competent in making the artificial things. The excellent Hippocrates put forward, concerning nature, a view in which he distinguished between nature and the soul, as follows (*d*): 'Nature' is the principle of movement from the inside, which strengthens the body, prepares for it food and other things which it needs, and keeps harm away from it as far as possible. The soul is the principle of movement from outside; it pours some of its light and brilliance over the human bodies and makes them alive, and possessing movement and sense-perception. Isaac says: He means by this the animal soul, as it alone possesses movement and sense-perception.

COMMENTS

Before commenting upon the contents of this chapter, it ought to be pointed out that a parallel—one can even say identical—passage occurs in the *Ghāyat al-Ḥakīm* (or *Picatrix*), p. 284, where, after some other statements concerning nature, we read the following:

In truth, it is an equivocal term. It stands (1) for 'living being',[1] (2) for something which is peculiar to a thing, (3) for the humours, (4) for the world, for the heaven, and for the power made by the Creator, may He be exalted, to be the cause for the influence over coming-to-be and

10–11 *The philosopher . . . saying*: *Aristotle* Ibn Ezra. 15 *Plato . . . saying*: *Plato* Ibn Ezra. *Nature* &c.: *al-ṭabīʿatu jawharun ʿālimun bi-ṣināʿati 'l-ashyāʾi 'l-maṣnūʿāt* Ibn Ezra *al-ṭabīʿatu jawharun* (*tabīʿiyyun*, dele) *muḥkimun li-ṣanʿati 'l-ashyāʾ* Ghāya. 16–18 *The excellent . . . as follows*: *Hippocrates* Ibn Ezra. 23 *sense-perception*: a variant in L^{AC} reads: *locomotion with interposition and descent* (?). 24–25 *Isaac . . . sense-perception* LH^2 om. AH (homoioteleuton).

[1] *Sic*. It is, however, possible that *al-ḥayy*, 'living being', is a scribal error for *al-khalq*, 'constitution'.

passing-away, and the movement and rest in everything which moves and rests. On account of this (*a*) the ancients defined it as follows: the principle of movement and rest. (*b*) The philosopher also defined it: form belonging to the heavenly bodies (*ṣūra jismiyya*), which is in the human body through the mediation of the sphere between it and the soul. (*c*) Plato defined it by saying: nature is a natural[1] substance competent in making things. (*d*) Galen[2] gave it a technical definition, saying: it is an innate warmth which consolidates the body by keeping harm away from it as far as it is in its power and preparing for it food and other things.

As we have explained above (p. 8), it is probable that the *Ghāya* derived this passage from Israeli, rather than from an author who also served as a source for Israeli himself.

In interpreting Israeli's doctrine concerning nature, we must take into consideration the parallel passage in the *Book of Substances*, iii. 2ʳ. There he interprets 'nature' in four ways:[3] as the spherical power (= 5 in the present passage), the qualities, the elements (= 4), and the mixtures (= 3). (In the light of the passage in *BSubst*. we may interpret (2) as referring to the elemental qualities, hot, cold, humid, dry; for 'nature' as the designation of 'quality' see P. Kraus, *Jābir ibn Ḥayyān*, ii, Cairo, 1942, pp. 165–6.)

These meanings of the term 'nature' need no further comment, as they are the common acceptations inherited from elementary physics and medicine. It is the equation 'nature' = the power of the sphere which is important for Israeli, as he himself clearly says (*BSubst*., loc. cit.): 'Nature in reality is the spheric power appointed by its Creator to influence coming-to-be and passing-away.' This formula recurs also in *BDef*., § 2, ll. 40–44, § 6, ll. 22–24, *Mant*., § 1. It is obvious that this concept of nature is derived from the Neoplatonic theory of nature as the hypostasis coming after the universal soul; this Plotinian hypostasis is, however, identified with the sphere. Cf. § 6, and for a further discussion of this subject Part II, ch. III.

Israeli finds that the various definitions of 'nature' given by

1 This word is probably to be deleted.
2 *Sic*, for Israeli's 'Hippocrates'.
3 *BDef*.'s (1) is missing in *BSubst*.

the ancient authorities are all in harmony with 'nature' taken in the sense of the spherical power governing the world of coming-to-be and passing-away; the reason for the different definitions lies in the different points of view from which they were formulated: from the property, the essence, or the effect of 'nature' (cf. above, p. 16). The first definition (*a*), quoted in the name of 'the ancient philosopher', is the well-known Aristotelian definition; a slightly different variant is quoted in the parallel passage of *BSubst.* and is attributed to Aristotle. While, however, that definition is the only one used in *BSubst.* to explain the concept of nature as spherical power, in the present passage definitions by the philosopher (i.e. Aristotle), Plato, and Hippocrates are added, the provenience of which is not quite clear. (The one attributed to Aristotle, which takes the place of the genuinely Aristotelian definition, obviously comes from some Neoplatonic pseudo-Aristotelian source.)

The next stages in the process of emanation, which are on a purely corporeal plane, and are described in the manner of Ibn Ḥasdāy's Neoplatonist in *BSubst.*, *BSpirit*, and *Mant.* (see Part II, ch. V), are not dealt with in the *Book of Definitions*.

§ **10.** On reason (*nuṭq*). Reason is knowledge which attains the truth through deliberation and cogitation.

COMMENTS

§§ 10–19, 32–34 deal with various psychological notions. The definitions are short and abrupt. Such brief definitions were originally extracted from a coherent context (either textbooks or commentaries), but as they stand, the system underlying them is not always clear. In a few cases there obviously exists a relationship between Israeli's definitions and those of al-Kindī; it is possible that the rest are also derived from him, either from a longer version of his *On Definitions*, or from other lost works of his.

§ 10. 1 *On reason* AH *definition of reason* L^C (om. L^L, *def.* om. L^A; so perhaps L had *De racionalitate*, or ⟨*Sermo*⟩ *de racionalitate* = AH). Here ends the fourth fragment of H^2. *truth* A *truths* H *occulta* L (*al-ḥaqīqa*, 'truth', misread as *al-khafiyya*, 'hidden things').

§ **11.** Definition of absolute knowledge (*al-ʿilm al-mursal*): The soul's perception of the truths of things which are the objects of knowledge.

COMMENTS

Cf. al-Kindī, *On Definitions*, p. 169: 'Knowledge: Finding out the things according to their truths'; and Rabīʿ ibn Yaḥyā's edition of Nicomachus, in a passage immediately following that quoted in the Comments on § 3; 'He defined Knowledge by saying: "Knowledge is the perception of the things which are the objects of knowledge", i.e. the everlasting things which do not change in their existence are not affected by change in their being and do not cease from their movement, i.e. the genera.' Rabīʿ, as noted above, loc. cit., was a pupil of al-Kindī.

§ **12.** Definition of true knowledge (*al-ʿilm al-ṣādiq*): True cognition confirmed by syllogism and established by demonstration.

§ **13.** Definition of cognition (*maʿrifa*): An established opinion which does not cease.

COMMENTS

An identical definition occurs in al-Kindī, p. 176.

§ **14.** Definition of opinion (*ra'y*): Belief in some thing.

COMMENTS

Cf. al-Kindī, p. 168: 'Opinion: Estimation (*ẓann*) which is manifested by word or by writing. It is also said: The belief of the soul

§ 11. 1 *absolute knowledge*: *ha-maḥshābhā ha-shĕlūkhā* H (*maḥshābhā* is otherwise the translation of *fikr*, not of *ʿilm* (*ḥokhmā*).

§ 12. 1 *true knowledge*: in L read *cognicio vera* (with L^{AL} = AH) for *cognicio veri*.

§ 13. 1 *established opinion*: in A read *ra'y thābit* (*th'bt* for *br'y*), as also in al-Kindī.

§ 14. in L om. *vel firmitudo* (with L^{AL}); gloss.

in one of two opposite statements, but in such manner that the belief can cease. It is also said that it is estimation with the judgement established: thus opinion is the resting of the estimation.'

§ **15.** Definition of cogitation (*fikr*): An intellectual faculty which roves among the things. It is one of the faculties of reason, on account of which every cogitative being is rational.

COMMENTS

'Cogitation' corresponds to *διάνοια*; the exact source of Israeli's definition, which is in rather general terms, is not known. For the interpretations given to this term by later Arabic philosophers see H. A. Wolfson, 'Isaac Israeli on the internal senses', *Jewish Studies in Memory of George A. Kohut*, New York, 1945 (pp. 583–98), p. 588; cf. also the same author's 'The internal senses in Latin, Arabic, and Hebrew philosophic texts', *Harvard Theological Review*, 1935, pp. 69 ff. (Some of Wolfson's comments on Israeli's paragraph are occasioned by the false reading *taḥillu* instead of the correct *tajūlu* and should therefore be disregarded.)

§ **16.** Definition of memory (*dhikr*): The apprehension of the things which are in the soul through investigation and research.

COMMENTS

The various aspects of memory are dealt with in §§ 16, 17, and 19, to which we may add a passage in *BEl.*, p. 55 (below, p. 137): 'Once the imaginative faculty has received them [the material impressions of the senses] from the *sensus communis*, it transmits them to the memory and deposits them there.' There is hardly anything in these texts beyond the most commonplace notions concerning memory; the exact sources of Israeli's definitions could not be identified. Wolfson (in the article quoted in the Comments on § 15) tried to connect Israeli's definitions with the passage on

§ 15. 2 *roves*: in A read *tajūlu* (*tjwl* for *tḥl*).
§ 16. 2 *are in the soul*: in A read *al-kā'ina* (*'lk'ynh* for *'lḥ'ṣh*).

memory in John of Damascus, *De fide orthodoxa*, ii. 20 (or rather in Nemesius, *De natura hominis*, ch. xiii, copied by John); one can, however, find no specific connexion.

§ 17. Definition of recollection (*tadhakkur*): The coming-back of a thing which had been forgotten.

COMMENTS

Cf. the definition of ἀνάμνησις in Elias's commentary on the *Isagoge* (*CAG* xviii/1. 2): 'The renewal of lost memory'; this seems to be even nearer to Israeli's definition than that of Nemesius and John of Damascus: 'The re-acquisition of memory which has grown pale.'

§ 18. Definition of deliberation (*rawiyya*): Letting opinion explore among the thoughts.

COMMENTS

Cf. al-Kindī, p. 168: 'Deliberation: Letting explore among the thoughts [read *khawāṭir*] of the soul' (the word 'opinion' is missing in al-Kindī's text).

§ 19. Definition of retention (*ḥifẓ*): A continuous and uninterrupted memory.

§ 20. Definition of discernment (*tamyīz*): Putting everything together with its similars.

§ 17. *recordacio est inquisicio adventus rei iam oblitae a virtute cogitativa* L (similarly L^{ab})—it is not clear how *i. a.* renders 'coming-back' (*ikhtilāf*) and *a v. c.* has nothing corresponding in AH.

§ 18. 1 *deliberation*: in A read *al-rawiyya* (*'lrwyh* for *'lḥyh*). 2 *thoughts*: the variant in L^{C}: *sensibus* (which is wrongly attached to § 19) attests a corrupt variant *al-ḥawāss* for *al-khawāṭir*.

§ 19. *in alio sensibus* in L^{C} seems to belong to § 18, as a variant to *praecordiis* (see note to § 18).

§ **21.** DEFINITION OF SYLLOGISM (*qiyās*): Referring the cause to the caused.

The dialecticians defined it as follows: Syllogism is a statement in which various things are put together in such a way that one thing necessarily results. Isaac says: This is not an independent definition, as it is impossible for one of the different things to come out as the result without clarification and proof of its truth, otherwise the claims will be equal. On the other hand, demonstration cannot be established without referring the cause to the caused, because the syllogism supports and reinforces the true deliberation.

COMMENTS

The definition seems to refer, strangely enough, not to the Aristotelian syllogism, but to the analogical reasoning of the Muslim jurists: Saʿadya, as quoted by al-Qirqisānī, ed. Nemoy, pp. 82–83, 358 ff., calls 'referring the cause to the caused' the syllogism of the dialecticians, as opposed to the logicians'. (See also G. Vajda's translation of the passages, *Revue des études juives*, 1946–7, pp. 69–70, 1948, pp. 70 ff., and his study of the Muslim background, 1946, pp. 55 ff.)[1] The second definition, quoted in the name of the 'dialecticians', is rejected by Israeli. The term 'dialecticians' (*jadaliyyūn*, which can simply mean 'those fond of controversy') was in contexts similar to ours mostly understood in a more technical sense: 'those satisfied with dialectical —as opposed to apodictical—syllogisms'. It was widely used by the philosophers in a pejorative sense to denote the dogmatic theologians (*mutakallimūn*). Israeli uses the same term in § 24. (Both passages are quoted by I. Goldziher, in *Revue des études juives*, 1903, p. 178; and a rich collection of passages illustrating this usage is to be found in Goldziher, *Kitāb maʿānī al-nafs*, *Buch vom Wesen der Seele*, Berlin, 1907, notes, pp. 13–16.) The definition, however, which is put into the mouth of the 'dialecticians'

§ 21. In L ll. 23–27 of p. 321 are to be omitted; they form a gloss. Similarly, ll. 4–5 of p. 322: *cum non sit causa nisi in causato neque causatum nisi causae.* 4 *one thing* (bis) *one true thing* L (L^A states with reference to the first occurrence that *vera* is a variant).

[1] It is worth while to draw attention to a passage in Ammonius's commentary on the *Prior Analytics* (*CAG* iv/6. 25): 'Syllogisms show the caused through the causes'. Cf. also S. van den Bergh, *Averroes' Tahafut al-Tahafut*, ii. 145.

is doubtless a slightly altered variant of the definition of the syllogism by Aristotle himself, *Posterior Analytics* i. 1, *Topics* i. 1: 'Syllogism is a form of speech in which, certain things being laid down, something follows of necessity from them.' Israeli thus seems to have attributed the philosophical definition to the theologians and himself adopted the one of the theologians!

§ **22.** DEFINITION OF CERTAINTY (*bayān*): The resting of the understanding when the proposition is established by demonstration.

COMMENTS

An identical definition occurs in al-Kindī, p. 171. (The lemma is, however, *yaqīn*, not *bayān*.)

§ **23.** DEFINITION OF DEMONSTRATION (*burhān*): A scientific norm which must contain a subject, a predicate, and a premiss which has no middle term.

§ **24.** DEFINITION OF 'TRUE' (*ḥaqq*): That which the thing is.

The dialecticians defined it as follows: Truth is a statement which is established by demonstration, either through the intellect or the senses. Isaac says: This definition gives the quality, not the quiddity, of truth, because if someone asks what truth is, the answer will be: that which a thing is; if he then asks how this is, we shall answer: because it is a statement established by demonstration, either through the intellect or from the senses.

COMMENTS

It ought to be noted that a definition of truth, wrongly attributed to Israeli, enjoyed some fame among the scholastics. It is quoted by Thomas Aquinas in the *Summa Theologica* (i, q. 16, a. 2, ad 2):

§ 22. 1 *certainty*: in L read *manifestacionis* for *meditacionis*; H has *bi'ūr*, which in § 21 stands for *īḍāḥ*. 2 *proposition*: *cleverness* AH (*fiṭna*, *'ormā*) *argumentacio* L; I reconstruct *qaḍiyya* (*qḍyh* for *fṭnh*) after al-Kindī.

§ 23. In L *in qua non removetur subiectum et praedicatum et proposicio cui medium non est* (L^L = AH) must be the correct reading; *a subiecto praedicatum quod est accidens quaesitum cum proposicione* (L) is an interpolation.

§ 24. In L om. p. 322, l. 9–p. 323, l. 6; gloss. In A read (l. 4) *al-ḥaqqi lā 'an* (*'lḥq l'* for *'l'ql'*); also (l. 7) *'aqlan* (*'ql'* for *'lm'*).

'Praeterea, Isaac dicit in libro *De definitionibus*, quod "veritas est adaequatio rei et intellectus"'; and in the *De veritate* (q. 1, a. 1): 'Et sic dicit Isaac, quod "veritas est adaequatio rei et intellectus".' J. T. Muckle, 'Isaac Israeli's definition of truth', *Archives d'histoire doctrinale et littéraire du moyen âge*, 1933, pp. 5–8, has already pointed out that such a definition is not to be found in the *Book of Definitions*. The history of the definition was elucidated by D. H. Pouillon in his study on Philip the Chancellor's *Summa de Bono*, in *Revue néoscolastique de philosophie*, 1939, p. 59. He shows that the definition is derived from Avicenna and was quoted anonymously by authors such as William of Auxerre, Philip the Chancellor, Alexander of Hales, and others. Philip also quotes Isaac's definition (Pouillon, pp. 57–58): 'Item Augustinus in *Libro soliloquiorum* [ii, c. 5, n. 8, *Patr. Lat.* xxxii, 889] "verum est", inquit, "id quod est". Item Augustinus in libro *De definitionum collectione* idem dicit.' The second 'Augustinus' is obviously an error for 'Isaac'; this is borne out by Albert the Great (*Summa*, i, tr. 6, q. 25, m. 2, p. 206): 'secundum Isaac et secundum Augustinum verum est id quod est.' By some error Thomas attached Isaac's name to the wrong quotation.

The definitions of 'true' and 'false' (§ 25) are closely related to those of truth and falsehood (§§ 26, 27) which are taken from Aristotle, and seem to be derived from them. We have seen that Augustine quotes a corresponding form; and so does John of Damascus, in the opening paragraph of the *De fide orthodoxa*. The second definition of 'true' again looks more like one used by philosophers than by theologians (cf. Comments on § 21).

§ 25. Definition of 'false' (*bāṭil*): That which the thing is not. Others say: The description of a thing in a manner in which it is not.

§ 26. Definition of truth (*ṣidq*): Attributing to some thing something which it possesses in truth, or to deny to some thing something it does not possess in truth.

§ 27. Definition of falsehood (*kidhb*): Attributing to some thing something which is denied to it in truth, or denying to some thing something that it possesses in truth.

COMMENTS

The following definitions in al-Kindī, p. 169, evidently correspond to §§ 25 and 26: 'Veracity: A statement which affirms that which is and denies that which is not. Lie: A statement which affirms that which is not and denies that which is; it is also either attributing ⟨to some thing⟩ something that it does not possess, or denying to some thing something that it does possess.'

The ultimate source is Aristotle (*Met.* iii. 7): '. . . we start by defining truth and falsehood. Falsehood is saying of that which is that it is not, or of that which is not that it is; truth is saying of that which is that it is, or of that which is not that it is not.'

§ 28. Definition of the necessary (*wājib*): That the absence of which is impossible.

§ 29. Definition of the impossible (*mumtani'*): That the existence of which is impossible.

§ 30. Definition of the absurd (*muḥāl*): The simultaneous presence in a thing of two opposites, according to one name and description, at the same time, in the same part, and according to the same relation, as we have explained before in this book.

COMMENTS

The definition is identical with the one by al-Kindī, p. 169: 'The absurd: the simultaneous presence in a thing of two opposites, at the same time, in the same part, and according to the same relation.' The two further qualifications ('according to one name and description') may be additions by Israeli, in accordance with his full treatment of the qualification of the impossibility of the simultaneous presence in a thing of two opposites, to which he expressly refers (above, the second half of § 3). Al-Kindī's definition occurs also in al-Khuwārizmī's glossary of technical terms, *The Keys of Sciences*, ed. van Vloten, p. 140.

§ **31**. Definition of the possible (***mumkin***): 'Possible' can be said in two ways, viz. in the proper and the improper sense. (1) In the proper sense: that which stands at the two ends of contraries, when it is not yet known which one of the sides will appear. (2) In the improper sense, it can also be said in two ways. (*a*) Firstly, the possibility of something which has not yet occurred, but which must necessarily occur; for instance, the rise of the sun tomorrow from the east—though it has not yet risen, its rise tomorrow occurs necessarily. (*b*) Secondly, the possibility of what has already occurred and become actual, but the occurrence of which was not necessary by nature—for instance a hunter who becomes caliph or a barber who becomes a general. Isaac says: I have seen something of the sort with my own eyes in Egypt: one of the Ṭūlūnid generals, called Ibn al-Khalīj, seized power and became very mighty, his fame rose, and his army was numerous; the commander of his army was a black barber, called Bilāl.

COMMENTS

The division of the possible seems to be connected with the discussion by the commentators of the passage in Aristotle's *De interpretatione*, ch. xiii. 22^{b} 29 ff. The elements of Israeli's division are present in Ammonius's comments (*CAG* iv/5. 238 ff.), though Ammonius's division is more complicated. There are, moreover, serious discrepancies between him and Israeli. One has to assume therefore that Israeli's passage goes back, through some intermediary, to another commentary of the Alexandrian school. I give the relevant parts of Ammonius's comments (p. 240, ll. 1 ff.):

He says that (*a*) the possible can either already be actual—thus we say that the man who walks has the potency of walking, or that the sun has the potency of giving light or of moving; or (*b*) it can be *in potentia* and have the ability only—thus we say that a man who sits has the potency of walking, and a man who walks has the potency

§ 31. 3 In A read *ḥāshiyatay* for *ḥāshiyatayn*. 15 *Bilāl* (pronounced in Hispano-Arabic: Bilēl): *bl'ls* A *Bel'el* H *Bibel* L^{C} *Lilel* L^{AB} *Bidel* A^{L}.

of not walking. But also that which is actual (*a*) can either (a^1) naturally belong to, and be a formal principle of, the thing which we say it has in potency, or (a^2) it is something which is acquired and not always present in the substratum. [There follow further subdivisions.]

It is clear that (a^2) corresponds to Israeli's (2) (*b*), (*b*) to Israeli's (1), though already the different formulation is apparent. (a^1) looks different from Israeli's (2) (*a*), as it deals with a necessary concomitant already actualized, while Israeli speaks of a necessary occurrence which has not yet taken place. But the two cases are very similar (one would only have to change Israeli's example 'the rise of the sun tomorrow' into 'the sun which has risen today', and we should have the case envisaged by the commentator). At any rate it seems obvious that Israeli's division goes back to the same discussion as that of Ammonius.

Israeli's example for (2) (*b*) is rather queer, but we owe to it the only autobiographical reference in his work. Ibn al-Khalīj was an officer of the deposed Ṭūlūnid dynasty who was carried into exile by the ʿAbbāsid authorities but was proclaimed as *amīr* in Syria by the partisans of the Ṭūlūnids in Shaʿbān 292 A.H./June 905. He managed to return to Egypt, captured the capital, Fusṭāṭ, on 16 Dhu'l-Qaʿda of the same year (19 Sept. 905), but was defeated by the ʿAbbāsid armies sent against him, on 3 Rajab 293/30 May 906. After this he went into hiding, but was arrested on 6 (or 8) Rajab (2 or 4 June) and taken to Baghdad. He ruled, as the historians sum up, for seven months and twenty (or twenty-two) days. (The main authorities are: al-Kindī—who is not identical with the philosopher—*Governors and Judges of Egypt*, ed. Guest, pp. 251–63; Ibn Taghrībirdī, *al-Nujūm al-Zāhira*, Cairo, 1932, iii. 147–55; al-Maqrīzī, *Khiṭaṭ*, Cairo, 1270 A.H., i. 327.) The name of the black general mentioned by Israeli does not recur in the accounts seen by the present writer.

§ **32.** DEFINITION OF IMAGINATION (*wahm*): A faculty which roves among the things possible and uses the psychical faculty; be-

§ 32. 2 *uses the psychical faculty*: mistranslated in H *wĕ-yaʿăseh zeh ba-kōaḥ ha-ḥiyyūnī*.

cause those forms which are communicated to us by the senses with their matter are communicated to us by the psychical faculty abstracted from their matter.

Imagination is also said of the faculty which is resting in the things concerning which one seeks to find out whether it is so-and-so or not.

COMMENTS

A rather obscure paragraph. 'Imagination' has as its objects possible beings, in contrast to 'estimation', which has as its objects impossible notions (§ 33). (N.B. I use 'imagination' and 'estimation' as merely conventional renderings of the terms.) 'Psychical faculty' must stand for fantasy, the function of which is to abstract the forms from the matter (cf. *BEl.*, pp. 53–54, below, pp. 135–6). 'Imagination', then, stands for a certain faculty which is related to, or is a subdivision of, fantasy; similarly 'estimation'. The second definition is even more obscure. (A re-examination of the psychological doctrines of the earlier Islamic philosophers will perhaps elucidate these matters. Wolfson's studies quoted above, on § 15, where he also discusses §§ 32 and 33, have not yet solved the problems.)

§ 33. DEFINITION OF ESTIMATION (*ẓann*): Estimation is a faculty which roves among things impossible. It is also said that it is a judgement concerning a thing with reference to what it appears to be and not with reference to what it is in truth. For this reason brute animals are estimating beings, and not imaginative beings; they are said to be imaginative only in a figurative and metaphorical sense.

COMMENTS

The second definition is derived from al-Kindī; cf. al-Kindī, p. 171: 'Estimation: it is a judgement concerning a thing with reference to what it appears to be—it is also said: not with reference to what it is in truth—and an explanation without proofs or demonstration; so that this judgement may cease.' The first definition

§ 32. 5 *in their matter* (expressed by a hendiadys) (*fī ṭīnihā wa-ʿunṣurihā*) A *in their nature and matter* HL (both misreading *ṭīnihā* as *ṭabīʿatihā*, a not infrequent mistake.

correlates 'estimation' with 'imagination' (see § 32). For estimation as a property of the animal soul cf. § 5, Comments.

§ **34.** Definition of sense-perception (*ḥiss*): The impression of the trace of the object of sense-perception in the senses; thus the object is the agent, as it stimulates and moves the senses towards the knowledge of its essence. For instance: a book which moves its reader by stimulating him to strive for the science and the stories contained in it; or the beloved who moves the lover and stimulates him to meet him, look at him, and be in his company. Sometimes, the opposite is said, viz. that the senses are the agents and the objects are passive. But all this is not said in the proper sense, as in most cases there is no passiveness, and therefore no agent in the proper sense of the word, only metaphorically, not in the meaning, but in the expression only. Similarly, it is sometimes said that a man knows the Creator, may He be exalted, viz. that He is the creator and the 'maker-anew'; yet the Creator is not affected by passiveness in any sense, but He is the agent of everything which is acted upon and the cause of everything caused, and as He is not affected by passiveness, man does not, on account of his knowledge, of Him, become an agent. 'Action' is said in two ways: (1) spiritual, and (2) corporeal. (1) Spiritual action is also said in two ways: (*a*) some action does not go beyond its agent to another thing; (*b*) others pass beyond it to another thing. A case of an action (*a*) which does not pass beyond the agent to something else is man's cogitation and deliberation, in order to distinguish things that are useful or harmful for him; of one (*b*) which does pass beyond the agent to something else is the action of the object of sensation upon sense, as the action of the object passes beyond itself and reaches sense; another example is the action of the beloved upon the lover or of the book upon the reader. Neither of these two kinds of action, viz. that which passes and that which does not pass beyond the agent to something else, is an opposite of, or is incompatible with, its agent, but is on the contrary similar to it and adds something to it; thus the man who cogitates and deliberates about what is useful or harmful for himself is not opposed to, or incompatible with, his essence, but adds something to it, and similarly the object of sense-perception is not opposed to, or incompatible with, sense, but is similar to it and adds something to it, viz. by stimulating it to acquire knowledge. (2) Corporeal action is one which is due to the will, e.g. the action of the bodies which are moving and move others, such as the beast which moves itself and through its movement moves the wheel of the mill, or the air which is moving itself and catches the ship's sail and moves it. In addition there is also composite movement, as for instance that of a man who moves and sets in motion the oars of a ship, so that the ship moves through the movement of both.

§ **35.** Definition of coincidence (*ittifāq*): The coexistence of different things in one, e.g. the coexistence of man, horse, and the other animals in 'animal' and their coincidence in receiving the same name and definition.

§ **36.** Definition of contact (*ijtimāʿ*): The approach of bodies to each other.

COMMENTS

No corresponding definition is to be found in the Istanbul manuscript of al-Kindī's *On Definitions*, but there is one quoted in Abū Ḥayyān al-Tawḥīdī's *al-Muqābasāt* (Cairo, 1929, p. 313), in a chapter containing many definitions derived from al-Kindī (without mentioning his name); thus it can be assumed that it stood in the full text of the book.

§ **37.** Definition of touch (*mumāssa*): The contact of limits in space.

COMMENTS

Cf. al-Kindī, p. 170: 'Touch: the continuity of two bodies between which there is nothing, either belonging to their nature or different from it, except what is not apprehended by the senses. Also: the approach of the limits of two bodies in a line common to both.'

§ **38.** Definition of adherence (*mulāṣaqa*): One body joining another.

§ **39.** DEFINITION OF LOVE (*maḥabba*): The desire of the soul for the object of its seeking by completing the cause of contact.

COMMENTS

Cf. al-Kindī, p. 175: 'Love: the object of the soul's seeking and the complement of the power which is the ⟨cause of the⟩ contact of things'; and p. 168: 'Love: the cause of the contact of things.'

§ **40.** DEFINITION OF PASSION (*'ishq*): Excess of love.

COMMENTS

Identical definition in al-Kindī, p. 176; the definition recurs in Miskawayh's 'Ethics' (tenth century; *Tahdhīb al-Akhlāq*, Cairo, 1904, p. 45).

§ **41.** DEFINITION OF DESIRE (*shahwa*): Longing (*shawq*) for and seeking the object of desire.

COMMENTS

Cf. al-Kindī, p. 176: 'Desire: the object of the power which gives life and the cause of its perfection; it is derived from "desire", i.e. will directed towards the object of sense-perception. [The text seems corrupt.] It is also said: Desire is a longing, in an affective way, to add what is missing in the body and to take away what is superfluous; by saying "in an affective way" we mean: in a way which is different from that of cogitation and discernment.'

§ **42.** DEFINITION OF 'INNOVATION' AND 'MAKING-ANEW' (*al-ibdā' wa'l-ikhtirā'*): Making existent existences from the non-existent (*ta'yīs al-aysāt min lays*).

§ 39. 2 *by completing the cause of contact* (*bi-tatmīmi 'illati' l-ijtimā'i*) A, H mistranslates: *bi-shĕlēmūth bĕ'ēth ha-ḥibbūr* (but probably we have to read *sibbath ha-ḥibbūr*).

§**43.** Definition of creation: Bringing into being existences from the existing.

Someone may think that the non-existent (*al-lays*) is the same as privation (*al-ʿadam*); we let him therefore know that this is wrong, for the following reason. Privation only occurs after existence (*wujūd*); for instance, if a thing exists, and is then deprived, it is said that such a thing has been deprived: thus if a man has his sight and then loses it, it is said that he is deprived of his sight. In the same way it is said about everything that exists and is then deprived that such-and-such a thing is deprived; it cannot, however, be said that the non-existent is deprived as the non-existent has no form in the imagination whereby it could be described by existence or privation.

§ **44.** Definition of coming-to-be: The passing of corporeal substances from privation to existence. Everything which is caused-to-be has a natural coming-to-be; nature, however, does nothing out of nothing, but creates and causes-to-be by the spheric power appointed and ordained by its Creator for the action of coming-to-be and passing-away; e.g. the causing-to-be of animals and plants. For this reason its action is creation, not 'innovation' and 'being made anew', as there is no 'innovator' and 'maker-anew' except the Creator, may He be praised and may His name be sanctified; there is no God except Him, and no one is to be worshipped except Him.

§ 43. 1–2 Ibn Ezra: *fa-ḥaddada 'l-khilqata annahū dhātun lam takun mawjūdatan wa-huwa aysun*—correct the text as follows: *annahū* ⟨*ījādu*⟩ *dhātin lam takun mawjūdatan wa-huwa* ⟨*ījādu aysin min*⟩ *aysin. definition . . . existing*: *om.* A *definicio conditoris et creatoris*: *creator est faciens esse essencia ex non esse* L *definition of creation*: *bringing into being existences from the non-existent.* H and L misread the second *ays* as *lays* (cf. note to l. 3). The reconstruction of the text is confirmed by the last sentence of § 44. 3–8 are only briefly paraphrased by Ibn Ezra. 3 *non-existent*: read in A *al-lays* (*'llys* for *'l'ys*). 5 *privation*: in A read *al-ʿadam* (*'lʿdm* for *'l'ys*). 10 *it cannot, however, . . . non-existent*: *et neque potest aliquis de eo quod fuit inventum et postea privatum est dicere quod sit privatum ex non est* L. Ll. 5–7, 10–11 are quoted by Ibn Laṭīf (cf. above, p. 7). In 5 his text has: *its existence*—but *mĕṣī'ūthō* may be an error for *mĕṣī'ūth*. In 10–11 his text reads: *as the non-existent has no existence in the intellect, and even less outside the intellect,* but this seems to be but a paraphrase.

§ 44. 3 *nature*: *natures* L (mistaking *ṭibāʿ* for plural). 6 *and plants*: *from the four elements* adds L. 7 *creation*: *making and creation* L.

§ 45. DEFINITION OF PASSING-AWAY: The passing of a substance from existence to privation; thus, for instance, the bodies of the animals and plants pass-away when they are transformed into the elements from which they had been caused-to-be.

COMMENTS

The distinction between God's creation from nothing and nature's 'creation', i.e. coming-to-be and passing-away, as well as the terminology, derive from al-Kindī. The following passages can be quoted from his extant writings.

On Definitions, al-Kindī, p. 165: '"Innovation" (*ibdāʿ*): manifesting a thing from the non-existent (*lays*).'

The treatise, *The Agent in the proper sense, being first and perfect, and the agent in the metaphorical sense, being imperfect* (al-Kindī, pp. 182 ff.), is partly devoted to the discussion of the concept of *ibdāʿ*. The following is a complete translation of the short treatise.

We must explain what is action (*fiʿl*) and in which senses it is used.

The first kind of action in the proper sense is making existent existences from the non-existent (*ta'yīs al-aysāt ʿan lays*). It is clear that this kind of action belongs properly to God, who is the end of every cause, because making existent existences from the non-existent does not belong to anybody except Him. To this kind of action belongs properly the name of 'innovation' (*ibdāʿ*).

The second kind of action in the proper sense, coming immediately after the preceding, is the influence (*athar*) of one who influences the thing that is influenced. The true Agent is one who influences[1] without being influenced by any kind of influence; the true Agent is therefore one who makes what he makes without being acted upon in any way. One who is acted upon is one who receives some influence, i.e. who is acted upon by an agent.

Therefore, the Agent in the proper sense of the word, who is not acted upon, is the Creator, the maker of the universe, may He be praised. On the other hand everything beneath Him, i.e. all His creations, are only called agents in a metaphorical, not in the proper, sense; because in the proper sense they are all acted upon. The first of them is acted upon by the Creator, the rest by each other: the first is acted upon, and through this passiveness the next is acted upon, from the passive-

[1] Omit *fīh* in the text.

ness of the latter another is acted upon, until we reach the last thing which is acted upon. The first among these is called 'agent in a metaphorical sense' of the first thing which is acted upon, and is the near cause of its passiveness; similarly, the second is the near cause of the passiveness of the third, until we reach the last thing which is acted upon. The Creator, however, is in the proper sense the first cause of all things that are acted upon, both those that are acted upon through an intermediary and those without an intermediary, because He is active, never passive; only He is the near cause of the first passive thing, and a cause through intermediaries to those things that He acted upon after the first.

This kind of action, viz. that belonging to a thing which is acted upon —which is action in a metaphorical sense, not in the proper sense (as none of the agents which are also acted upon is exclusively active but exclusively passive, as its passivity is the cause of the others' passivity)— can be divided into two kinds. One is that kind to which this general name, viz. action, belongs in the proper sense, to wit those things in which the influence ceases simultaneously with the passiveness caused by its agent. For instance, the walking of a man, which ceases when the man ceases to walk, as the passiveness of the walker ceases and no influence remains to be perceived by sensation. The second kind is where the influence remains in the thing acted upon even after the source of the influence ceases to cause passiveness; for instance, the impression of a seal, or an edifice, and similar products of the crafts. This kind of action is more particularly known by the name of 'work' (*'amal*).

This is a sufficient answer to your question.

End of the epistle, praise be to God.

A precious fragment from a lost work of al-Kindī, which elucidates the concept of *ibdā'* from yet another point of view, is preserved in Abū Ḥayyān al-Tawḥīdī's *al-Imtā' wa'l-Mu'ānasa*, iii. 133. Abū Ḥayyān relates there 'Isā ibn Zur'a's enumeration of the six kinds of movements posited by Aristotle (locomotion, coming-to-be, passing-away, growth, decrease, change) and continues as follows:

Al-Kindī says: There is yet another kind of movement, viz. the movement of 'innovation' (*ibdā'*). There is a difference between it and the movement of coming-to-be, because the former is without a substrate, while the movement of coming-to-be is from the passing-away of a substance, which takes place when the coming-to-be occurs. For this reason it is said that coming-to-be is the passing from a viler to a more precious state.

It can be shown that this doctrine of creation from nothing was not an innovation of al-Kindī himself, but was already professed in the Neoplatonic circles which stood behind the nascent Islamic philosophy. The book of Ammonius *On the Opinions of the Philosophers*, a compilation in which Neoplatonic doctrines are put into the mouth of the ancient philosophers,[1] contains a discussion of the problem the importance of which is emphasized by the fact that it is the subject with which the book opens. The problem is treated in the author's self-imposed manner as one discussed by the ancients. The following is the translation of the first three paragraphs of the book.

Ammonius says:

The first subject about which we want to find out the opinions of the ancients concerns the Creator, and whether he created (*abdaʿa*) this world and the form contained in it from something or from nothing (*min shay'in am min lā shay'*). If from something, then that thing is eternal together with the Creator, which is not permissible; if from nothing the question arises whether the form of the thing was with Him, or whether He created things without having their forms with Him in essence.

Thales said: The incontrovertible view is that the Creator had no created thing with Him and He created what He created without having its form with Him in essence; because before creation (*ibdāʿ*) only He existed, on account of which there were then no different aspects, but 'He', and 'how He is', 'in what He is', 'in which state He is' are all included in 'He is He'; *ibdāʿ* is making existent a thing which

[1] I have discovered this important Neoplatonic pseudepigraph of late antiquity in MS. Aya Sofiya (Istanbul), no. 2450. It was known to al-Bīrūnī (tenth–eleventh century), who quotes it twice (*India*, ed. E. Sachau, pp. 41–42, transl. Sachau, p. 85; *Chronology of Ancient Nations*, missing in ed. Sachau, ed. H. Taqizade, in *Bulletin of the School of Oriental Studies*, 1935–7, p. 949), and served as one of the main sources for al-Shahrastānī in his account of the ancient philosophers in his *Religions and Sects*. (Also the paragraphs translated here recur in al-Shahrastānī, though in shortened form, and dispersed in various chapters.) I have made use of Ammonius in my article 'Anbaduḳlīs' (= Empedocles) in the new edition of the *Encyclopaedia of Islam*; I hope to publish and translate the full text in the future.

did not exist (*ta'yīs shay'in mā lam yakun*). Making a thing existent is not . . .; thus that which is brought into existence (*al-mu'ayyas*) has no form at all, otherwise it is not brought into existence. As He is the one who brings the existents into being (*mu'ayyis al-aysāt*), and 'bringing into existence' means from no pre-existent thing and from nothing, but bringing it into existence—on account of this, the one who brings the existent into existence need not have the form of the existents with him in order to bring them into existence. Otherwise it would follow that He would be together with the form, because if someone has with himself a separate form, he is different from the form. As the first Creator has the utmost excellence, it follows that He cannot have forms with Him, otherwise He would not be the Creator.

Plutarch said: The Creator, may He be exalted, always existed in eternity, which is the eternity of eternities, and He is the Creator (*mubdiʿ*). Every created being, the form of which appears at the limit of the creation (*ibdāʿ*), had its form present in His fore-knowledge; the forms present with Him are infinite. [There follows the proof.] This was the opinion and doctrine of Plutarch; it is however a wrong opinion.

Xenophanes said: The first Creator (*mubdiʿ*) is an eternal essence (*anniyya*); he is the source of everlastingness and eternity. He cannot be perceived by logical and intellectual attributes; He is the creator of every attribute and logical and intellectual description. This being so, it is absurd to say either that a certain form in this created world had not been, or had been, with Him; it is equally absurd to say how and why He created. The reason is that the intellect is created; what is created has something preceding it; what is preceded can never perceive that which precedes it—so how could that which is preceded describe that which precedes it? What we must say is that the Creator created what He wanted, and as He willed; He was He, and nothing existed together with Him. This statement: 'He and nothing else', is a simple and not a compound statement, and contains all we seek of knowledge, because if you say 'and nothing with Him', you deny concerning Him the eternity of form and matter, and of everything else.

These paragraphs are sufficient for our purpose; in the following ones the emphasis is less on the problem of creation from nothing. We may note that the special turn given to the problem in the paragraphs quoted, viz. the question whether creation from nothing is compatible with the pre-existence of forms in the mind of the

Creator (denied by 'Thales', affirmed by 'Plutarch', while 'Xenophanes' offers an intermediate solution), does not recur in al-Kindī. But the similarity between the terminology of creation from nothing used by Ammonius in the paragraph on 'Thales' and that of al-Kindī is rather striking.

The distinction established by Israeli between God's creation from nothing and the creative power of nature, producing out of previously existing things, does not occur in the extant texts of al-Kindī. There is, however, a striking parallel in a text by John Philoponus, viz. his refutation of Aristotle's doctrine of the eternity of the world, extracts of which are quoted by Simplicius in his commentary on the *Physics* (*CAG* x. 1145). The text—the knowledge of which I owe to R. Walzer—reads as follows): '. . . *τὸν θεὸν ταύτῃ διαφέρειν τῆς φύσεως . . . καθ' ὅσον αὕτη μὲν ἐξ ὄντων, ὁ δὲ θεὸς ἐκ μὴ ὄντων ποιεῖ τὰ γινόμενα*', '. . . the difference between God and nature lies in the following: . . . it [nature] makes things out of what exists, God out of that which does not exist'. It is very likely that this distinction was reflected in a text of al-Kindī now lost, whence it was taken over by Israeli. (The difference between God's activity of 'innovation' and the causality of nature which is operated through the sphere is also stressed in *BSubst.* v. 12^{v}.)

For the part played by this distinction in the context of Israeli's metaphysical scheme see Part II, ch. IV.

A few words have to be said about the influence of al-Kindī's and Israeli's doctrine of creation from nothing. This is, of course, not the place to treat of the idea of creation in Islamic and Jewish philosophy, nor even of the history of the term *ibdāʿ*[1]; I only wish to show that the terminology of al-Kindī and Israeli can be clearly recognized in several authors.

When we find in the Ikhwān (iv. 11): 'Innovation and making-anew, i.e. bringing into existence something from nothing' (*al-ibdāʿ wa'l-ikhtirāʿ*, *fa-huwa ījādu shay'in min lā shay*'),[2] the juxtaposition of the two synonyms *ibdāʿ* and *ikhtirāʿ* alone indicates a

[1] As is well known, the term is employed by such early Arabic Neoplatonic documents as the *Theology of Aristotle* and the *Liber de causis*, as well as the Ismāʿīlī Neoplatonists.

[2] *Ibdāʿ* and *ikhtirāʿ* also occur together in other passages of the *Epistles* of the Ikhwān.

common source with Israeli.[1] Miskawayh (tenth century), in the course of his refutation of Galen's statement that everything existing is produced from another existence,[2] quotes the same definition of *ibdāʿ* (*The Smaller Book of Bliss*, i. 10, ed. Beirut, 1319 A.H., p. 32, translated in J. W. Sweetman, *Islam and Christian Theology*, i. 1, London and Redhill, 1945, p. 117; I have translated the passage afresh): 'If God, may He be exalted, had created existing things from something already existing, there would be no meaning in *ibdāʿ*, because there would be something existing before *ibdāʿ*, while the meaning of *ibdāʿ* is: bringing into existence something out of nothing (*ījādu shay'in lā min shay'*).' Ibn Sīnā, whose doctrine of *ibdāʿ* does not concern us, as it goes much beyond al-Kindī's ideas,[3] shows, nevertheless, his acquaintance with al-Kindī's formula, when he gives the following definition of *ibdāʿ* in his *Treatise of Definitions* (in *Tisʿ Rasā'il*, Istanbul, 1928, p. 69): '*Ibdāʿ* has two meanings: firstly, making existent a thing from nothing . . . (*ta'yīsu* [read so; ed. *ta'sīsu*] *'l-shay'i lā ʿan shay'*).' The addition: 'and not through the intermediary of something', as well as the whole of the second meaning, does not concern us.

Joseph ibn Ṣaddīq (*Microcosm*, pp. 55–56) distinguishes between *khalq* (the Hebrew version, in which the book has come down to us, has *yĕṣīrā*, which no doubt renders the original *khalq*) and *ibdāʿ* (the Arabic word is preserved in the translation). The first term denotes the composition of the elements and coming-to-be; while *ibdāʿ* is reserved in the terminology of the philosophers to the creative act of God, i.e. the bringing into existence of something

[1] *Ikhtirāʿ* does not appear in al-Kindī as a synonym of *ibdāʿ*. The fact that Israeli as well as the Ikhwān use the two synonyms together as a stereotyped formula shows that they were following an earlier usage. It is likely that al-Kindī himself used this formula in some of his lost works.

[2] Miskawayh knew the views of Galen from a polemical treatise by Alexander of Aphrodisias, who refuted Galen's thesis 'that a thing can only come into being from another thing'. This treatise is evidently identical with the treatise by Alexander: 'The refutation of the one who says that a thing can only come into being from another thing', preserved in an Arabic translation in MS. Escurial, no. 794. (It is obvious from the argument as reproduced by Miskawayh that the problems discussed in that treatise did not concern *creatio ex nihilo*, which was, of course, entirely foreign to Alexander.)

[3] For Ibn Sīnā's theories see L. Gardet, *La Pensée religieuse d'Avicenne*, Paris, 1951, pp. 62–66.

from nothing. There can be no doubt that here, as in other passages of Ibn Ṣaddīq (cf. above, p. xiii), we have a direct influence of the *Book of Definitions*.[1]

§ **46.** Definition of growth: The lengthening of the limits of bodies after they have been near to each other.

§ **47.** Definition of decrease: The nearing of the limits of bodies after they have been remote from each other.

§ **48.** Definition of locomotion: Locomotion is change in space by interval and stopping.

§ **49.** Definition of time: An extension separated by the movement of the sphere.

§ **50.** Definition of eternity: An extension separated by no movement.

§ **51.** Definition of perpetuity: Perpetuity is a perpetual extension which is not separated or interrupted.

COMMENTS

We have a number of invaluable studies on the ideas of the Islamic philosophers about time: H. A. Wolfson, *Crescas' Critique of Aristotle*, Cambridge (Mass.), 1929, pp. 638 ff.; Tj. de Boer, article 'Zamān', in *Encyclopaedia of Islam*; S. Pines, *Beiträge zur islamischen Atomenlehre*, Berlin, 1936, pp. 48 ff.; id., *Nouvelles Études sur Awḥad al-zamân Abu-l-Barakât Al-Baghdâdi*, Paris, 1955, pp. 21 ff., 63 ff. Israeli's passage is not quoted in these

§ 48. 2 *by interval and stopping*: doubtful (*cum interposicione et descensione* L *bĕ-emṣāʿiyyūth dābhār she-ḥāl lihyōth* H).

[1] I think that the conclusion of G. Vajda ('La Philosophie &c.' [cf. above, p. 21], p. 144) that here Ibn Ṣaddīq follows Ibn Sīnā has to be abandoned.

studies, although the definition which corresponds to his and is to be found in several Arabic texts is discussed. Moreover, one can find out about the Greek antecedents of this definition some details which complete and modify the result reached in these studies.

The definition recurs in various authors: Ikhwān, ii. 13 (Dieterici, *Naturanschauung*, pp. 14–15): 'It is said: Time is the number of the repeated movement of the sphere [this is the Aristotelian view]; others say it is an extension counted by the movements of the sphere (*muddatun taʿudduhā ḥarakātu'l-falak*)'; al-Tawḥīdī, *Muqābasāt*, Cairo, 1929, p. 278: 'some people say it is an extension, &c.'; al-Khuwarizmī, *The Keys of the Sciences*, ed. van Vloten, pp. 137–8: 'Time is an extension counted, i.e. measured, by movements, for instance of the celestial bodies or other moving things; according to others [al-Rāzī, see Pines, *Beiträge*, loc. cit.] *mudda* is the "absolute time" [= eternity, in the terminology of al-Rāzī] which is not counted by movement'; ʿUbayd Allāh ibn Bukhtīshūʿ, *al-Rawḍa al-Ṭibbiyya*, ed. P. Sbath, Cairo, 1927, p. 44. With the help of these parallels we can reconstruct the Arabic original of Israeli as: *ḥaddu'l-zamān*: *muddatun tafriquhā* ['separated'; the Arabic parallels have *taʿudduhā*, 'counted'] *ḥarakatu'l-falak*.

The authors of the studies quoted above have drawn attention to the Neoplatonic parallels of the definition of time as *mudda*, 'extension' = διάστημα or διάστασις. The exact source of the definition is, however, a definition which is attributed in Greek authors to Plato. Pseudo-Plutarch, *Placita Philosophorum*, i. 21 (H. Diels, *Doxographi Graeci*, p. 318), gives as the Platonic definition of time: 'The moving image of eternity [see *Timaeus*, 37D] or the interval of the movement of the universe' (διάστημα τῆς τοῦ κόσμου κινήσεως). The Arabic translation of Qusṭā ibn Lūqā probably had: *mithālun li'l-dahri mutaḥarrikun aw muddatun li-ḥarakati'l-ʿālam* (the passage is corrupt in the edition of Badawī). The same definition is attributed to Plato by Galen, according to the testimony of Alexander, contained in his refutation of Galen's views on space and time, which is lost in Greek, but is quoted after an Arabic translation (not known in its entirety) by Yaḥyā ibn ʿAdī (see Pines, *Beiträge*, p. 75): Alexander refutes Galen's view 'according to which time is eternal in itself and is in no need of movement for its existence. He

(Galen) says that Plato was of the opinion, i.e. he held that time was a substance—he means by this the *mudda*—and that movement measures it and marks it off.'[1] The definition was given a Neoplatonic turn by combining it with the idea of 'eternity' (*dahr*, *αἰών*, see the studies quoted above), which appears here as a corollary of that of time. When Ibn Sīnā (*al-Shifā'*, i. 81) and al-Lawkarī (see Pines, *Nouvelles Études*, p. 63) refute an opinion according to which '*dahr* is the *mudda* of immobility, or a time not numbered by movement', they no doubt refer to the same distinction between 'time' and 'eternity' which is expressed by Israeli and is implied in the definitions of 'time' quoted above (rather than to the doctrines of al-Rāzī, as assumed by Pines).

The third definition (the Arabic term underlying 'perpetuity' was perhaps *sarmad* or *azal*) is not clear to me.

§ **52.** Definition of decision: Decision is the readiness to accept something and the interpenetration of action and will.

§ **53.** Definition of sadness: Sadness is the solicitude and the worry caused by the privation of something beloved and the absence of the object of one's desire.

§ **54.** Definition of fear: The frightening affliction of somebody.

§ **55.** Definition of creature: Creature is the coming-to-be of a thing resulting from the corruption of the form from which it comes-to-be and its change into another form; e.g. the coming-to-be of bodies of animals and plants from the four elements, resulting from the corruption of the form of the elements and its change into the form of the animal or the plant.

§ 52. 1 *decision*: doubtful (*arbitrii* L *ha-da'ath* H). 2 *and the interpenetration . . . something* (§ 53): om. H (homoioteleuton).
§ 53. 2–3 *and . . . desire* L om. H.
§ 55. 1 in L om. *vel factura* (with LAL = H).

[1] The definition is in reality Stoic and often quoted; see H. von Arnim, *Stoicorum Veterum Fragmenta*, ii. 164–5.

§ **56.** DEFINITION OF ARTIFICE: Artifice is the application of a form in the matter without the corruption of the matter and of the form of the thing formed in the matter after the artificer finishes his work; as for instance the form of the ring or the *dirham* which obtains in silver without the corruption of the silver or the loss of its nature and essence; nor is the form of the ring and the *dirham* corrupted after the artificer has finished his work. Similarly, the form of the *dīnār* and the bracelet and other forms made of gold are obtained without the corruption of the gold or the loss of its essence and nature, and the form of the *dīnār*, and the other forms, are not corrupted when the artificer rests.

§ **57.** DEFINITION OF OPERATION: In an 'operation' the form of the thing, which is its object, disappears when the operator rests; e.g. walking, which disappears and is deprived and of which no trace remains when the walker rests; similarly speech, which disappears and is corrupted when the speaker rests.

If someone contradicts us and says: Why do you say that the form of speech disappears and no trace of it is left when the speaker rests, while we find that everything said is deposited in the heart of the listeners, and everything written is deposited in the writing?—we answer: Your objection is wrong, since that which remains in the heart of the listeners is only the form of the account and not the form of the speech; the speech is interrupted, finished, and is not heard after the speaker has rested; and similarly, the walk is interrupted, destroyed, and finished after the walker has rested. On account of this the walker, if he is very tired and interrupts his walk and rests, finds rest from his tiredness; if the form of the walk was fixed and remained after the walker's rest, the fatigue would also be fixed and would remain after the walker's rest; experience, however, shows the contrary.

COMMENTS

Israeli distinguishes three kinds of action: the natural (§ 55) and the artificial (§ 56)—both of which produce some lasting result—and finally the 'operation' (§ 57), which leaves no trace after its cessation. The distinction between actions which have lasting

§ 56. 4, 6 *dirham*: *denarii* L *dīnār* H. 5 *silver*: in L omit full-stop after *argenti*. 7, 10 *dīnār* H *drachmae* L. 7–8 *and the bracelet* L om. H.

results (*ʿamal*) and those which have none (*fiʿl*) goes back to al-Kindī; see the last paragraph of the text translated above, p. 69, and al-Kindī, p. 179: ' "work" (*ʿamal*): a trace which remains after the cessation of the movement of the agent.'

A parallel passage by Israeli is to be found in *BEl.*, p. 8:

Things are generated in three ways: In the way (1) of 'innovation', (2) of nature, and (3) of artifice. (1) By 'innovation' existing things are generated from non-existing; this is peculiar to the action of the Creator. (2) Those things which are generated by nature lose their form, change, and are transformed from their being into the form of those things which are generated from them; as, for instance, food, which changes and is transformed into the form of flesh, bone, &c. (3) Artifice gives the things an accidental and foreign form; at the same time they do not lose their natural form and character; for instance silver, which acquires the form of the ring, without losing the form and the character of silver.

This text distinguishes between 'innovation' and natural creation (see above, Comments on § 45) and between these and artificial generation; it does not mention the distinction between action and 'operation'.

End of the Collections of Isaac the Physician Son of Solomon the Israelite concerning the Definitions of Things and the Difference between Description and Definition

Colophon. The physician . . . Solomon H om. L. *definition*: H adds: *which I have written for myself, I Isaac the son of Solomon the priest, the Spaniard, may God grant me to study it, I, my children, and the children of my children, to the last generation, Amen.*

II

THE BOOK OF SUBSTANCES

PRELIMINARY NOTE

THE existence of the *Book of Substances* and a very general account of its contents have been known for some time. The first mention of it occurs as early as 1876, in A. Neubauer's account of the Second Firkovitch Collection of Hebrew and Judeo-Arabic manuscripts, mostly derived from the Genizah, in which he mentions 'Isaac Israeli's unknown treatise, called *Kitāb al-Jawāhir*' (*Oxford University Gazette*, vii, 1876–7, 100). This short allusion, however, passed unnoticed. The text to which Neubauer referred is no doubt that contained in a fragment of three folios numbered 2nd Firk. coll., hebr.-arab. nova, no. 1243; the identification of the fragment was a simple matter, as it included the title-page which gives the full title and the author's name. In 1929 A. Borisov succeeded in finding, among the fragments of the same collection, a number of further folios from the same manuscript. Borisov reported his discovery in an article which constitutes something of a literary problem. Offprints of the article came into the possession of various scholars, but the identity of the periodical to which it belongs cannot be established. In a bibliographical survey, incorporated in *Revue des études islamiques*, 1936: 'Abstracta Islamica', p. 318, it is stated that the article appeared in *Bibliografia Vostoka*, viii–ix (1936), 621–8; but an examination of that periodical showed that it contained no such article, either on the pages given in the reference or elsewhere. It is not improbable that the offprints were made from sheets destined for some publication which never actually appeared.[1]

[1] The article of Borisov, written in English, bears the title 'Some new fragments of Isaak Israeli's works'. The article consists of a short introduction about Israeli, and of three chapters. (i) Deals with the *Book of Substances*, and contains a short analysis of its system of emanation. (The analysis was reprinted in *Journal of Jewish Studies*, 1955, pp. 137–8, as at that time the full text of the extant fragments was not yet available; the edition of the full text and the present translation make it superfluous to reprint it again.) (ii) Contains the edition of the fragment

The pressmark of the large fragment discovered by Borisov is 2nd Firk. coll., hebr.-arab. nova, no. 1197. In 1949 I found two folios of the treatise among the Genizah fragments of the British Museum, Or. 5564 B, fols. 8–9. The text contained in these folios runs parallel with part of the text of the Leningrad manuscript.

At the request of the Institute of Jewish Studies, Manchester, photographs of the Leningrad manuscript were obtained by the John Rylands Library and the Manchester Central Library, and the text of the fragments of the *Book of Substances* was published, on the basis of the Leningrad and British Museum manuscripts, in the *Journal of Jewish Studies*, vii (1956), 13–29. For the problems connected with the original text the reader is referred to that publication.

The text as preserved by these fragments is incomplete and, moreover, does not run in an uninterrupted sequence. We have altogether eight disconnected pieces, shorter or longer.

(i) Leningrad, fol. 1 (title-page and beginning).
lacuna.
(ii) Len., fol. 17.
lacuna.
(iii) Len., fol. 12.
lacuna.
(iv) Len., fols. 4–11 (partly identical with Brit. Mus.).
lacuna.
(v) Len., fols. 2–3.
lacuna.
(vi) Len., fol. 14.
lacuna.
(vii) Len., fols. 15–16.
lacuna of one folio (which can be filled with the help of the parallel text in Ibn Ḥasdāy).
(viii) Len., fol. 18.

of the Arabic original of the *Book on Spirit and Soul* discovered by Borisov; see below, p. 106. As explained there, the text was reprinted in my edition of the Hebrew version of the book. (iii) Announces the discovery of a fragmentary manuscript of a second Hebrew translation of the *Book of Definitions*, cf. above, p. 7.

The order of the various fragments as given in the list is partly uncertain. The following are the firmly established points:

(i) is the beginning of the book;
(vii) and (viii) are consecutive (with a short lacuna between them);
(iv) is posterior to (iii), as fol. 4^{v}, 'as we have promised', refers back to 3^{r}, 'we shall quote the necessary proofs later'.
(v) is posterior to (iii), as fol. 12^{r}, 'we have established', refers back to 2^{r}.

For the rest, the order adopted above is only conjectural.

Both the Leningrad and the British Museum manuscripts are written in Hebrew characters; but, as I have shown in the publication referred to above, they most probably go back to manuscripts written in Arabic script; it is very likely that Israeli originally published the book in Arabic characters. The book is on general, not specifically Jewish, philosophy, and the author wrote it for the general, not specifically Jewish, public interested in philosophy. (We may assume that Israeli published his works on general philosophy in Arabic characters (cf. also above, p. 4), but works like the *Book on Spirit and Soul*—collecting biblical passages, quoted in Hebrew, to support certain philosophical doctrines—which was evidently meant for a Jewish public, in Hebrew characters.)

TRANSLATION OF THE FRAGMENTS

FRAGMENT I

[*fol.* 1^{r}] *The Book of Substances collected from the Sayings and Texts of the Ancients by the Accomplished Master the Physician Abū Yaʿqūb Isaac the Son of Solomon, the Israelite, God's Mercy and Blessing upon him*

[*fol.* 1^{v}] In the name of God the Merciful and Compassionate. O God assist us.

A question put by a certain dialectician, explained and clarified by the physician Isaac, son of Solomon, the Israelite, concerning the substance which is generic in reality and that which is generic by way of metaphor and relation. This is the book better known as the Book of Substances.

The questioner asked: Why did the philosopher call the simple substance genus of the compound substance, while both of them are species of the first substance which is the genus of genera? Now he has postulated in the book of logic that species are divided under their genera in an equal way, without one preceding the other, or having precedence over the other in receiving the name of the genus exclusively, or being superior to the other, or its being said . . .

FRAGMENT II

. . . [*fol.* 17^{r}] and does not want any of this, I say that it is affected by alteration, because impotence is the absence of power, and if you say power and no power, will and no will, this implies alteration, in respect of quality. We say to him: You have made an absurd objection and your assertion is erroneous on three counts.

Firstly, you have compared an alteration of action, affecting the object of the action, and an essential alteration, affecting the agent. This is a quite manifest error, because an alteration of action which affects the object of an action is the movement of the object of action and its motion and its passing from potentiality to actuality, while an alteration affecting an agent is the motion of its essence to the opposite of its condition; e.g. its motion from being 'non-active', or 'impotent', or 'non-willing' to being active, potent, and willing, or from the existence of these things to their absence and privation. If the agent is always potent, willing, and active, alteration and change cease and impotence is altogether absent. It is established [*fol.* 17^{v}] that if the object of the action does not pass from potentiality to actuality at all times, this is not due to the impotence of the agent to effect this, but to the impossibility of its passing from potentiality to actuality except at the time when it does pass. For example, there are many generations and ancestors between Adam and Moses, peace be upon them, but the fact that it was impossible for Moses, peace be upon him, to appear at the time of Adam is not due to the impotence of the Creator to achieve that, but to the fact that such a thing would not belong to wisdom but to absurdity, as the only alternative to his appearance after the passing of the generations and ancestors between them would be for this to happen by the way of 'innovation' and 'making-anew' [creation from nothing], which would abolish natural procreation, and some of the characteristics and effects of wisdom would disappear.

Secondly, the power of the Creator, may He be exalted, is infinite and its scope cannot be comprehended. The whole of an infinite thing cannot pass into actuality, as an infinite thing cannot pass into actuality in a finite time, because . . .

FRAGMENT III

. . . [*fol.* 2r] Its light is the least bright and that farthest removed from spirituality, because it is at the farthest distance from the true light and pure brilliance, as it merely receives its light from the vegetative soul. For this reason its light is weak and its powers are dispersed and the matter which carries it acquires bodily shape and receives length, width, and depth. It executes the perfect and simple circular movement. For this reason the philosopher says that the word 'nature' has various meanings. It is applied to the sphere and the other heavenly bodies, as they are a fifth nature, affecting coming-to-be and passing-away; as the philosopher has said: 'Nature' is the beginning of movement and rest, meaning by movement coming-to-be, and by rest passing-away. 'Nature' is also applied to the qualities, viz. warmth, coldness, moisture, and dryness, because these are the qualities and simple natures of things. For this reason everything possessing nature is either warm, or cold, or moist, or dry. 'Nature' is also applied to the [*fol.* 2v] elements, viz. fire, air, water, and earth, because these are the natures and elements of things. It is also applied to the mixtures of the bodies, composed of the elements, viz. the bodies of animals and plants. 'Nature' in reality, however, is the spheric power appointed by its Creator to influence coming-to-be and passing-away.

Someone may object and say: What is the proof to show that the first created things are two simple substances and that the intellect is brought into being from them? We answer: Indeed, you have asked a question which ought not to be neglected, even without your asking. Nevertheless, we prefer to postpone the answer for the present, until we finish the subject which we have begun; after that, we shall quote the necessary proofs, which are clear and which do not come under the head of probability or rhetorical conviction, but under the head of necessity and compulsion.

We have explained and made clear that the form of nature and its specificality which establishes [*fol.* 3r] its essence is brought into being from the shade of the vegetative soul and its ray. The form of the vegetative soul and its specificality is brought into being from the shade of the animal soul and its ray. The form of the animal soul and its specificality is brought into being from the shade of the rational soul. The form of the rational soul is brought into being from the shade of the intellect. Thus it is evident that the ray and shade of the intellect are the specificality of the rational soul, the ray and shade of the rational soul are the specificality of the animal soul, the ray and shade of the animal soul are the specificality of the vegetative soul, the ray and shade of the vegetative soul are the specificality of nature. This being so, the intellect is the specificality of all substances, and the form which establishes their essence, as its ray and light, which emanate from its shade, are the fountain of their substantiality and the root of their forms and specificality.

Someone may say: Why do you not add that the power and the will are the specificality of all substances, as it is the power and the will that bring into being wisdom, which is the form and specificality of the intellect and that which perfects its essence? The answer is as follows: You have made an absurd objection, because you have compared an influencing and [*fol.* 3^{v}] acting thing to one substantial and essential. The light of wisdom is brought into being from the power and the will by way of influence and action, while the light which emanates from the intellect is essential and substantial, like the light and shining of the sun, which emanate from its essence and substantiality. Specific form is not brought into being from an influencing and acting thing, but from an essential one—like reason which establishes the essence of man, and which does not come from the soul in the way of influence and action, but is essential.

Having reached this point in our discourse, let us return and continue the discussion of our subject. When the nature of the sphere and the other heavenly bodies was established and they executed their perfect and simple circular movement, from their movement there came into being a warmth which combined with matter and spread out in it. Matter contracted itself at it, and the spherical power, which was appointed by its Creator for influencing coming-to-be and passing-away, accompanied it. From this there came into being the nature of the four elements, viz. fire, air, water, and earth. . . .

FRAGMENT IV

. . . [*fol.* 4^{r}] he is differentiated from 'horse' by the substantial reason which establishes his essence, and is differentiated from himself, with respect to his own various states, by his various voluntary movements, such as eating and drinking, sleeping and waking, &c. Man, while he is eating, is not the same as while he is drinking, awake not the same as asleep; but one cannot say that while he is rational he is not the same as while he is irrational, as by abolishing his rationality he is abolished altogether.

If someone says: We did not wish to contradict your statement that man is differentiated from animal by his substantiality and essence, but only wanted to make you admit that reason is an accident in the 'living being', as it can cease without the destruction of the 'living being': the proof is that the horse is a living being, but not rational—we answer as follows: The answer is the same as the one which we gave before when replying to a similar objection, saying that an accident is what perishes when separated from its substratum. Reason does not perish after being separated from its substratum, as it is identical with the rational soul, [*fol.* 4^{v}] for it exists while the latter exists and is abolished when the latter is abolished; now it is established by manifest proofs that the soul survives after its separation from its substratum—thus reason remains in existence after it is separated from its substratum.

Having reached this point in our discourse, let us return to our promise to bring a proof for the statement that the first of created things are two simple substances, out of which is established the nature of the intellect. We say as follows: This is proved by the difference in the degrees of the substances, which are either simple or compound, spiritual or corporeal. This we see by examining the actions and the properties of the substances. We find that the vegetative soul's properties are nourishment, growth, and reproduction. We then rise a step higher and find that the animal soul is of a higher degree, because, in addition to nourishment, growth, and reproduction, it also has the property of movement and sensation, [*fol.* 5^{r}] by which it is distinguished from the vegetative soul. We then rise another step upwards and find that the rational soul is higher and nobler, because in addition to growth, reproduction, sensation, and movement it also has the property of reason, investigation, and discrimination, by which it is distinguished from the two dull souls. We then rise a third step upwards and find no other condition towards which we could rise except the perfect wisdom, pure science, and unmixed knowledge which, we find, is the property of the intellect, as it is impossible that intellect should exist except in wisdom, or that wisdom should be created except in intellect, the existence of one implying that of the other, the abolition of one that of the other. This being so, it is clear that the intellect is the most noble of all substances, of the highest degree and loftiest rank, and the one nearest to 'innovation' and 'making-anew' [creation from nothing] and most particularly affected by the action, without mediation, of the power and the will—as the perfect wisdom, pure knowledge, and true science is its form and the perfection of its substantiality. Having [*fol.* 5^{v}] found that this is so, we inquire about the intellect and find that it must be one of the following three things: a material substance, or a formal substance, or a substance composed of matter and form; as the intellect has no fourth possibility in the way of substance in addition to the above-mentioned. If someone thinks that it is a material substance we shall easily show his error. Matter can be either universal and general or particular and special. If it is universal, it is the substratum for the universal forms which constitute the essence of the species, as for instance the universal substance, which is one in number, exists by itself, and is the substratum for diversity absolutely. If it is particular, it is the substratum for a special form which constitutes the essence of a particular single species, as for instance 'living being', which receives reason and thus constitutes the essence of man. If the intellect were matter, it would receive a certain form and constitute the essence of a certain species; but we do not find that the intellect has a form for which it serves as a substratum in order to constitute [*fol.* 6^{r}] the essence of a certain species; thus the intellect is not a material substance.

If the opponent says: Why do you deny that wisdom is a form for which the intellect serves as substratum, so that the rational soul arises from both of them?—we say to him: If this were so, wisdom would be the form of the rational soul, constituting its essence, and the intellect would be its matter. Wisdom being the form, and the intellect the matter, of the soul, it would follow that wisdom was alien to the intellect, as every form which is in matter is alien to its matter and the latter can exist without it. For example reason, which is predicated of 'living being'; 'living being' exists also without reason, because the horse and the other species of 'living being' are alive, but have no reason. Thus it is clear that wisdom, if it is a form constituting the essence of the intellect, is alien to the latter. If it is alien to the intellect, it can be absent from it; if it is absent, the intellect lacks knowledge and cognition and turns into ignorance, as wisdom is the true knowledge of the eternal, everlasting things and acting [*fol.* 6^{v}] according to knowledge; if the intellect lacks wisdom, it lacks knowledge and cognition and turns into ignorance. Thus it is clear that wisdom is not the form of the soul, nor is the intellect its material substance.

If someone says: What do you say about the following statement? Ignorance is a form, and when it is in the intellect as in a substratum, the nature of the rational soul is established; the proof for this is that we find that the soul is ignorant, and acquires knowledge when it is taught—we answer: The objection is wrong, on three counts. Firstly, because ignorance has no form or existence; it cannot be a thing's form and cannot be predicated of a thing, because it is privation, and privation has no existence or form; for instance blindness, which has no form or existence, because it is the privation of sight. Similarly, darkness has no form or existence, because it is the privation of light. The proof is that if someone were sitting during the night, a shining candle before him, and then [*fol.* 7^r] the candle were taken away, he would not find that anything happened beyond the privation of light. In the same way, if water got into someone's eyes, he would not find that anything happened beyond the privation of his sight. If he says: Is not the entrance of water something which exists?—we answer: Its entrance is not a form for the privation of sight, but one of the causes that bring it about; as for blindness, it has no form, because it is the privation of sight. Secondly, if ignorance were a substantial form, it would preserve the nature of the matter which serves it as a substratum and perfect the substantiality of that for which it is the form. For instance, the light of the sun, which preserves the nature of the air and perfects its light and brilliance; or the soul, which preserves the nature of the body and perfects the form and substantiality of man. Ignorance, however, does not preserve the nature of the intellect and does not perfect the form and the substantiality of the soul, as discrimination, investigation, and the knowledge of the truths of things belong to the substantiality of the soul, while ignorance is the privation of all these. Thirdly, if ignorance were [*fol.* 7^v] the substantial form of the soul, then man, if ignorance were absent from him, would be deprived of soul and an animal would claim soul with better right, because ignorance belongs more properly to it. Thus it is clear that the intellect is neither the material nor the formal substance of the soul, because if the intellect were the form of the soul, it could not be absent from it, as the absence of the substantial form implies the destruction of the thing of which it is the form; as for instance reason, the abolishing of which implies abolishing man. The soul, however, is not like that, because we see that it is always ignorant and deprived of intellect until it learns and acquires knowledge. Thus the intellect is in it a final form (which, through training and teaching, makes what is potentially present in it pass into actuality), not a substantial form; as we find it in the soul in potentiality, before it passes into actuality. It is like the light of the sun which perfects the air by making it brilliant and perfect light. Thus the intellect is [*fol.* 8r] a final, not a substantial, form in the soul.

Thus it is manifest that the intellect is neither the material nor the formal substance of the soul; it only remains, therefore, to say that it is a substance composed of matter and form, as the division of the intellect has been carried out and no fourth possibility remains. As the intellect is composed of matter and form, it is clear that matter and form precede it by nature; thus it is clear and manifest that the first of created things are two simple substances and that the intellect is composed of them.

Having reached this point in our discourse and having accomplished our aim, which was to answer our opponent and prove that the first of created things are two simple substances, let us return to the subject which we had promised to clarify, viz. the reasons for the difference between the substances and for one taking precedence of another in their spirituality and degree. I say that this is for three reasons. Firstly, the quality of the emanation of the light which is created from the power and the will [*fol.* 8v]. Secondly, the quality of the reception of the light by one substance from the other. Thirdly, the difference existing between that which bestows and that which is bestowed, the bestowing and the reception of the bestowal. Regarding the quality of the emanation of the light from the power and the will, we have already made it clear that its beginning is different from its end, and the middle from both extremes, and this for the following reason: when its beginning emanated from the power and the will, it met no shade or darkness to make it dim and coarse—while its end met various imperfections and obscurities which made it dim and coarse; the middle partook of both extremes.

If someone objects and says: Is the Creator, may He be exalted, unable to create a light which has equal power, so that its beginning should be equal to its end and middle its to its extremes?—we answer: We have answered a similar question above; that answer is quite satisfactory, but we add a further explanation [*fol.* 9r] here, as follows: All things come-to-be according to the ability of matter to be affected by action, not according to the power of their Creator and Maker. It is impossible that the light which issues from the shade of a substance should be in its entirety similar to the light which emanates from the power and the will without shade and dimness—except if it is by way of 'innovation' and 'making-anew' [creation from nothing]; but in that case all created things would be the same, the distinction between the general and the particular would be abolished, wisdom would miss the substances which are below the intellect, the sphere and its movement would be lacking, coming-to-be and passing-away, mixing and being mixed, junction and composition, justice and equity, truth and falsehood, reward and punishment would cease. It is clear that what the Creator, may He be exalted, does is the most faultless and excellent, may our Lord and Creator be praised.

The difference between the substances arising from the quality of their reception of the light is of more than one kind. Some of the substances themselves receive the light from the power and the will without mediation, [*fol.* 9v] such as the intellect which itself receives the light of wisdom without the mediation of another substance between itself and wisdom (on account of which wisdom is its essence and substantiality). Others receive the light through one intermediary, or two, or three, or more. For instance, the rational soul receives the light of wisdom through the single intermediary of the intellect; the animal soul receives it through the intermediaries of the ⟨rational soul and the intellect; the vegetative soul receives it through the intermediaries of the⟩ animal and rational souls and the intellect; nature receives it through the intermediaries of the two dull souls and the substances above them; corporeal matter and corporeal form, by which I mean the elements and their qualities, receive it through the intermediaries of nature and the substances above it. This being so, I say that the intellect, as it receives the light of wisdom by itself without mediation, is altogether deprived of ignorance, and its knowledge is perfect and its cognition pure and unmixed, for its light and brilliance are also [*fol.* 10r] the same as they came forth from the power and the will, since no shadow or darkness intervened to dim them; on account of which it beholds the truth of the knowledge of the eternal and everlasting things. The rational soul, since it derives its light through the mediation of the shade and the shadow of the intellect, is coarse, affected by ignorance, and in need of instruction and training in order that that which it has potentially should pass into actuality. The animal soul, since it receives its light from the rational soul, has even more shadow and dimness, lacks investigation and discrimination, and is in need of the bodily senses, on account of which it has estimation and imagination, as it is overcome (?) ⟨. . .⟩ the senses not towards (?) the intellect. The vegetative soul, since it receives its light from the animal soul, has more shadow and dimness than the other souls and lacks psychical sensation and only has natural sensation, by which I mean the sensation of the reproductive desire; [*fol.* 10v] for this reason it is heavy and keeps to its place on the surface of the earth. Nature, since it is at a great distance from the true light and the unmixed brilliance, on account of the numerous intermediaries between them, has heavy shadow and darkness, assumes bodily shape and is delimited, and executes the perfect, viz. circular, movement and is confined to the action of coming-to-be and passing-away—we have already referred to the saying of the philosopher: Nature is the principle of movement and rest. The elements and their qualities, as they receive their light from the shade of corporeal nature, are mere shadow and unmixed darkness, are affected by mixing and being mixed, coming-to-be and passing-away; out of them the compound bodies come-to-be. The bodies composed of them lack action and influence and are organs and instruments for the souls which are attached to them and which act in each one according to what its nature is and bring that which belongs to its essence from potentiality [*fol.* 11r] to actuality. A body to which the rational soul is attached becomes rational, discriminating, and investigating. A body to which the animal soul is attached is mobile and has sensation; one to which the vegetative soul is attached takes food, grows, and reproduces itself.

If someone says: Has not rational man movement, sensation, and reproduction as well?—we answer: We have said above that the rational soul derives the light from the intellect and passes it on to the animal soul, the animal soul derives it from the rational soul and passes it on to the vegetative soul, the vegetative soul derives it from the animal soul and passes it on to nature. This being so, and the rational soul desiring to be attached to bodies in order to manifest the power which is in its essence and which it derived from the intellect, it was in need of the faculties of sensation; it moved the animal soul [*fol.* 11v] to attach itself to bodies so that its movement and sensation might appear in them. When the animal soul wanted to do so, it was in need of the faculties of feeding, growing, and reproduction so as to replace that which bodies continually lose through movement; it moved the vegetative soul to attach itself also to bodies and make growth and reproduction appear in them. Having this intention, it was in need of natural faculties, i.e. the faculty of taking in, by which it takes in food to every part of the body, of retention, digestion, and excretion, by which it excretes the remains of the food from the parts of the body. It moved nature to attach itself to bodies and bring forth the natural faculties which belong to its essence. Having this intention, nature was in need of warmth . . .

FRAGMENT V

. . . [*fol.* 12^{r}] from what precedes that the vegetative soul is the specificality of trees and plants, as their form which separates them from other things is perfected by growth and procreation; that the animal soul is the specificality of living beings, as the form of all living beings is perfected by movement and sensation; that the rational soul is the specificality of man, as his form and specificality is perfected by reason and discrimination. We have also explained that it is the intellect that gives to all these substances their substantial form which is their specificality and perfection; it also became clear that it is these substances that perfect the genera of the animals and plants, as they are their substantial forms and the perfection of their specificality. This being so, it is clear that the intellect is the specificality of all things; on account of which the philosopher has defined the intellect as the specificality of the things, meaning to inform us that the specificality of the things is found in it in a simple, not compound, manner. For this reason one sees things in sleep as in a simple form without [*fol.* 12^{v}] matter and without organs because one sees the colours without the eye, one hears the sounds without the ear, and perceives things without the senses; this is the manner of the angels. For this reason the intellect when it wants to know its objects has recourse to its own essence and finds its contents to be spiritual and simple. It is clear from what we have said before that the sphere and the substances above it are intelligibilia of the Creator, may He be exalted, as they are generated from the power and the will without the mediation of any agent except the Creator, may He be exalted; while the compound and sensible bodies under the sphere are made by nature. On account of this the higher substances are firm, lasting, and affected perpetually by action, as their agent affecting them, the Creator, may He be exalted, is acting perpetually and in acting is in no need of things outside Him; while the compound corporeal substances are subject to dissolution and disappearance and their action is deficient—because the agent affecting them is deficient in acting and in its action is in need of things outside itself . . .

FRAGMENT VI

. . . [*fol.* 14^{r}] each of the intermediaries and things which are caused partakes of the two extremities according to its nearness or remoteness from the first cause. The nearer one of them is to the first perfect cause, the pure brilliance and the perfect beauty, the greater is its light and brilliance, the nearer it is to perfection, the less is its movement and the more its rest, as it can reach its goal and perfection from a place near. The remoter one of them is from the first cause and the perfect beauty, the less is its light and the more its shadow and ignorance, the stronger its movement of search, as it has to reach its goal from a very remote place. On account of this, that which is caused by the first perfect cause has, of all caused things, the least movement and trouble and the most rest, because of its nearness to its goal and perfection; its Maker's generosity and bestowal are perpetual, as He has no need of others, and want and dependence are absent from Him. Because of this, that which is caused by Him perceives the objects of its knowledge by its essence immediately without [*fol.* 14ᵛ] the help of anything outside itself. I mean to say that in order to know the objects of its knowledge it has no need of the help of the bodily senses nor of anything else, as it has the objects of its knowledge present in itself, and when it has recourse to its own form, i.e. the perfect wisdom, it finds the objects of its knowledge immediately, without cogitation or deliberation, in the same way as one of us knows that two is an even number or that the part is less than the whole.

If someone says: Does one of us know that the part is less than the whole before we experience it by our senses and find that the whole is divided into parts and the parts together form the whole?—we answer: What we say only refers to learned men, not to the ignorant. Man is composed of soul and body; the soul, on account of its attachment to the body, the division of its thoughts, and its preoccupation with the events that continually happen to it, forgets what it possessed; when it remembers it by learning and . . .

FRAGMENT VII

. . . [*fol.* 15ʳ] its essence. Also, if animals could do without food, growth, and decay, increase and decrease would disappear, wisdom would lack the elements, and mixing and being mixed, and would thus fall short of perfection.

Secondly, the power of the Creator, may He be exalted, is infinite, and its scope has no limits and intellects do not encompass it with their knowledge; while things which come-to-be and are made are finite by nature and are contained and delimited by the intellect. Were the coming-to-be of that which comes-to-be according to the power of the Creator, it would be infinite, just as is the power of the one Who causes it to come-to-be; this is, however, manifestly absurd and obviously wrong.

Having thus explained the opponent's argument, we return to the subject which we had discussed and say as follows: The beginning of every light which emanates from a source of light, or of a brilliance which emanates from a source of brilliance, is more powerful than its end, and the middle partakes of both extremities. On account of this the light which emanates from the shade of the intellect also has three degrees: a higher degree which is near to the horizon of the intellect and is joined [*fol.* 15^{v}] to the true light and the pure brilliance; a lower degree which is near to the horizon of the animal soul and remote from the true light and the pure brilliance; and a middle degree between them. Those rational souls, the light of which is of the higher degree, near to the horizon of the intellect, are spiritual and near to perfection, and resemble the spirituality of the angels in apprehending truth and recognizing the divinity of the Creator and acknowledging His majesty, in doing what is dictated by the intellect: thanking, praising, and sanctifying the Creator, following justice and equity, and always doing good—like the souls of the prophets, peace be upon them, and teachers guided aright. Souls the light of which is of the lower degree, remote from the true light and pure brilliance, are affected by ignorance, neglect goodness and deviate from truth, and choose bodily pleasures and vile desires. [*fol.* 16^{r}] Those the light of which is of the middle degree partake of both extremities to a greater or a lesser degree according to the deviation of their light from the middle degree towards one of the extremities. Regarding the animal soul, one which is of the higher degree, near to the horizon of the rational soul, is perfect, has perfect senses and even some understanding, thanks to which it can imitate much of what it hears and sees, according to its ability and capacity; as, for instance, the parrot, which can imitate much of what it hears and sees, according to its ability; and the monkey imitates much of what it sees according to its ability and capacity. Those souls which are of the lower degree, near the horizon of the vegetative soul, are less perfect, have coarser senses, and are nearer to the nature of plants—on account of which they are deprived of all senses except the sense of touch; as, for instance, shells, which have the sense of touch which is near to the natural sense found in plants. Plants have the natural sense, on account of which [*fol.* 16^{v}] they prefer sweet water and sweet soil and have a distaste for salty water and soil which contains natron. Those souls which are of the middle degree partake of both extremities to a greater or lesser amount according to the inclination of their light from the middle degree towards one of the extremes, or to its being right in the middle. If it keeps the middle between the two extremes in a balanced manner, it acquires, in addition to the sense of touch possessed by the shells, the sense of taste, of smell, and of hearing; but it lacks that of seeing, because that is the most refined and spiritual of all the senses. If it inclines from the middle degree towards the higher, it becomes more perfect and acquires in addition to the afore-mentioned senses that of sight; as for instance fish, which have the sense of sight, but in a weak and imperfect manner only, as they

[*Lacuna, which can be filled in with the help of the parallel text in Ibn Ḥasdāy, as follows. The parallel also shows that no more than one folio is missing.*]

perceive of colours only the white and the black, because of their lack of eyelids which prevents them from closing their eyes and collecting enough light to perceive the true shades of the colours. This is shown by the fact that if one keeps one's eyes open continuously without shutting one's eyelids, the particles of the light by the help of which one sees are divided through the force of the outside light so that one's sight becomes confused and one sees all colours as one. If the soul inclines even more towards the higher degree, its senses grow even more perfect and strong and acquire from the perfection of the senses also the faculty of swift movement—as for instance the horse and similar animals. If it inclines even more towards the higher degree, it also acquires some understanding through which it is enabled to perform human actions, such as walking and grasping—as for instance the monkey which even imitates man, in eating and sitting and other actions.

Concerning the vegetative soul—if it is of the higher degree

FRAGMENT VIII

[*fol.* 13r] near to the horizon of the animal soul, it is more brilliant, better, and more colourful and fragrant. The reason is that the vegetative soul attaches itself to bodies out of its desire to make manifest the shining colours and pleasant fragrance which are in its essence, to bring them from potentiality to actuality, and so derive pleasure from them in this world, since it does not reach the next world (as we shall explain, if God wills). This being so, it is clear that a brighter colour and a better smell in a plant indicate the power of the soul's influence upon it and its manifestation and brilliance. The opposite indicates the weakness and smallness of the soul's influence over it. Sometimes this varies and is compound in certain plants, so that they have a perfumed smell and ugly colour, or a brilliant colour but bad smell; this indicates an influence [*fol.* 13v] which is in the mean between strength and weakness. This too may vary and incline from the middle degree towards one of the extremes, according to the intermediate stages which exist between the middle degree and the extremities.

If someone contradicts us and mentions food, saying: Why is it that food does not serve as an indication of the influence of the soul upon plants in the same way as smell and colour?—we answer as follows: The reason is that the generation of the food is in most cases an action of nature, on account of which the kinds of food serve as indication of the nature of the plants and of the amount of warmth, coldness, humidity, and dryness which they have, be they simple or composite. The case is different with smells and colours, which are mostly generated through the influence of the soul, and but rarely through the action of nature; because that which belongs to the influence of nature, and for this reason becomes . . .

COMMENTS

For the understanding of the *Book of Substances* it is necessary to give a short account of the text which I propose to call 'Ibn Ḥasdāy's Neoplatonist', which was one of the main sources of Israeli's philosophy. Isolated traces of this text were already encountered in the *Book of Definitions* (§§ 2 and 5); but the *Book of Substances* in its entirety stands in the most intimate relation to that Neoplatonic treatise. The problems connected with the latter have been exhaustively dealt with in my article 'Ibn Ḥasdāy's Neoplatonist—a Neoplatonic treatise and its influence on Isaac Israeli and the longer version of the Theology of Aristotle', to be published in *Oriens*, 1959; here I confine myself to a brief description.

Abraham ibn Ḥasdāy's Hebrew book *The Prince and the Ascetic*, like the Greek *Barlaam and Joasaph*, is an adaptation of the Arabic book *Bilawhar wa-Yūdāsaf*, which goes back, as is well known, to the legend of the Buddha as it was transformed in a Middle-Persian version. In the last chapters (xxxii–xxxv) of Abraham ibn Ḥasdāy's version the ascetic gives the prince a long philosophical lesson on emanation and its various grades and on the destiny of the soul after death. It is obvious that this text, which does not occur in any other version of the story, was added by Ibn Ḥasdāy himself.

There are various passages in these chapters which occur in

Israeli's writings. In two cases Israeli expressly describes the passages in question as quotations: in the *Book on Spirit and Soul*, § 14, he names as his authority the 'philosophers' (see below, p. 113), and at the beginning of the Mantua text 'Aristotle' (see below, p. 119). In the article referred to above I tried to make out a case for the view that Ibn Ḥasdāy derived the text from a source common to himself and Israeli, rather than from Israeli. This means that he had at his disposal an Arabic treatise, ascribed to Aristotle (as is suggested by the Mantua text), which he translated into Hebrew; and that this treatise served as a source for Israeli not only in the two passages which are expressly marked as quotations but also in all the passages which are common to him and Ibn Ḥasdāy.

The *Book of Substances* has many such passages and is thus heavily indebted to the treatise of 'Ibn Ḥasdāy's Neoplatonist'. The following analysis will show that the whole of it revolves in a sense round that treatise. Partly, but to a lesser degree, it contains explanatory material for certain passages of the treatise; the greater part consists of excursuses, 'problems and solutions' occasioned by various points in the doctrine of pseudo-Aristotle.

Thus for the proper understanding of the *Book of Substances*, as well as of the *Book on Spirit and Soul* and the Mantua text, an acquaintance with Ibn Ḥasdāy's Neoplatonist is necessary. For full information the reader is referred to my article. On the other hand, the passages which have left direct traces in Israeli's writings will be quoted *in extenso* in the course of the comments. Nevertheless, I should like to give a cursory survey of them here so that the reader may be acquainted with the general outline of the Neoplatonic treatise. (It is assumed that Ibn Ḥasdāy followed the original arrangement in the order of his chapters.)

Ibn Ḥasdāy's ch. xxxii contains a general statement about the degrees of emanation which are determined by the distance of the various substances from the source of the emanation. (An excerpt from this chapter is given below, p. 102.) Ch. xxxiii, first half, contains an exposé of the process of emanation in its various degrees: matter and form, intellect, the three souls, sphere, elements. (A reconstruction of the Neoplatonist's text is given *in extenso* below, pp. 98–100.) The second half of the chapter contains an account of the different degrees of souls according to their greater or lesser participation in the light of emanation. (This is quoted *in extenso* by Israeli, see below, p. 105.) These are the sections which were used by Israeli in the *Book of Substances* (and in the Mantua text). Ch. xxxiv deals with the immortality of the soul. (A faint echo is found in the *Book on Spirit and Soul*, see below, p. 115.) Ch. xxxv describes the fate of the soul after its separation from the body (extensively used in the same treatise, see below, pp. 115–16).

We turn now to a detailed analysis of the *Book of Substances*, always keeping in mind its dependence on Ibn Ḥasdāy's Neoplatonist. As, however, we do not possess the text in its entirety, it is not always possible to discern the course of the argument.

Fragment i. By 'first substance' Israeli no doubt designates primary matter, which according to Ibn Ḥasdāy's Neoplatonist is the highest genus (*jins al-ajnās*, 'genus of genera'). Israeli quotes the philosopher, i.e. Aristotle, for the statement that simple substance (viz. the spiritual substances, intelligence, and the souls) is the genus of compound substance (viz. the corporeal substances); we may conclude that such a statement was also found in the pseudo-Aristotelian treatise in question, though it is not attested in the other extant reproductions of it. The question asked is: If both simple and compound substance are species of the first substance, how can the one be the genus of the other? None of the extant fragments contains the solution; if we are justified in taking our clue from the heading of the book, 'concerning the substance which is generic in reality and that which is generic by way of metaphor and relation', we might venture the suggestion that the answer was—only spiritual substances are substances in the proper sense of the word, while bodily substances are so called only metaphorically. This is, however, no more than a guess.

The context of the short *Fragment ii* is not certain; it may come from a general discussion of the principles of emanation. It aims at solving the problem of creation: God's decision to create involves a change in Him, viz. the change from lack of power to create to the acquisition of it. To this there are three answers: (1) The change is not in the Creator, but in the object of creation.

(For comment see Part II, below, pp. 152–3.)[1] (2) The power of the Creator is infinite. Here the fragment breaks off, so that the rest of the argument, as well as the whole of the third argument are lost.

With *Fragment iii* we are in the middle of the discussion of the process of emanation according to the doctrine of Ibn Ḥasdāy's Neoplatonist. For the understanding of Israeli's argument in this and the following fragments it is necessary to give in full the text of the Neoplatonist which forms its basis. We do not, of course, possess that text in a direct transmission, but it can be reconstructed with some degree of accuracy with the help of the various quotations from it. I have attempted such a reconstruction of the section on emanation in the article on 'Ibn Ḥasdāy's Neoplatonist' referred to above. There I have given a full account of the evidence which permits the reconstruction, and a detailed collation of the divergent authorities; here it will be sufficient to give the text as established in an eclectic manner and to refer the reader for the full evidence to that publication. (As in the last two paragraphs the divergence of the various versions does not allow the reconstruction of the original text, I have reproduced the different versions in parallel columns, omitting, however, various obvious interpolations in the different versions.)[2]

The first created things are two simple substances: primary matter which is the substratum for everything, i.e. the first hylic matter which is the substratum for all forms, and is called by the philosophers the genus of genera; and form which precedes that which is found with it, i.e. the perfect wisdom, by the conjunction of which with matter the nature of the intellect came into being, so that the intellect, being composed of it and of matter, is a species of it.

After the nature of the intellect was established, a brilliant flame went forth from it and a light like the flame which goes forth from crystal and glass and the mirrors which are put in the windows of baths and houses when the ray of the sun falls upon them. From this flame arose the rational soul, the light and brilliance of which is less than the light of the intellect, because the light of the intellect is nearer to the power

[1] The argument that it is against wisdom that the whole creation should depend on God's immediate creative act recurs in fragment iv, fols. 8^v–9^r; cf. also a similar argument at the beginning of fragment vii, fol. 15^r.

[2] For the Aristotelian elements in the following account see the references contained in the footnotes to *Mant.*, §§ 1–2 (below, pp. 119–21).

and the will, without being met by the shade, cloud, and mist of darkness and being thickened and obscured by the shade. Hence the rational soul requires learning and memory, while the intellect is never affected by ignorance, because nothing intervenes between it and the power.

After the nature of the rational soul was established, another flame went forth from it and a light from which the nature of the animal soul came into being, in which the brilliance of the light is still less, because it received its light from the rational soul, not the intellect; its darkness and density are so great that learning and understanding are denied to it, and, on account of the great distance between it and the intellect, it possesses only the faculties of movement, sense-perception, and estimation.

After the nature of the animal soul was established, a flame went forth from it again, and the nature of the vegetative soul came into being. Its light is dimmer than that of the animal soul, because of the great distance between itself and the perfect light, i.e. the intellect; on account of which it became coarse and was deprived of movement and sensation and had only growth and reproduction.

(*Mantua text*)

After the nature of the vegetative soul had come into being, a radiance and splendour went forth from it like the radiance and splendour which had gone forth from the other substances, and from this the nature of the sphere came into being. Its radiance and splendour are less than the radiance of all those we have mentioned before, on account of which it is corporeal, and its motion is circular, perfect, and simple, as its Creator, blessed be He, appointed it for the sake of influencing coming-to-be and passing-away in this world.

(*Longer Theology*)

From its light nature came into being. On account of the distance of that substance from the unmixed light, it became dense and coarse and lacks the pure refinement; it acquired corporeality and is confined by circumferences and dimensions, such as length, width, and depth, and moves with a circular, simple, and fixed movement, which is the spherical movement appointed by the first Creator for the sake of coming-to-be and passing-away.

(*Ibn Ḥasdāy*)

After the nature of the vegetative soul was established, other lower natures went forth from it, such as minerals, &c.

From the motion of the sphere the warmth of fire came into being. When as a result of the motion of the sphere the nature of fire had come into being and the

(*Book on Spirit and Soul*)

As the nature of the sphere is movement, one part collided with the other, and fire came into being from its movement, and from

(*Book of Substances*)

When the nature of the spheres and the other heavenly bodies was established and they executed their perfect

(*Mantua text*)

warmth moved away from its radiance and root, it diminished and dissipated. From this the nature of air came into being. After the nature of air had come into being and after it had moved away from the root of fire, its warmth continued to diminish, dissipate, and moisten, and from this the nature of water came into being. After the nature of water had come into being and after it had moved away from the air, its warmth and moisture diminished, coldness befell it, and it lowered itself to the production of sediment, refuse, and dry mud. From this the nature of earth came into being. After the natures of the four elements which are the first roots had come into being as a result of the perfect, circular, and simple motion of the sphere, they mixed, combined, and penetrated one another. From this, combinations of coldness, warmth, dryness, and moisture, i.e. composite bodies and substances, came into being, and the natures of animals, plants, and minerals arose.

(*Book on Spirit and Soul*)

fire air, from air water, from water earth. Out of these elements the animals and the plants came-to-be.

(*Book of Substances*)

and simple circular movement, from their movement there came into being a warmth which combined with matter and spread out in it. Matter contracted itself at it, and the spherical power which was appointed by its Creator for influencing coming-to-be and passing-away accompanied it. From this there came into being the nature of the four elements, viz. fire, air, water, and earth. [Here there is a lacuna in the text.]

Fragment iii starts in the middle of the description of the sphere, corresponding to the last paragraph but one of the passage of Ibn Ḥasdāy's Neoplatonist. I think there can be no doubt that in the preceding pages, now lost, Israeli quoted and discussed the whole passage of the Neoplatonist on the process of emanation. This is strikingly confirmed by the next paragraph of the fragment: 'Someone may object and say: What is the proof that the first created things are two simple substances and that the intellect is brought into being from them?' This evidently refers to the opening sentence of the Neoplatonist's passage which must have occurred previously. The description of the sphere taken from the Neoplatonist is combined with definitions of nature, the sphere being identified by Israeli with nature: cf. the Comments on *BDef.*, § 9. The definitions are apparently taken from some doxographical source enumerating the views of various ancient authorities; a similar, but not identical, passage is also found in *BDef.*, § 9.

The author interrupts the argument with a question about the proofs for the statement that primary matter and form are the first created things, but only to postpone the discussion; the promised proof is given in fragment iv (fol. 4^v).

The author then draws the conclusion that, as each of the substances figuring in the Neoplatonist's chain of emanation is the 'specificality' of the one immediately beneath it, the intellect is the 'specificality of all the substances', viz. the simple, spiritual substances of the chain of emanation. The further conclusion that the intellect is the 'specificality of all things' is drawn in fragment v.

Next a problem is resolved: why is not the hypostasis of the 'power and the will' included in the ascending series and described as the specificality of all the substances? (For the distinction between 'influence and action' of the 'power and the will' and the 'essential' causality of emanation see Part II, ch. IV.)

After these various interruptions the author returns to the text of the Neoplatonist and continues with the next phase of the emanation, viz. the generation of the elements (cf. Part II, ch. V). With this the subject of the Neoplatonist's section on emanation is exhausted and we may assume that Israeli then turned to the discussion of various problems connected with the text.

Fragment iv opens in the middle of an argument about the rational soul. The opponent obviously tried to make out a case for the view that reason is an accident, while Israeli proves that it is a substance.

At this point Israeli, fulfilling his promise (fragment iii, fol. 3^r), begins his lengthy discussion of the proof that the first of created things are two simple substances, matter and form, and the refutation of other alternative theories accounting for the mutual relations of wisdom, intellect, and soul and dispensing with matter and form as first hypostases. (The characterization of the various degrees of emanation in 4^v–5^r is derived from Ibn Ḥasdāy's Neoplatonist. For an analysis of the concept of 'Wisdom' see Part II, ch. II.)

On fol. 8^{r} another important topic is initiated—the reasons for the differences between the various substances. These reasons are said to be three in number: (1) the quality of the emanation of the light; (2) the quality of the reception of the light by the various substances; (3) the difference between that which bestows the emanation and that which receives it. (1) is discussed on fols. 8^{v}–9^{r}. For the differences in the quality of the light at the various levels of emanation the author refers to a previous passage where he had said about the light that 'its beginning is different from its end, and the middle from both extremes'. The idea of the light gradually diminishing as it passes downwards through the degrees of the emanation underlies the whole of the Neoplatonist's section on emanation. Moreover, a general statement announcing the principle of gradation was probably placed by the Neoplatonist at the beginning of his treatise. At least Ibn Ḥasdāy starts his excursus with such a statement (ch. xxxii):

> The purity or the coarseness of every substance is according to its nearness to, or its remoteness from, the root. The nearer a substance is to the root and the source, the power and the will, the more brilliant and the more pure it is and the greater right it has to the name of spirituality as compared with a substance more remote from that place. The greater its remoteness, the weaker and the darker it becomes, the more remote from the spirituality of the intellect and the nearer to absolute corporeality.

A few examples are given, from the realm of the sublunar world, in order to serve as analogies for the spiritual world. Israeli's formulation of the principle does not, however, coincide with the above passage, but corresponds literally with another passage, at the beginning of a section (Ibn Ḥasdāy, ch. xxxiii, second half) where the principle is more particularly applied to the different degrees of spirituality possessed by the various souls. The whole section is reproduced by Israeli in fragments vii and viii of the present book, and the sentence in question does in fact recur there (fragment vii, fol. 15^{r}). One might then take the present reference as alluding to that passage and deduce that what we call fragment vii must come before the present fragment. But I think it more likely that Israeli dealt with the principle of gradation in a previous, now lost, passage of the book, and on that occasion used the same formula. My main reason is that while the section in ch. xxxiii, reproduced in fragment vii, speaks of a special application of the principle, in the present context what is in question is the general principle as such and the reference is more likely to be to another general argument. The brief treatment of (1)—consisting of no more than a reference to a previous passage of the book—is rounded off by the rebuttal of the objection: why did not God create an unvarying light?[1] Reason (2) is discussed on fols. 9^r–11^v;[2] the text breaks off in the middle of an argument; thus (3) is missing altogether.

Fragments v and *vi* both deal with problems connected with the intellect. I must admit that there is no cogent reason for arranging the order of the fragments as I have done; one could, for instance, put v and vi before iv, assuming that the author, after having reproduced in full the section of the Neoplatonist on emanation, first discussed problems connected with the intellect (v–vi), then problems connected with the rational soul (ending with the opening lines of iv), and finally returned to the postponed discussion of matter and form and the reasons for the gradation of the emanation (the rest of iv). I have assumed that the problems of the intellect were treated after the more general problems of matter and form and of gradation. Altogether, we have not enough evidence to reconstruct with any certainty the course which the argument took in the book, so that the arrangement of the fragments, hypothetical in any case, is not of great importance.

In fragment v, Israeli, pursuing an argument in fragment iii (fol. 3^r), where it was established that the intellect is the specificality of 'all the substances'—i.e. evidently the spiritual substances—makes a further step and states that the intellect is the specificality 'of all things', i.e. of corporeal as well as spiritual substances. The definition of the intellect as the 'specificality of all things' comes, as we have seen (see Comments on *BDef.*, § 4, above, pp. 37–38), from al-Kindī. Here Israeli, on the one hand,

[1] Here Israeli repeats the argument with which he had 'answered a similar question above' (in fragment ii); cf. above, p. 98, n. 1.

[2] The characterization of the various degrees of emanation again follows closely the text of Ibn Ḥasdāy's Neoplatonist.

combines this definition with the system of Ibn Ḥasdāy's Neoplatonist, and, on the other hand, explains the different relations of the intellect to spiritual and to corporeal substances. An argument is initiated to show that the intellect, when it wants to know its object, has recourse to its own essence and finds its contents to be spiritual and simple (cf. *BDef.*, § 4); it is, however, interrupted by the lacuna in the text. Fragment vi has a related argument. It explains that the nearer a substance is to the first cause, the more perfect it is (cf. the Comments on fragment iv); and therefore the first caused substance, viz. the intellect, is the most perfect substance and derives its knowledge from itself. The problem why some intellects are imperfect is solved by reference to their association, through their souls, with the bodies, through the influence of which they forget their original perfect knowledge and are in need of ἀνάμνησις. (The whole fragment may have stood in a context in which Israeli discussed the statement of Ibn Ḥasdāy's Neoplatonist that 'the intellect is in no need of instruction'.)

Fragments vii and *viii* belong together. The text begins in the middle of an answer to a problem, which seems to be again: why could God not make the various kinds of being of an equal perfection (cf. fragment iv, fols. 8^v–9^r)?[1] It is impossible to guess the context in which this argument stood; I have put these fragments after those connected with the Neoplatonist's exposé of emanation, because according to the sequence of the chapters in Ibn Ḥasdāy's excursus, the long section on the degrees of the various souls, the textual citation of which fills the greater part of the fragments, comes after the section concerning emanation. The sentence which introduces the quotation: 'Having thus explained the opponent's argument, we return to the subject which we had discussed and say as follows', seems to indicate that after long excursions the author is returning to the text which serves as his main guide; and if we may rely on Ibn Ḥasdāy's having faithfully retained the order of the Neoplatonist's argument, we may assume that, while all the preceding fragments were centred round the exposition of the emanation (= Ibn Ḥasdāy, ch. xxxiii, first part),

[1] The argument concerning the infinity of God's power is akin to that which occurs in fragment ii, at the end.

with fragments vii–viii Israeli was starting an argument centred round the exposition of the grades of soul (= same chapter, second part).

The text itself, commencing with 'The beginning of every light', is identical with Ibn Ḥasdāy's version, and thus is to be assumed to be a textual quotation from the Neoplatonist. There is, therefore, no need to illustrate the relation of the two versions by a reproduction of that of Ibn Ḥasdāy. (The textual variants, which concern minute details only, are fully registered in the article on Ibn Ḥasdāy's Neoplatonist mentioned above, p. 95.) The quotation ends with the words 'and the extremities' on fol. 13^{v}.[1] The next paragraph contains a problem and its solution, which is, however, interrupted in the middle.

We have, of course, no means of determining the further contents of the *Book of Substances*, as, for example, how many of the other sections of the Neoplatonist were commented upon; or how much is missing from the end of the book; nor do we know whether the author ended by finally giving the answer to the problem to which, according to its opening words, the book was devoted in the first place.

[1] On fol. 13^{r} the words from 'The reason is' to 'as we shall explain if God wills' do not occur in Ibn Ḥasdāy and are evidently interpolated by Israeli. The promised argument is not found among the extant fragments; cf., however, the similar theory about the attachment of the rational soul to the bodies, fragment iv, fol. 11^{r-v}.

III

THE BOOK ON SPIRIT AND SOUL

PRELIMINARY NOTE

OUR knowledge of this text is mainly based on the Hebrew version, of which two manuscripts are known. One was discovered by M. Steinschneider in a miscellaneous manuscript in Munich (Steinschneider's Catalogue, no. 307, fols. 47 ff.; the manuscript contains philosophical texts, written by various hands of the late Middle Ages). The existence of a second manuscript was revealed by J. L. Teicher, who found the work in another philosophical miscellany in Cambridge (Add. 1858, fols. 113^{v} ff.; Spanish hand of the late Middle Ages).[1] The text was first published from the Munich manuscript by Steinschneider in the Hebrew periodical *Ha-Karmel*, 1871, pp. 400–5;[2] I have re-edited the text on the basis of both manuscripts together with the Hebrew version of the *Book of Definitions*, see above, p. 6. A small fragment of the Arabic original has been found and published by A. Borisov. As the article in which Borisov published the fragment is practically out of reach (for the reasons explained above, p. 79), I have reproduced the text as published by Borisov (together with those sentences of his account which are relevant) in the introduction to my edition of the Hebrew version.

As one moves on somewhat insecure ground, owing to the relative scarcity of the evidence, one cannot expect to be able to reach more than approximative answers to the literary problems connected with the treatise. In the Hebrew version it is headed: 'The Book on Spirit and Soul and the difference between the two.' As no such title is otherwise mentioned among Israeli's books, Steinschneider put forward the suggestion that the text was but

[1] See J. L. Teicher, 'The Latin-Hebrew School of Translators in Spain', *Homenaje a Millás-Vallicrosa*, ii, Barcelona, 1956, p. 424. Teicher's suggestion, expressed in the passage quoted, that Israeli is not the author of the treatise is entirely unfounded.

[2] A short account of the text is also to be found in his *HebrÜb.*, § 226*b*.

part of a larger book, possibly of the 'Treatise on "Let the waters bring forth abundantly" ', which was a disquisition on Gen. i. 20.[1] One could quote in support of this hypothesis a passage from Moses ibn Ezra's *al-Ḥadīqa*, p. 92,[2] which reads as follows: 'The philosopher Isaac the son of Solomon the Israelite, may he find pleasure in the sight of God, says in his treatise on "Let the waters bring forth abundantly" that it was concerning the rational soul that Abigail said to David: "The soul of my lord shall be bound in the bundle of life", expressing her wish that it should survive for ever in its eternal and everlasting world.' If this does refer, as it could, to §§ 8 and 14 in the present text, then our text would belong to the treatise on the verse of Genesis, but the biblical verse containing Abigail's words may well have been quoted by Israeli in more than one of his works; that it was a favourite *versus probans*

[1] Of this treatise a short fragment only is preserved in a Munich manuscript, ed. S. Sachs, in *Literaturblatt des Orients*, xi (1850), 168–9 = *Ha-Tĕḥiyyā*, 1850, p. 39. The problem posed is the apparent contradiction between Gen. i. 20, according to which birds were generated from the water, and ii. 19, according to which they were generated from the earth. After discussing two exegetical solutions which he found in the literature before him, Isaac proceeds with his own philosophical solution. 'Having mentioned the arguments of the disputants, we say as follows about this problem: If each of the disputants had examined the natural senses created by God in this world, knew their nature and mixture [the last words are corrupt in the original and the translation is conjectural], and weighed the passages of the Torah which caused them difficulty, they would have understood that the Creator, by saying at one place that birds were created from the water, and at the other that they were created from the air, only wanted to inform us that they are composed of both, viz. the four elements. [The next sentence is incomprehensible to me: *ū-ma she-'ārakh ōthō li-qĕṣāthām hāyā 'erekh amittī*.] A conclusive proof of this is the consideration that if a compound substance were composed of one element only, there would be no need of another element.' Here ends the fragment. The argument in fact tallies well with Israeli's manner in his other works; the closest parallel is to be found in *Mant.*, §§ 4–5. There is, of course, no indication to connect the Mantua text with the 'Treatise on "Let the waters bring forth abundantly" '. (That *BSpirit* and *Mant.* cannot both of them have formed part of the same treatise is abundantly clear from the duplication of *BSpirit*, § 11, and *Mant.*, § 1.) Another complication is that Israeli probably wrote a commentary on the account of the creation in Genesis (referred to by Abraham ibn Ezra, in his introduction to his commentary on the Pentateuch, and by David Qimḥī, in his comments on Gen. i. 2 and 10; see Fried, pp. 46–47), either identical with the treatise on Gen. i. 20 or containing similar matter. Israeli evidently had the habit of repeating the same points in various works.

[2] For the book cf. above, p. 7; the Arabic original of the passage is to be found in S. D. Sassoon, *Ohel David, Descriptive Catalogue of Hebrew and Samaritan MSS. in the Sassoon Library*, pp. 410–11.

for the survival of the soul is shown by the fact that Israeli's pupil, Dūnash ibn Tamīm, also quotes it for the same purpose in his commentary on the *Sēfer Yĕṣīrā*.[1] Thus even this passage is not conclusive;[2] nor is Steinschneider's other argument, viz. that the title does not fit the contents, as it is the first lines only that deal with the difference between the spirit and the soul. To conclude, the nature of the work cannot be ascertained with certainty.

The discovery of the second manuscript made it possible to establish a much improved Hebrew text, and in the case of the short passage which it covers, the Arabic original remedies several remaining errors of the Hebrew text. For a discussion of the textual problems the reader is referred to the introduction of my edition of the Hebrew version. I only repeat the conclusion reached there. The comparison of the Arabic fragment with the text of the Hebrew version as now established shows that one can rely much more on its trustworthiness than one might have expected on the basis of the sole Munich manuscript. This does not, however, mean that the Hebrew text does not contain various omissions, due either to the translator himself or to the archetype of the two extant manuscripts of the translation.

The Book on Spirit and Soul and the Difference between the Two, compiled by Rabbi Isaac, the Son of Solomon, known as the Israelite, the Physician, may his Soul rest in Peace

§ **1.** Isaac, the son of Solomon, the physician, says: Know that the soul is a resplendent simple substance; 'simple' means: exempt from composition and the qualities, viz. warmth, coldness, humidity, and

[1] See Vajda, *Commentaire*, cvii. 20.

[2] There is a further reference to the treatise in another work by Moses ibn Ezra (*al-Muḥāḍara wa'l-Mudhākara*, MS. Oxford 1974, fol. 140, reproduced in Steinschneider, *Cat. Libr. in Bibl. Bodl.*, col. 1116; cf. the Hebrew translation by B. Halpern, *Shīrat Yisrāēl*, Leipzig, 1924, p. 189). Ibn Ezra is refuting the thesis according to which the Messianic prophecies will only be fulfilled after the destruction of this world; he then adds: 'The philosopher Isaac, the son of Solomon, the Israelite, has refuted this view with valiant arguments in his treatise on "Let the waters bring forth abundantly".' This passage is even less conclusive than that in *al-Ḥadīqa*: on the one hand, the *Book on Spirit and Soul* does in fact deal with eschatological subjects, on the other, it contains no passage to which the reference could actually apply.

dryness, and not falling under the sense of sight. The spirit, on the other hand, is humid, and is in the cavity of the heart, on the left-hand side. The heart has two cavities, one on the right side, in which is the vital spirit, called by the philosophers 'natural warmth', which is found in animals and birds.[1]

§ **2.** The soul is divided into three parts: rational, animal, and vegetative. The intellectual soul is not found in animals, while the two others, viz. the vegetative and the sensitive, are. Only the vegetative soul is found in plants; for this reason it is said that the plants grow in soil with sweet water, but avoid salty soil, sulphurous . . . and natronic water.

§ **3.** Death is the absence of the spirit, i.e. the natural warmth, from the heart; we live through the warmth, but die of coldness.

§ **4.** The soul is a splendour, as the prophet says: 'The spirit of man is the lamp of the Lord' (Prov. xx. 27). It is in its world, i.e. above the sphere, while its faculty is attached to us, because it is not a body and its substantiality is the substance of the intellect, on account of its being a part of the intellect.

§ **5.** The intellect is a splendour, and is wisdom, discernment, and understanding. If we say wisdom, understanding, discernment, knowledge, correct thinking—they all belong to the faculty of the intellect. A proof from Scripture for its being a splendour is: 'The wise man's eyes are in his head, but the fool walketh in darkness' (Eccles. ii. 14), which shows that the intellect is light; similarly: 'They know not, neither do they understand; they walk to and fro in darkness' (Ps. lxxxii. 5).

§ **6.** If the light of the rational soul is inclined towards the highest excellence which can be reached by reason, it becomes intellectual and its excellence is according to its conjunction with that thing. If, on the other hand, it inclines towards the lower degree, like the animals, it becomes ignorant and pursues vile things.

§ **7.** The intellect is not affected by ignorance, because it derives its wisdom from its Creator, and causes it to emanate to the rational soul. The rational soul receives the emanation from the intellect and causes it to emanate to the animal soul. The animal soul receives the emanation from the rational soul and causes it to emanate to the vegetative soul.

[1] For the difference between soul and spirit cf. *BDef.*, § 8. The text of § 1 is no doubt corrupt—the 'vital spirit' of the physicians, which was identified with the 'natural warmth' of Aristotle, is always said to have its seat in both cavities of the heart (cf. the references quoted in the Comments on § 8 of *BDef.*).

The vegetative soul receives the emanation from the animal soul and causes it to emanate to the sphere. The sphere receives the emanation from the vegetative soul and causes it to emanate to the elements. The elements receive the emanation from the sphere and their power causes it to emanate to the animals and plants.

§ **8.** The intellectual soul is nobler than anything else and it is for this reason that man only, of all living beings, receives a reward, because he only, of all living, possesses this noble substance. It is on account of this that the prophet says: 'If a soul sin' (Lev. v. 15); 'If a soul commit a trespass' (verse 17); 'And when a soul offereth a meal-offering' (Lev. ii. 1). The spirit is the natural warmth which is in the heart; as the prophet says: 'Then shall the dust return to the earth as it was' (Eccles. xii. 7), i.e. the body will return to its component elements. But the soul returns upwards to the place of retribution; for this reason he says: 'and the spirit shall return unto God who gave it',[1] in order to inform those who have intelligence that the spirit returns to air, the phlegm and the humidities to water, the flesh and bones, which are earthly, to dust —as Scripture calls them 'dust'. The soul, however, is the most noble of things, and is with the angels above the sphere, as he says: 'And I will give thee a place of access among those that stand by' (Zech. iii. 7), showing that its reward is to be with the angels, as these are granted bliss by God. This happens if the soul inclines towards the intellect and towards wisdom; if, however, it inclines towards the degree of the animal soul, it deserves punishment, according to the words of Scripture: 'The soul of my lord shall be bound in the bundle of life with the Lord thy God; and the souls of thine enemies, them shall he sling out, as from the hollow of a sling' (1 Sam. xxv. 29). The wife of Nabal did not say this thing following her own reason, but following a tradition generally known amongst all the Israelites, the believers, i.e. the prophets. This establishes that reward and punishment belong to the soul; we see that Scripture says: 'The spirit passeth away and cometh not again' (Ps. lxxviii. 39)—it does not attribute reward and punishment to the spirit, but describes it as something which passes away and does not come again.

§ **9.** The ancients also compared the soul to a splendour and said as follows: God created the intellect as a splendour; when its nature and essence were established, a radiance and brilliance went forth from its

[1] In this verse Israeli obviously interprets the word *rūaḥ*, 'spirit', as standing for 'soul', as was commonly done by philosophical exegetes of the Bible. He ought, however, to have drawn attention to this, as in the same sentence he uses the word 'spirit' in the sense of 'vital spirit'.

shade like the radiance which goes forth from the shade of the glass balls and the mirrors which are set in windows of baths and houses, when the ray of the sun falls on them; from this the nature of the rational soul comes into being. Its splendour and brilliance are less than the splendour and brilliance of intellect; the reason being that the degree of intellect is intermediate between the soul and its Creator, so that the soul acquired shadow and exhaustion, i.e. darkness, as the intellect intervened between it and the light of the Creator, the absolute brilliance, i.e. the perfect wisdom and the pure brilliance. On account of this it was affected by ignorance and is in need of instruction; while the intellect is not affected by ignorance, because it is near to the wisdom, the pure brilliance and the absolute light. When the nature of the intellectual soul was established, a radiance went forth from its shade, and the nature of the animal soul came into being. On account of this it became estimative and imaginative, and does not subsist in what it is, i.e. in itself. Between it and the pure light intervene the degrees of the intellect and of the intellectual soul. Likewise a splendour went forth from the animal soul, and the nature of the vegetative soul came into being. Its splendour was further dimmed, and its movement became restricted to the movement of growth only, and it was thus deprived of locomotion, owing to the intervening degrees and its distance from the splendour. Likewise, a splendour went forth from the vegetative soul, and the essence and the nature of the sphere came into being. It was coarse and fell under the sense of sight. As the nature of the sphere is movement, one part collided with the other, and fire came into being from its movement, and from fire air, from air water, from water earth. Out of these elements came-to-be the animals and the plants.

§ **10.** Each compound returns into its components; the soul, however, does not fall under composition and under the senses, and therefore does not perish.

§ **11.** On account of this there are two kinds of action, perfect and imperfect. Perfect actions pass beyond the sphere, i.e. the everlasting sphere. These perfect actions are those which are in accordance with the demands of the intellect, while the imperfect are those which are in accordance with the demands of the animal soul. The proof is from the passage in Scripture: 'What profit hath man of all his labour wherein he laboureth under the sun?' (Eccles. i. 3). By 'under the sun' are meant the works of ignorance, such as eating, drinking, and sexual intercourse, which are the desires of the animal soul, together with the quest for eating drinking, and sexual intercourse. The noble works are the desires of the rational soul, such as worship, purity, and sanctity. Scripture compares the intellect to the angels, on account of the praise of God which it produces: 'And I will give thee a place of access among those that stand by' (Zech. iii. 7). About the imperfect one it is said: 'She is clamorous and wilful, now she is in the streets, now in the broad places' (Prov. vii. 11–12). These are the vulgar actions which remain under the sun, while the perfect actions ascend above the sphere and do not remain under the sun, as it is written: 'The fear of the Lord is clean, enduring for ever' (Ps. xix. 9). This means that the fear of the Lord, if it is pure from the ways of the hypocrites and those who think themselves pious, endures for ever, and He rewards it—as is shown by the end of the verse which says: 'The judgements of the Lord are true, and righteous altogether.' God is just in His judgement and does not allow those who labour fare like those who do not. Similarly, it is written: 'In keeping of them there is great reward. Who can discern errors, &c.' (verses 11–12).

§ 12. If someone says: this reward is given in this world, ⟨we answer that this is wrong for two reasons. The first is that this world⟩ is the opposite of the next, as this world is the place for work, the next the place for reward,[1] and it is fit that the righteous ones and the prophets should abide there, but not the sinners; as it is written: 'Your fathers, where are they? and the prophets, do they live for ever?' (Zech. i. 5)—meaning that they have been raised to a nobler state. Similarly: 'But the wicked shall be cut off from the land' (Prov. ii. 22), meaning: from the enduring 'land', i.e. the next world. Another proof is: 'The word which he commanded to a thousand generations' (Ps. cv. 8); now a generation normally lasts for forty years, as it is written: 'And saw his sons, and his sons' sons, even four generations' (Job xlii. 16), four times forty, a hundred and sixty years;[2] this can occur in the case of a righteous man, but a thousand generations is quite impossible in this world, so that it is proved that it refers to the next world.

[1] 'Place for work' and 'place for reward' are Islamic expressions for this and the next world (*dār al-'amal* and *dār al-jazā'*); see M. Gruenbaum, *Gesammelte Aufsätze zur Sprach- und Sagenkunde*, Berlin, 1901, pp. 419 ff.; I. Goldziher, in *Revue des études juives*, 1903, p. 181.

[2] The beginning of the verse, however, reads: 'And after this Job lived a hundred and forty years.' As S. J. Finn, the editor of *Ha-Karmel*, has pointed out in a footnote to Steinschneider's edition of the text, the passage seems to be quoted in Abraham ibn Ezra's commentary on Job xlii. 16 in a different form: 'Here erred Isaac the confused one, who said that a generation is thirty-five years'; this calculation conforms to the text of the Bible.

§ 13. A proof from the Torah for the existence of reward is: 'And the Lord commanded us to do all these statutes, to fear the Lord our God, for our good always, that he might preserve us alive, as at this day' (Deut. vi. 24); and also the end of the passage: 'And it shall be righteousness unto us, if we observe to do all this commandment' (verse 25), which shows that the keeping of these commandments is the good and the righteousness. If one wishes to say ⟨. . .⟩; and the explanation of righteousness in this passage is 'the good'. Another proof: 'Gather not my soul with sinners' (Ps. xxvi. 9), which refers to the resurrection. Concerning reward it is written: 'Return unto thy rest, O my soul' (Ps. cxvi. 7), referring to the bliss of the soul. There are many similar passages in Scripture: 'Keep my commandments, and live' (Prov. iv. 4; vii. 2), i.e. be blissful. Concerning punishment: 'And from the wicked their light is withholden' (Job xxxviii. 15), i.e. their bliss, which is light with the angels. There are also mentioned, in the passage: 'Then shall thy light break forth as the morning' (Isa. lviii. 8), two kinds of bliss: one which occurs without delay, the other remote. The one which occurs without delay: 'He shall satisfy thy soul in dry places' (verse 11), and: 'I will feed thee with the heritage of Jacob thy father' (verse 14); the remote one: 'And thy righteousness shall go before thee' (verse 8), meaning union with the excellent splendour.

§ 14. The philosphers compared this to a man who left his country and stayed abroad for some time. When he was near achieving his desire concerning his children and relatives and afterwards went on his way, when he was near to achieving it, he was deprived of it and remained naked in heat and cold, and hungry.[1] As it is said: 'And the souls of thine enemies, them shall he sling out, as from the hollow of a sling' (1 Sam. xxv. 29); concerning bliss: 'The soul of my lord shall be bound in the bundle of life' (ibid.).

§ 15. The work of righteous actions passes above the sphere and reaches its own world, the world of the soul being the 'coming world'. Man in this lower world is a wanderer,[2] as it is written: 'For I am a

[1] The text seems slightly corrupt, probably owing to some mistranslation. With the help of the parallel passage of Ibn Ḥasdāy (see below, p. 116), the original can be approximately reconstructed as follows: 'The philosophers compared this to a man who left his country and stayed abroad for some time. When he was near achieving his desire [to meet again] his children and relatives, having spent a long time on his way and being filled with desire to reach his home, he was deprived of it and remained naked in heat and cold, and hungry.'

[2] For the idea of the sage being a stranger in this world cf. G. Vajda, *Juda ben Nissim ibn Malka, philosophe juif marocain*, Paris, 1954, p. 11.

stranger with Thee, a sojourner, as all my fathers were' (Ps. xxxix. 12); and: 'O spare me that I may recover strength, [before I go hence]' (verse 13). A wise man is satisfied with a little of this world, rather than with much of it; may God make us one of the pious; may He do so.

The End.

COMMENTS

The arrangement of the argument in the present treatise is not conspicuous for its order or clarity, but from his other works we are used to Israeli's somewhat incoherent and rambling manner. (This quite apart from the (remote) possibility that the treatise may have been part of a larger work; see the Preliminary Note.) It seems that the main subject of the treatise is eschatology, or the problem of reward and punishment, which occupies the second half of the text. The exposé of the process of emanation (§ 9) serves as a preparation for the description of the soul's fate after death. As this exposé is one of the fundamental texts of Ibn Ḥasdāy's Neoplatonist and is repeatedly reproduced by Israeli (see *Mant.*, § 1; *BSubst.*, *passim* and Comments; *BDef.*, § 5; cf. also Part II, chs. II–V), there is no need for a repeated confrontation between its text as given by Ibn Ḥasdāy, ch. xxxiii, and our present treatise. We may draw attention to the words by which it is introduced and which characterize it as a literal quotation: 'The ancients also compared the soul to a splendour and said as follows.' In addition, we have to point out the somewhat puzzling feature that the beginning of the exposé, concerning universal matter and form, is here omitted.

The eschatological doctrines themselves are also derived from Ibn Ḥasdāy's Neoplatonist: the evil souls cannot pass beyond the sphere of fire surrounding the atmosphere, while the good souls pass to the light of the Creator. In effect, § 14, which contains a textual quotation from the Neoplatonic text, acknowledges this expressly by the words: 'The philosophers compared this, &c.' A reproduction of some sentences from Ibn Ḥasdāy's ch. xxxiv, and the whole of his ch. xxxv, alongside the corresponding passages of Israeli's treatise, will form the best commentary on the eschatology of the *Book on Spirit and Soul*.

Ibn Ḥasdāy, ch. xxxiv

The soul does not pass-away; for the passing-away can occur in three ways: firstly, by perishing . . .; secondly, by the division of that which had been united . . .; thirdly, by changing a thing into something else. . . . All these cases, however, only occur in bodies or in what exists in bodies. The soul, however, is not a body, that it should perish and disappear or that its component parts should disintegrate, nor an accident, that it should pass-away when a new thing comes-to-be in its substratum.

As the soul is not a body, it is clear that it has no sorrow, except when it is found in a body. When it is separated from the body, it becomes strong and powerful in its actions . . . Thus it has become clear that the soul, when it is separated from the body, becomes perfect, wise, brilliant, resplendent, knowing, and discriminating.

BSpirit, § 10

Each compound returns into its components; the soul, however, does not fall under composition and under the senses, and does not therefore perish.

Ibn Ḥasdāy, ch. xxxv

If the rational soul is righteous, understands the truth of things, is purified from the defilement of this world, and not soiled by its evil and blameworthy desires, but acts according to truth, it is then worthy of receiving its reward and goes to the world of the intellect and reaches the light which is created from the power, its pure brilliance and unmixed splendour and perfect wisdom, from whence it had been derived; it is then delighted by its understanding and knowledge. This delight is not one of eating, drinking, and other bodily delights, but the joy of the soul in what it sees and hears, a delight which has nothing in common with other delights except the name.

If the sinful soul is not righteous and is not cleansed from the defilement of this world and its desires which destroy every goodness, and its delights which carry with them all evil, and does not act in accordance with truth and does not understand it—it is then worthy of remaining in

BSpirit

Perfect actions pass beyond the sphere, i.e. the everlasting sphere. These perfect actions are those which are in accordance with the demands of the intellect. . . . The perfect actions ascend above the sphere and do not remain under the sun. [§ 11]

. . . Their bliss, which is light with the angels . . . Union with the excellent splendour. [§ 13]

The work of righteous actions passes above the sphere and reaches its own world. [§ 15]

Ibn Ḥasdāy, ch. xxxv

exile from the world of the intellect and removed from the light and the splendour of its Creator and His great bounty which is treasured up for such as fear Him. It remains sad and despondent and joins the fire which comes-to-be by the power of the movement of the sphere; that fire prevents it from passing to the great good—instead, it must revolve with the sphere's revolution, perplexed and full of desire, hungering and thirsting to find a way to go home to its country and return to its native place. It resembles a man who travelled away from his house, brothers, children and wife, relatives and family, and stayed abroad for a long time. When finally he was on his way back and approached his country and the goal of his desires, having passed through seas and rivers, forests and deserts, and was filled with the strongest desire to reach his home and rest in his house—obstacles were put in his way and the gates were shut and he was prevented from passing. He called, but it was of no avail, and he had to remain outside, hungry, thirsty, suffering from the heat of the day and the cold of the night, in continuous fear of the wolves, lions, and other wild beasts. He wandered about, perplexed how to find a refuge, weeping bitterly and sorrowfully bewailing the great good which he had lost and the evil which had befallen him. The soul, if this is its fate, is sufficiently punished by the everlasting fire which is its lot.

BSpirit

The philosophers compared this to a man who left his country and stayed abroad for some time. When he was near achieving his desire concerning his children and relatives and afterwards went on his way, when he was near to achieving it, he was deprived of it and remained naked in heat and cold, and hungry. [§ 14]

Finally, it may be noted that the combination of the themes of the process of emanation and of eschatology is also in accordance with the example set by Ibn Ḥasdāy's Neoplatonist. Thus the *Book on Spirit and Soul* is manifestly inspired, in its whole structure, by that Neoplatonic source of Israeli. (We can, in addition, point to an incidental quotation: § 2 closely follows a sentence in Ibn Ḥasdāy, ch. xxxv, second half, which is also contained in the extensive quotation in *BSubst.*, fragment vii.)

The first part of the *Book on Spirit and Soul* (§§ 1–8) deals in a desultory way with psychological matters, no doubt as a kind of introduction to the treatment of eschatology. Part of the statements are, in effect, anticipations of the exposé of emanation borrowed from Ibn Ḥasdāy's Neoplatonist: the intellect and the soul described as light (§§ 4, 5); the three souls (§ 2; this paragraph contains, as has been noted above, a quotation from another part of the Neoplatonist). Similarly, § 6, explaining the idea of the inclination of the rational soul towards either the intellect or the animal soul, reproduces an idea expressed in the same context of the Neoplatonist: see Ibn Ḥasdāy, ch. xxxiii, beginning of the second part, and cf. *BSubst.* vii. 15^{v}–16^{r}. § 7 is in fact an abbreviation of the account of emanation in § 9.

The aim of the *Book on Spirit and Soul* was not, however, simply to reproduce the doctrines of the Neoplatonist, or, like that of the *Book of Substances* and the Mantua text, to comment on and discuss various problems connected with them; it was to collect biblical passages to prove the correctness of these doctrines. The *Book on Spirit and Soul* is thus a theological work providing a biblical foundation for the Neoplatonic teaching of Israeli. While the *Book of Substances* was addressed to the general philosophical public (as is also shown by an external feature: see above, p. 81), the *Book on Spirit and Soul* was no doubt addressed to specifically Jewish theological readers. Israeli finds such biblical *loci probantes* for the statements that the soul (§ 4) and the intellect (§ 5) are splendours, that reward and punishment concern the soul, while the spirit does not survive death (§ 8). The main text invoked for proving that the good soul survives in bliss and the bad one receives punishment is 1 Sam. xxv. 29 (§§ 8, 14; cf. also Preliminary Note, above, pp. 107–8). A copious store of quotations is contained in the paragraphs concerning the question of reward and punishment (§§ 11–15).[1]

[1] The eschatology of Israeli (combined with elements derived from other sources) recurs in the *Microcosm* of Joseph ibn Ṣaddīq (pp. 76–79): The happiness of the soul consists in returning to its original world and being illuminated, without intermediary, by the light which emanates from God, after having left this world of misery, 'jail of the just, paradise of the wicked'. If it is not, however, purified from earthly desires, it is unable to return to its world or to come back to this world; it is carried along with the movement of the sphere of fire. Also some of the biblical verses employed by Israeli to prove that reward and punishment concern the soul recur in Ibn Ṣaddīq's text (Eccles. xii. 7; Zech. iii 7; 1 Sam. xxv. 29). [Cf. also below, pp. 194–5.]

IV

THE MANTUA TEXT

('CHAPTER ON THE ELEMENTS')

PRELIMINARY NOTE

THE *Chapter on the Elements* is known from a single manuscript (28*c*) preserved in the Bibliotheca Comunale di Mantova (Mantua) as part of a miscellaneous volume, and written in an Italian hand of about the sixteenth century. It comprises five pages (16^{r}–18^{r}) and is ascribed to Aristotle. Steinschneider mentions it in his *Die hebräischen Übersetzungen des Mittelalters* (§ 123, p. 234), and quotes the opening and concluding passages. He regarded it as a pseudo-Aristotelian chapter from some lost encyclopaedic work similar to the pseudepigraphical *De causis proprietatum elementorum*, a Latin version of a lost Arabic treatise which is extant in editions of Aristotle's *Opera*. The Mantua text does not, however, bear out this assumption. It is described as a commentary on a work by Aristotle, for it is stated in the *explicit* that the aim of the text is 'to explain the words of the philosopher [sc. Aristotle] by way of arguments and proofs'. It is therefore clear that we are dealing here with a treatise by an author who had some pseudo-Aristotelian text before him, the propositions of which he deemed it necessary to support by arguments and proofs. The ascription of the work to Aristotle is therefore incorrect and due to the copyist who probably inferred from the *incipit*, 'Aristotle . . . said', that the treatise in its entirety was by Aristotle.

G. Scholem was the first to suggest that the Mantua text represents the Hebrew version of a work by Isaac Israeli, the Arabic original of which is lost, and his surmise has been substantiated in a detailed analysis by the present writer who published the text, with an English translation and notes, in the *Journal of Jewish Studies*, vii (1956), 31–57.

The significance of the Mantua text lies not only in the addition it presents to the *corpus* of Israeli's extant writings but also, and primarily, in the light it throws on the source of his metaphysical doctrine. From it we learn that our author based his view of creation and the series of emanations on a pseudo-Aristotelian text which offers a doctrine somewhat different from other known types of medieval Neoplatonism. (See above, pp. 95 ff.; Comments, p. 127; Part II, below, pp. 161 ff.)

Blessed be God.

THE CHAPTER ON THE ELEMENTS

§ **1.** Aristotle the philosopher and master of the wisdom of the Greeks said: The beginning of all roots is two simple substances: one of them is first matter, which receives form and is known to the philosophers as the root of roots. It is the first substance which subsists in itself and is the substratum of diversity. The other is substantial form, which is ready to impregnate matter. It is perfect wisdom, pure radiance, and clear splendour, by the conjunction of which with first matter the nature and form of intellect came into being, because it [intellect] is composed of them [matter and form]. After the nature, form, and radiance of intellect had come into being, a radiance and splendour went forth from it like the radiance that goes forth from mirrors of glass set in the windows of baths and palaces when the radiance and splendour of the sun fall upon them. From this the nature of the rational soul came into being. Its radiance and splendour are less than the radiance and splendour of the intellect, on account of which this soul is ignorant and needs instruction and memory. After the nature of the rational soul had come into being, a radiance and splendour went forth from it like the radiance that goes forth from mirrors of glass, and from this the nature of the animal soul came into being. Its radiance and splendour are less than the radiance and splendour of the rational soul, on account of which this soul possesses estimation and imagination. After the nature of the animal soul had come into being, a radiance went forth from it like the one which had gone forth from the first ones, and from this the nature of the vegetative soul came into being. Its radiance and splendour are still less, and dimmer than the first radiances. For this reason the animal soul is capable of locomotion and sensation,[1]

[1] Cf. Aristotle, *De anima*, iii. 9. 432^a, 15.

whereas the vegetative soul is restricted to the motions of growth and generation only.[1]

In discussing the subject of the soul, the philosopher therefore said that because growth has not the strength to subsist in itself, it requires nourishment in order that its being be sustained.[2] But it is necessary for us to return to our first subject, and we will therefore say as follows:

After the nature of the vegetative soul had come into being, a radiance and splendour went forth from it like the radiance and splendour which had gone forth from the other substances, and from this the nature of the sphere came into being. Its radiance and splendour are less than the radiance of all those we have mentioned before, on account of which it is corporeal, and its motion is circular, perfect, and simple, as its Creator, blessed be He, appointed it for the sake of influencing coming-to-be and passing-away in this world.

§ **2.** From the motion of the sphere the warmth of fire, i.e. the elemental fire, which is one of the four elements, came into being.[3]

Proof of our assertion may be seen in the testimony of corporeal objects such as stones and iron which when held and rubbed against each other produce fire as a result of the friction.[4] We need not, however, prolong this discussion and thereby deviate from our line of inquiry.

When as a result of the motion of the sphere the nature of fire had come into being and the warmth moved away from its radiance and root, it diminished and dissipated. From this the nature of air came into being, the nature of fire being warm and dry, and the nature of air being warm and moist. After the nature of air had come into being and after it had moved away from the root of fire, its warmth continued to diminish, dissipate, and moisten, and from this the nature of water came into being. After the nature of water had come into being and after it had moved away from the air, its warmth and moisture diminished, coldness befell it, and it lowered itself to the production of sediment, refuse, and dry mud. From this the nature of earth came into

[1] Ibid. ii. 3. 415^{a}, 432^{b}.

[2] Cf. Aristotle, *De part. animal.* ii. 3. 650^{a}, 1: 'Everything that grows must take nourishment.' See also *De anima*, ii. 4. 416^{b}, 10–19.

[3] Cf. Aristotle, *Meteor.* i. 3. 340^{b}, 12: 'The circular motion of the first element [ether] and of the bodies it contains . . . generates heat.' *De caelo*, ii. 6. 289^{a}, 30 ff.: 'The air underneath the sphere of the revolving body is . . . heated by its motion.'

[4] Cf. Aristotle, *De caelo*, ii. 6. 289^{a}: 'The warmth and light which proceed from them [the stars] are caused by the friction set up in the air by their motion. Movement tends to create fire in wood, stone, and iron.'

being.[1] The ancients are therefore agreed in saying that the nature of fire is warm and dry, the nature of air warm and moist, the nature of water cold and moist, and the nature of earth cold and dry.[2]

It follows that the air which is attached to the sphere became fire as a result of the friction caused by the perpetual, unceasing motion.[3] The ancients therefore called the air which is attached to the sphere 'moving fire' on account of the perpetuity of the motion and the revolving movement around it. . . . The reason for the progressive degradation is that every force which emanates from something strong, and every motion caused by a moving agent, and every stroke delivered by one who strikes will be very powerful when near the source but will fail or weaken when remote from it. This will serve to illustrate what has been said.

After the natures of the four elements which are the first roots had come into being as a result of the perfect, circular, and simple motion of the sphere, they mixed, combined, and penetrated one another. From this, combinations of coldness, warmth, dryness, and moisture, i.e. composite bodies and substances, came into being, and the natures of animals, plants, and minerals arose.

§ **3.** Every animal inclines towards the element which predominates in it. Thus fire and air predominate in fowl whilst the other elements in them are feeble. On this account they [fowl] incline towards that which is predominant in them. Those animals in which water and earth predominate incline towards the former; such as fish, in the nature of which water predominates. For this reason they swim and dive in water precisely as fowl incline towards their own nature and fly in the air. Those animals in which earth predominates incline towards that particular nature; such as cattle, in which earth predominates. For this reason they are four-footed and their face is continually turned towards the earth. Their being is not balanced and their limbs are disposed facing the earth. The nature of man, however, is balanced and blended, and no one element holds sway over him more than the other. Hence the fire takes its path upward towards his head, and, similarly, the earth drops downward towards his feet.[4] His being is therefore balanced and

[1] Cf. Aristotle, *Meteor.* i. 3. 339^{a}, 36; *De gen. et corr.* ii. 4; *De caelo,* iii. 6 and 7; see, however, *De gen. et corr.* ii. 5. 332^{b}, where Aristotle proves that since the elements are transformed into one another, it is impossible for any one to be an 'originative source' of the rest. [2] Cf. Aristotle, *De gen. et corr.* ii. 3. 330^{b}, 4–6.

[3] See p. 120, n. 3. On the difficulty of assuming that air is ignited whilst the uppermost element is fire, cf. J. L. Stocks's note on *De caelo,* ii. 6. 289^{a}, in *The Works of Aristotle,* ed. W. D. Ross, 1922.

[4] Cf. Aristotle, *De part. animal.* ii. 7. 653^{a}, 30 ff.: 'Man alone stands erect. . . .

blended by virtue of the equality of the elements and roots in him. But no one lacking such equality can be perfect in being and existence.

Proof of the correctness of our statement lies in the fact that fish are not perfect in being and existence in spite of water being predominant in them. Those in which water and earth predominate and which also contain the other elements possess red bile and blood. They also possess, besides the heart, lungs and the faculty of respiration by which to 'draw' cold air, pump it into the lobes of the lung, and expel the respired, hot air by contraction and relaxation. But fish have neither lungs nor heart.[1] For this reason they are able to exist in water. They possess but a little of the nature of air in their blood. They therefore perish when out of water. When fishes fill their belly with water, they shut their mouth, open their ears, and expel the water that way. The beasts of the field have no such faculty. For this reason their belly swells and they perish when entering water and swallowing it. For when water fills their belly, no passage is available by which to expel it, as they do not possess the faculty of fish. Frogs exist in water and we find that their development takes place therein. They possess two faculties combined. Likewise, water-birds such as the *agron*[2] and their like possess respiration by which to exist in the air, and an additional faculty by which to exist in water, to swim, and dive therein. They therefore exist both in air and water.

§ **4.** Proof of the fact that all created beings are composed of the four elements lies in their behaviour. For man who belongs to the order of created beings depends on food, drink, and respiration. Moreover, it is the characteristic of every nature to return to its nature. The first nature is simple, as we have said. But the nature found in man is composite and mixed, not simple. It consists of red bile, blood, black bile, and phlegm. These natures correspond to the first simple natures: red bile to fire, blood to air, phlegm to water, and black bile to earth. For red bile is warm and dry, blood warm and moist, phlegm cold and moist, and black bile cold

For the heat . . . makes growth take its own line of direction, which is from the centre of the body upwards.' See also ii. 10. 656ᵃ; iii. 1. 662ᵇ, 20; iii. 7. 669ᵇ, 5; iv. 10. 687ᵃ, 1. iv. 10. 686ᵃ says of man's upright stature that it is 'in accordance with his godlike nature and essence'.

[1] This contradicts Aristotle's statement that 'no sanguineous animal is without a heart' (*De part. animal.* iii. 4. 666ᵃ). Aristotle says, moreover, distinctly, that even in fishes the heart holds the same position as in other animals. See ibid. 666ᵇ; *De resp.* 16. 478ᵇ, 2.

[2] Unfortunately, we have not been able to establish the identity of this water-bird.

and dry. The composite natures which enable us to grow require something from the first natures to sustain and nourish them. All animals and plants depend on them, and in the end return to them. Proof of this may be seen in man. For if he lacks one of the four natures, his being and existence is not complete. Moreover, if he does not eat food which is of the nature of earth, and if he does not imbibe fluids which are of the nature of water, and if there is absent from him the elemental warmth which is of the nature of fire, or if there occurs a suspension of breathing which is of the nature of air, he immediately dies since his being is incomplete. The plants likewise, although restricted to the motion of growth, are nevertheless, like man, capable of an elemental perception. They therefore grow if supplied with sweet rain water, and dry up and perish in salty and sulphuric waters. It is also their behaviour that if one of the natures, e.g. water, is denied to them their growth is incomplete. Similarly, if they are supplied with water but subsequently denied the warmth of the sun —the equivalent of the elemental warmth in man—their growth and existence will be incomplete. Likewise, if wind and air do not blow on them, they fail to grow. Likewise, if they grow within water or in places such as the basement of a house where the warmth of the sun cannot reach them, their being will be incomplete. It is therefore clear that all created beings are composed of the four natures and return to them.

§ **5.** Should one argue that created beings are made from one single nature,[1] we say that in that case they would not be liable to corruption and decay. The cause of their corruption is their return to the elements which are their root and origin. Another proof: if man were made of one single nature, he would not be divisible into parts. Moreover, he would have to derive his nourishment and growth from one single thing. The cause of his divisibility into parts and of diseases lies in the preponderance of certain elements and natures over others. For this reason, simple, uncompounded substance such as the celestial bodies, i.e. the heavens and all their host, neither change nor decay but exist perpetually. The cause of their perpetuity is the fact that they are of one single nature and therefore perpetually remain in their original being. They are not, as is the case with us, composed of the four elements which are liable to return to their original place and being, i.e. the great elements, causing

[1] Cf. Aristotle, *De gen. et corr.* ii. 3. 330^{b}; ii. 5. 332^{a}, 5 ff.; *De caelo*, iii. 4. 5. Al-Shahrastānī, *Religions and Sects*, p. 343, reports Themistius as having said that according to Plato, Aristotle, Theophrastus, Porphyry, and Plutarch the world consists of one single nature.

man to be overwhelmed by death and corruption. Another proof: such beings as do not contain a large amount of composition and mixture do not readily submit to corruption and decay as man does. A case in point is trees, for their amount of composition is small. Therefore they enjoy a somewhat prolonged existence and endure for some length of time, provided their nourishment is balanced and well blended. For when they are supplied with too much water they immediately perish.

§ 6. We further want to know why some animals more than others are endowed with cognition and discretion like man; also why some plants more than others possess a fragrant scent. Instances are musk, amber, and suchlike, and dogs, doves, and similar beasts and birds which are endowed with discrimination and cognition approximating to the cognition of man. All this is due to the inclination of the souls towards one another. We mean that the rational soul sometimes inclines in its actions towards the actions of the animal soul which desires to eat, drink, and be glad. Likewise, the animal soul inclines in its actions towards the rational soul when instructed and influenced by it. Similarly, it is the nature and faculty of the vegetative soul in this world to sustain the plants. A plant, however, which is capable of receiving the influence of the spiritual substances thereby becomes more fragrant than others. Similarly, animals differ from one another in the way they receive the influence of the spiritual substances and the degree of their mixture, be it large or small, as we explained above. For the spiritual natures influence and are influenced in the same way as the small natures depend on the great ones and are influenced by them. As to man, who is a species of animal, we find that when that soul of his which is nearest to intellect achieves perfection, he becomes perfect, clear-minded, and truthful, and will pursue the things which are good and true such as knowledge and understanding, purity and holiness, the worship and nearness of his Creator, blessed be He, and that which attaches the creature to the Creator, like the souls of the prophets, peace be upon them, which are joined to Him. All this derives from the influence of the uppermost substance. When, however, the rational soul inclines towards the lower substance, i.e. the animal soul, it will pursue the things which are vile, evil, and corrupt such as homicide, theft, falsehood, and lust. It will abandon the good things, despise the pious and just, love the foolish and wicked, despise also those possessed of understanding, knowledge, and goodness. This is due to the lower influence. When both the rational and animal souls incline towards the vegetative soul, man will thereby be prone to pursue unworthy things such as excessive eating and drinking and the desire for the enjoyment of this world only. When the vegetative soul inclines towards the animal soul, and the animal soul in turn inclines towards the rational soul, and the rational soul in turn inclines towards intellect, man will thereby be balanced in his actions and pursue the good things such as the quest for wisdom and knowledge. His desire for food and drink will be balanced and moderate, and likewise his desire for the pleasures of this world. Whenever a man's soul inclines excessively towards some particular soul, he will incline towards the actions peculiar to the soul attracting him. For this reason it was necessary for the Creator to create man as a perfect creature and to endow him with the rational soul and intellect. He ordained and appointed it [intellect] to support him in order that he might abandon all lower influences which are of an earthly nature. He who is possessed of intellect will know and consider that the Creator, His Name be blessed, did not create it [intellect] without purpose but for the benefit of man. Every wise man is therefore obliged to seek and examine the truth, and those possessed of intellect must join in discussion with one another in order to clarify the truth. He therefore made it incumbent upon man to receive reward for good and punishment for evil. Likewise, when the souls of animals . . . incline towards the rational soul, some cognition will be found in them according to the degree of their inclination towards the rational soul, be it large or small. For we find that the hawk and similar birds listen to the voice of man calling them and return to him. Similarly, domesticated doves fly back to their cote in the evening, nest there, know their lodging-place, and always return to it. Likewise, the dog discriminates between his master and strangers. Similarly, a plant which has a balanced and proper mixture, and whose vegetative soul inclines towards the animal soul, will possess a fragrant scent according to the degree of the soul's inclination towards the [higher] soul. Each soul supports and instructs the other, as we have mentioned, and is instructed and supported by the other, as we have said. For intellect is strengthened and instructed by the Creator, His Name be blessed, and instructs and supports the rational soul. The rational soul is instructed and supported by intellect, and instructs and supports the animal soul. The animal soul is instructed and supported by the rational soul, and instructs and supports the vegetative soul. It is instructed and supported but does not itself instruct and support because there is nothing below it to be instructed and supported. For below it are the natures and the sphere.

§ 7. In speaking here of 'below' and 'above' we use these terms metaphorically in order to approximate the subject-matter to our comprehension. For in the sphere there is neither void nor fullness, neither place nor time. None of the simple substances and spiritual souls requires time or place. Nor are they in time or place but they are the place for time and place. The ancients had a profound understanding of the 'place' and described it as the place for what is below it.[1]

§ 8. We will further say that every cause has a cause. That cause must be either the first or second or third or fourth or fifth or a further cause. If the cause assumed to be first has a cause, and that other cause a cause and so *ad infinitum*, this cannot be true. For if we were to say that the first cause has a cause and the third is cause to it [the second] *ad infinitum*, this would be tantamount to affirming that things have no first cause or beginning.[2] If that were so, there would be no difference between such a statement and our saying that every agent has an agent and that agent an agent *ad infinitum*, from which it would follow that all agents are acted upon and that there exist only such agents as are acted upon, not such as are but agents. But this is not true, for that which is caused has a cause which is not caused, and that cause is one, not more, and it is the Agent who is not acted upon.[3] He is the Creator, His Name be blessed. Therefore the wise philosopher, Aristotle, said: 'Blessed and praised be God who is the cause of causes, the First without beginning, the Agent who is not acted upon.'

§ 9. Thus we have said here what we intended to explain of the words of the philosopher by way of arguments and proofs and where he

[1] Cf. Plotinus, *Enn.* iii. 7. 11: 'In fact, as the world moves in the soul (for the sensible universe has no other place than the soul) it also moves in the time which belongs to this soul.' See also pseudo-Empedocles, Kaufmann, p. 20, where the text reflects the same doctrine: 'There is, therefore, no doubt that it [the soul] is the place of the world, and not the world its place.' In the Jewish theological tradition God is 'the place of the world'. Cf. the Midrash *Bĕrēshīth Rabbā*, 68. 9; Philo, *De somniis*, I. xi. 63; *De fuga*, xiv. 75; *Legum Allegoriae*, I. xiv. 44. On the native Jewish origin of this concept see A. Marmorstein, *The Old Rabbinic Doctrine of God*, i, 1927, 92–93, quoted by H. A. Wolfson, *Philo*, i. 248, n. 44.

Occasionally Philo calls the *logos* a 'place'. Cf. *Somn.* i. 65–70. John of Damascus (*De fide orthodoxa*, ed. Migne, col. 852) follows Philo in calling both God and the *logos* a 'place'.

[2] The basis of this argument is the principle that 'If there is no first, there is no cause at all'. Cf. Aristotle, *Metaph.* ii. 2. 994^a, 18–19.

[3] The designation of God as the 'First Agent' instead of the 'First Cause' is characteristic of the Kalām. See Maimonides, *Guide of the Perplexed*, i. 69. Our text uses both terms. See, however, Comments, below, p. 129.

finished his words, by what other philosophers have mentioned, with the help of the Creator, Whose Name be blessed and Whose Remembrance be exalted, Amen.

End of the Chapter of the Elements, Praise unto God unto Whom it is good to render thanks.

COMMENTS

§ 1 (16r. 1–19, excluding the author's interpolation 14–16) gives an account of the coming-to-be of intellect from the conjunction of first matter and first form or wisdom, and of the series of emanations from intellect down to the sphere. This passage occurs with certain variations in *BSpirit*, § 9, Ibn Ḥasdāy, and *LTheol.*, and represents the text of the pseudo-Aristotelian source from which Israeli's metaphysical doctrine is derived. As the reconstruction of the parallel text of Ibn Ḥasdāy's Neoplatonist has been reproduced in the Comments on *BSubst.*, pp. 98 ff., there is no need to restate it here. For a discussion of the doctrine itself see Part II, chs. I–V.

The somewhat bizarre and characteristic simile describing emanation in terms of a 'radiance that goes forth from mirrors of glass set in the windows of baths and palaces when the radiance and the splendour of the sun fall upon them' is found, with some slight variations, in all three parallel texts. *BSpirit* (§ 9) speaks of a radiance 'like the radiance which goes forth from the radiance of glass balls and mirrors set in the windows of baths and houses, when the ray of the sun falls upon them'. *LTheol.* says briefly, 'like the splendour which, for instance, goes forth from crystal and glass'; and Ibn Ḥasdāy uses the phrase, 'like the flame which goes forth from the sun when it falls upon glass in a dark house'. This particular choice of illustration may have been occasioned by an apocryphal Plato passage, which is quoted in the preface to Moses of Narbonne's Commentary on Averroes' *On the Possibility of Conjunction*, MSS. Munich, 108 and 109 (see M. Steinschneider, *Letterbode*, ed. M. Roest, Amsterdam, 1883, p. 60). The passage reads: 'As Plato said, the soul resembles the light of the sun entering through a variety of windows, for if the immediate ones are removed, the ray will be delayed.'

§ 2 (16ʳ. 20–16ᵛ. 8, excluding the author's interpolation 16ʳ. 21–23 and 16ʳ. 29–16ᵛ. 5) describes how from the motion of the sphere the element of fire and subsequently the other three elements originated, and how from their mixture the composite bodies and substances such as animals, plants, and minerals came into being. It is probable that a short account of this process was contained in Ibn Ḥasdāy's Neoplatonist, which is reflected in *BSubst.* iii. 2ᵛ and *BSpirit*, § 9. In the Mantua text Israeli considerably enlarges this account in order to prepare the ground for the discussion on the influence of the elements in § 3. He may have found the material in some treatise utilizing Aristotelian doctrines from *De caelo*, *Meteor.*, and *De gen. et corr.* (See p. 120, nn. 3–4, and p. 121, nn. 1–3.)

§ 3 (16ᵛ. 8–17ʳ. 1) sets forth the doctrine that every animal inclines towards the particular element which predominates in its make-up, and that only man, in whom the elements are blended, is a perfect being. The allusion to his erect figure goes back to Aristotle (see p. 121, n. 4). It touches upon a theme which is still re-echoed in Gottfried Herder's *Ideen zur Philosophie der Geschichte der Menschheit* (Book V, p. 179): 'Man enjoys the royal prerogative of looking around him, his head high, upright. Man is the first freeman of creation; he stands erect.'

§ 4 (17ʳ. 1–20) proves from the behaviour of created beings that they are composed of the four elements. The proofs are as follows: (1) Their dependence on food (earth), drink (water), warmth (fire), and respiration (air). This applies even to the plants. They possess an elemental perception, and therefore grow if supplied with rain water, and perish in salty and sulphuric waters. The latter observation is also found in *BSpirit*, § 2, and in passages of Ibn Ḥasdāy and *LTheol.* which represent parallels to § 6 of the Mantua text. The argument stated in our passage is repeated in more elaborate fashion in *BEl.*, pp. 66–68. (2) The four natures (i.e. the two biles, blood, and phlegm) require to be sustained by the four elements, and they eventually return to them. The correspondence between the four natures and the four elements is also stressed in *BEl.*, pp. 20–21.

§ 5 (17ʳ. 20–17ᵛ. 2) refutes the statement that created beings are made from one single nature. Again, the problem is dealt with at some greater length in *BEl.* (pp. 64 ff.). The argument from man's liability to suffer disease is quoted in *BEl.*, p. 64, in the name of Hippocrates. The argument from the necessary variety of food is found in *BEl.*, pp. 65–67, and the argument from the divisibility of man into parts (i.e. members of the body) occurs in *BEl.*, pp. 67–68. A comparison between our text and the *Book on the Elements* suggests that the subject is much more fully dealt with in the latter teatise, and one may infer that the Mantua fragment belongs to an earlier phase in Israeli's literary activities.

§ 6 (17ᵛ. 2–18ʳ. 13) describes the various degrees of created beings in terms of the inclinations of their souls. This passage has its prototype in the passage used in Ibn Ḥasdāy and *LTheol.*, where similar or identical illustrations (e.g. the parrot) are used from a slightly different viewpoint. The guiding principle in these two texts is that of the distance of the souls from the source of emanation. In both Ibn Ḥasdāy and *LTheol.* the passage commences with the words: 'The beginning of every light which emanates from a light-giver is stronger than its end, and the middle partakes of both extremities.' In *BSubst.*, fragment vii, Israeli quotes this text. The Mantua text, on the other hand, adapts it to the purpose of proving the difference between the various beings as resulting from the various inclinations of their souls.

The classification of men in our text has a close parallel in the somewhat enlarged typology offered in *BEl.*, pp. 57–58 (see below, pp. 138–9).

§ 7 (18ʳ. 14–17) contains Israeli's comments on the terms 'below' and 'above' used in the preceding paragraph. For references see p. 126, n. 1.

§ 8 (18ʳ. 17–25) contains an excursus by Israeli on the Aristotelian notion of God as 'Cause of causes'. Cf. *BDef.*, § 34: 'The Creator is the Agent of everything acted upon and the Cause of everything caused.' Israeli's discussion may be indebted to al-Kindī's treatise, *On the Agent in the Proper Sense*, &c., reproduced in the Comments on *BDef.*, pp. 68–69.

§ 9 (18ʳ. 25–27) contains the *explicit*, from which it becomes perfectly clear that the treatise is intended to serve as a commentary on a psuedo-Aristotelian text. Interestingly enough, the *Book of Substances* represents a commentary on the same text, as shown in the Comments on *BSubst.*, above, pp. 98 ff. The difference between the two treatises can be briefly stated as follows. In the Mantua text Israeli put the emphasis on the doctrine of the elements, using the pseudepigraphical account of the series of emanations merely as a spring-board for a discussion of the elements (later elaborated in *BEl.*), whereas his chief interest in the *Book of Substances* was the metaphysical doctrine of his source.

The Mantua text was known to the Jewish mystics of the Gerona circle, one of the most important centres of the rising Kabbalah in thirteenth-century Spain. (Cf. G. Scholem, "Iqbhōtāv shel Gabīrōl ba-Qabbālā' ('Traces of Gabirol in the Kabbalah'), *Mĕ'assef Sōfrē Ereṣ Yisrā'ēl*, 1940, pp. 171–3, and the present writer's article, 'Isaac Israeli's "Chapter on the Elements" (MS. Mantua)', *Journal of Jewish Studies*, vii. 32.) It is quoted in Azriel of Gerona's *Commentary on the Aggādōt* (ed. J. Tishby, Jerusalem, 1945, pp. 83, ll. 12–27; 87, l. 25–88, l. 5). The passages cited are the major part of § 1 (16^{r}. 1–17, omitting the reference to Aristotle's *De anima*, l. 14), introduced as in the Mantua text in the name of Aristotle; a somewhat condensed account of § 2 (16^{r}. 20, 24–16^{v}. 8, omitting the author's comment 16^{r}. 29–16^{v}. 5); and the first sentence of § 3 (16^{v}. 8–9) in an abbreviated form. Azriel does not seem to have been aware that the Mantua treatise was by Israeli. He refers to the texts quoted as 'the words of the *ba'ălē ha-meḥqār* (philosophers)' (pp. 83, l. 28; 88, l. 5). Traces of the Mantua text can also be found in writings by other members of the Gerona circle, viz. in Ezra ben Solomon's *Commentary on the Aggādōt* (cf. Tishby, loc. cit., Introduction, p. 10, quoting the parallel to Azriel, fol. 57*a*); in Ezra's *Commentary on Canticles* (wrongly attributed to Moses ben Naḥman), Altona, 1764, pp. 5*b*–6*a*; in a fragment of the treatise, *The Mystery of the Sĕfīrōt and the Mystery of Colours*, quoted by G. Scholem, "Iqbhōtāv shel Gabīrōl ba-Qabbālā', p. 173; and in Ezra's Letter to Abraham ben Isaac Ḥazan (reproduced by G. Scholem, 'Te'ūdā ḥădāshā le-Tōlĕdōt Rēshīt ha-Qabbālā' ('A new document on the beginnings of Kabbalah') in *Sēfer Bialik*, ed. J. Fichmann, 1934, pp. 157–8).

The Gerona mystics were particularly intrigued by the doctrine of emanation put forward in Israeli's pseudo-Aristotelian source. They felt that it somehow corresponded with their own system of *Sĕfīrōt*, at least as far as the higher hypostases were concerned: 'The words of the wisdom of Torah [i.e. Kabbalah] and the word of the philosophers mentioned above [i.e. quoted from the Mantua text] are one. They follow the same method, and there is no difference between them, except in terminology' (Azriel's *Commentary*, ed. Tishby, p. 83, ll. 28–29). They consequently endeavoured to equate first matter, first form (wisdom), and the three souls with the three *Sĕfīrōt* following the supreme *Sĕfīrā* of *Keter* ('Crown'), which they held corresponded to the Divine Will. We quote the relevant passage in Azriel's *Commentary*:

They [the Kabbalists] called the radiance and splendour [denoting here both first matter and first form or wisdom, see Tishby, loc. cit., p. 84, n. 3] . . . Torah, which is light to illumine the ways of the creatures, as it is written, 'and Torah is light' (Prov. vi. 23), for it enlightens and teaches man how to do the will of God. And Torah is wisdom [= the *Sĕfīrā* Wisdom, *ḥokhmā*], which is the beginning of everything, and through which everything was created. . . . And thought (*maḥăshābhā*) which is the root of everything in truth and which is rightly called wisdom, for it is the potentiality [*koaḥ mā*, a play on the word *ḥokhmā*] of what may come-to-be. . . . And understanding (*tĕbhūnā* for the more common term *bīnā*) divides its paths and actions, and causes all beings to emanate from among its ways, for they are derived from its potentiality. And knowledge (*da'at*) establishes in the heart the perception of the potentiality of wisdom and understanding. And understanding [= the *Sĕfīrā* Understanding, *bīnā*] is the intellect, as it is written, 'He knoweth intellect and understanding' (2 Chron ii. 11). And the rational, animal, and vegetative souls convey the potentiality of wisdom and understanding, and the true scholars [sc. the Kabbalists] called it knowledge [sc. = the *Sĕfīrā* Knowledge, *da'at*] (p. 84).

It is clear from this passage that Azriel identified first matter and form (wisdom) with the *Sĕfīrā* Wisdom, intellect with the *Sĕfīrā* Understanding, and the three souls with the *Sĕfīrā* Knowledge. At the same time, it appears from this and other passages (notably pp. 107–8, see Tishby, p. 107, n. 9) that he interposed two more hypostases between God and Wisdom, viz. (1) the Will (*rāṣōn*), also called Spirit (*rūaḥ*) and identical with the supreme *Sĕfīrā* Crown, *Keter* (in some writings of the Gerona circle termed 'The Light which hides itself' (*ōr ha-mit'allēm*)), and (2) Intellection (*haskēl*) which 'causes' Wisdom to come into being. (For parallel texts cf. Scholem, "Iqbhōtāv shel Gabīrōl', p. 173, and Tishby's note, loc. cit.)

The concept of the supernal wisdom as the point from which the process of emanation started (see Mantua text, § 1) is identified with the haggadic motif of the 'garment' of God from which the primordial light was created. (Cf. the present writer's article, 'A note on the rabbinic Doctrine of Creation', *Journal of Jewish Studies*, vii (1956), 203–6.) Both Ezra and Azriel quote in the name of Isaac the Blind (referred to as the *Ḥāsīd*) an interpretation of the well-known Midrash of Samuel ben Naḥman to this effect (cf. Tishby, op. cit., pp. 10, 110–11), Ezra elaborating it still further in his *Commentary on Canticles* and his Letter to Abraham (see above, p. 130). The terminology used is strongly reminiscent of the description of wisdom and its emanations in the Mantua text. (For an English translation of the passages in Ezra and Azriel see the present writer's article quoted above, pp. 203–5.)

V

AN EXCERPT FROM THE 'BOOK ON THE ELEMENTS'[1]

PRELIMINARY NOTE

ISAAC ISRAELI'S *Book on the Elements* (*Kitāb al-Usṭuquṣṣāt*) is extant in one Latin and two Hebrew versions, the Arabic original being lost. The Latin translation was made by Gerard of Cremona (see M. Steinschneider, *HebrÜb.*, p. 393) and is published in *Omnia opera Ysaac*, Lyons, 1515. The first Hebrew translation was undertaken at the behest of David Qimḥī by Abraham ibn Ḥasdāy, the author of *The Prince and the Ascetic*, and was edited on the basis of a Leyden manuscript (Warner, 13) by S. Fried, *Das Buch über die Elemente*, Frankfurt a. M., 1900. According to Fried, the Hebrew version contained in a Munich manuscript (no. 43), though prefaced by Abraham ibn Ḥasdāy's Introduction, represents an entirely different translation, its Hebrew being more fluent and elegant than the language used in Ibn Ḥasdāy's text. Fried suggested Moses ibn Tibbōn as its author (pp. 75–83). In editing the version of the Leyden manuscript, he made use both of the younger Hebrew as well as of the Latin text. Unfortunately, he did not make sufficient use of the Latin version, and as a result many obscurities remain which could have been cleared up. Our present translation is based on Fried's edition and the Latin version.

The *Book on the Elements* is the most substantial in bulk of Israeli's extant philosophical writings. Summaries of its contents have been given by M. Steinschneider (op. cit., p. 225. 2), S. Fried (op. cit., pp. 36–43), and Guttmann, *Israeli*, pp. 56–58. It is composed of three chapters. The first chapter (pp. 5–39) describes the elements as the 'truly first principles of natural beings' and as 'simple' in contrast to composite beings (see below, p. 181). It

[1] Ed. Fried, pp. 51–60.

refutes the assumption that the four qualities (warm, cold, moist, dry) are prior to the elements, and interprets Hippocrates' view in this sense. The second chapter (pp. 40–61) discusses Galen's doctrine of the elements and establishes its identity with Aristotle's and Hippocrates'. It refutes at some length Democritus's atomic theory. Towards the end of the chapter, Israeli raises the question why Galen and Hippocrates expressed their views in a manner open to misunderstanding. This leads him on to an excursus on the nature of philosophical and prophetic allegory, and on the typology of men. The third and final chapter (pp. 62–77) deals with the various theories proposed by the ancients concerning the number of the elements.

The passage presented here is the excursus on philosophy and prophecy from ch. ii (pp. 51, l. 11–60, l. 5). It has been selected because of the important contribution it makes to our understanding of Israeli's doctrine of the Upward Way and, in particular, of his view on prophecy.

51 Hippocrates followed in his statement[1] the custom observed by the philosophers in their works and sayings. For it is the custom of the philosophers to use expressions, the plain meaning of which is different from their hidden one. They make wisdom precious in order that only those should wish to approach it who are worthy of it and labour for its sake, as Hippocrates said in the opening part of his *Aphorisms*, 'Life is short and Art is long'.[2] They speak in a subtle way, the plain sense of
52 their words expressing what relates | to the senses whilst hiding what relates to intellect. They do this for two reasons. Firstly, they desire to refine their disciples' intellect, and to keep them occupied by inquiry and research for the purpose of clarifying the premisses necessary for reaching correct conclusions and for the purpose of investigating spiritual matters by research and intellect. Secondly, the form of something corporeal and communicated by the senses impresses itself more

[1] On this same page Hippocrates is said to have described the four qualities (warm, cold, moist, and dry) as 'elements'. See J. Guttmann, *Israeli*, pp. 12, 60.

[2] Hippocrates' *Aphorisms* were translated by Ḥunayn ibn Isḥāq. As to the various Hebrew versions see *Encyclopaedia Judaica*, s.v. Hippocrates, viii. 77–78. The maxim quoted by Israeli is also mentioned in Ḥunayn ibn Isḥāq's *Ādāb al-Falāsifa*, translated by Judah ben Solomon al-Ḥarīzi under the title, *Sēfer Musrē Ha-Pilōsōfīm* (ed. A. Loewenthal, p. 129).

readily upon the anterior ventricle of the brain on account of its proximity to the corporeal sense. It will make it easier for people of rash disposition and hard understanding to bring it within their grasp until the form has settled and impressed itself upon their thoughts. It will then be possible to divest it of corporeality and interpret it in a spiritual sense by means of allegory and analogy.

In his book the philosopher uses an expression in Plato's name which illustrates this point. He said, 'Poke not fire with a knife'.[1] It could not have been his intention or the object of his wisdom to prevent people from poking fire with a knife, for no advantage can be derived from the plain meaning of this statement, since poking fire with a knife can neither yield any benefit nor ward off any damage. His intention was, however, to forewarn us not to tell a fool something that will enrage him, and he compared the fool with fire, and that which enrages him with a knife. He said, 'Poke not fire with a knife', meaning thereby, Do not tell a fool something that will enrage him lest you should be affected by his foolishness in the same way as you will be affected by fire when you poke it, kindle it, and come close to it.

In acting in this way, the Ancients followed in the footsteps of intellect as we find it acting during sleep. They wished to imitate it and its actions. For they observed that when intellect wishes to reveal to the soul what its Creator, blessed and exalted be He, has caused to emanate upon it [intellect], namely an understanding of the spiritual forms which it finds in itself, and of the spiritual things which belong to it, it shows the soul the spiritual forms and things which it finds in itself and imparts to them forms intermediate between corporeality and spirituality in order that they may be more readily impressed upon the *sensus communis*. For when the Creator wishes to reveal to the soul what He
53 intends to innovate in this world, He makes intellect | the intermediary between Himself and the soul, even as the prophet is an intermediary between the Creator, blessed be He, and the rest of His creatures. It is only the corporeal and imaginative form which will be impressed upon the *sensus communis*, thanks to the prevalence of the corporeal sense upon it. This is due to the proximity of the *sensus communis* to the corporeal sense, seeing that it [the *sensus communis*] is intermediate between the corporeal sense of sight and the imaginative faculty, which resides in the

[1] Transmitted in the name of Pythagoras. Cf. H. Diels, *Die Fragmente der Vorsokratiker*, 2nd edn., i, p. 281, ll. 19–21, *μαχαίρᾳ πῦρ μὴ σκαλεύειν*, quoted by J. Guttmann, *Israeli*, p. 14, n. 2. Al-Shahrastānī (p. 281, Cureton) reports it in the name of Socrates.

anterior ventricle of the brain and is called *fanṭāsiya.* It is for this
54 reason that it is called | 'common sense', for it receives from the corporeal sense, i.e. that of sight, the corporeal aspects of things and transmits them to the spiritual sense mentioned before, i.e. the imaginative faculty.

We mentioned that the forms with which intellect clarifies the spiritual forms are intermediate between corporeality and spirituality because they result from the imaginative representations of the corporeal forms, and are more subtle, spiritual, and luminous than the latter, which are found in our waking state and are full of darkness and shells. It is for this reason that the Ancients compared them to the forms in the higher world. Evidence of this may be seen in the fact that a man will behold himself during sleep as if endowed with wings for flying, and flying therewith between heaven and earth; and it will seem to him as if the heavens are open, and a voice is calling thence and speaking to him; and as if he is walking upon the waters of the sea and across great rivers; and as if the beasts are talking. The evidence lies in the fact that the character of these forms and images is spiritual, subtle, transcending the natural order, and contrary to what one experiences in waking condition. Otherwise they would be without purpose and meaning and inexplicable, seeing that they are beyond the ways of intellect. But this is not the case, for we discover that they do teach us certain truths once some really intelligent person interprets them.

Further evidence may be seen in the fact that when the prophets, peace be upon them, desired to stand out from the rest of men, and wished their proper qualities to become manifest, they armed themselves
55 with those spiritual forms and revealed | them to all and sundry in order that their fellow creatures might know their exalted qualities and their achievement of having passed from the flesh to a spiritual state, since that which they made manifest transcends the natural order. From this point of view, there is agreement between all authors of books on religion and all who believe in prophecy that dreams are a part of prophecy.

After having explained and verified this, we should have made it clear that during sleep the *sensus communis* sees forms intermediate between spirituality and corporeality—i.e. forms in which intellect has clarified the spiritual forms—but knows them only in their corporeal aspects. For it is not within its power and ability to know more of them than their image and imaginary form on account of its proximity to the corporeal sense, i.e. that of sight. But once it knows their corporeal aspects, it transmits them to the imaginative faculty which resides in the

anterior brain, and imagination receives them in a more subtle way since it is more subtle than the *sensus communis* and more remote from the corporeal sense, i.e. that of sight. Once the imaginative faculty has received them from the *sensus communis*, it transmits them to the memory and deposits them there. When the person awakes from his sleep, he claims these forms from the memory, and memory returns to him the remembrance of all their traces, impressions, and characteristics as received from imagination. Remembering them, one seeks to understand their spiritual meaning through the cogitative faculty, because the latter possesses the power to scrutinize, discern, and combine, and it discerns and distinguishes between the shells of a thing and its kernel. |
56 Having discerned and purified them, it returns them to the faculty of memory, and memory receives them and stores them away until such time as they are required.

When, therefore, the cogitative faculty of the person concerned is spiritual, pure, luminous, and hardly obscured by shells and darkness, intellect will cause its light and brilliance to emanate upon it and make known to it its own properties, forms, and spiritual messages; it will also enlighten it as to the properties and forms of the soul and its faculties, and as to the difference between its spiritual forms and corporeal ones. Then these forms will be completely purified of all shells adhering to them, and it [cogitation] will interpret those dreams without fault. Should the cogitative faculty, however, be obscured by a great many shells and much darkness, intellect will be unable to descend to its depth with its own light and brilliance, and cogitation will fail to know its own faculties and those of the soul. Nor will it be enlightened as to the spiritual forms and those of intellect and soul, nor will it be able to effect a complete and proper separation of the shells from the inner content of those forms in which some allegorical meaning is conveyed during sleep. For it will not have understood their spiritual meaning so as to distinguish it from its corporeal expression. For this reason his interpretation of the spiritual forms will take account only of their corporeal expression, not of the spiritual meaning behind it, according to the measure of the coarseness of the cogitative faculty and according to the measure of its shells and darkness. Hence his interpretation of dreams will be faulty, beset by errors, and bereft of correct and proper meaning. This being so, he will have to tell his dream to one of those intelligent interpreters upon whom intellect has already caused its light and
57 splendour to emanate, and who understand | the imaginative forms and their spiritual meaning so as to distinguish the meaning from the

corporeal expression; for unless he understands all these he will be unable to offer a correct interpretation.

In this operation intellect follows in the footsteps of the Creator, blessed and exalted be He, and seeks to imitate His activity according to its own power and ability. For when the Creator, blessed be He, willed to create the world, make visible His wisdom, and cause its content to pass from potency to actuality, He created and formed the world out of nothing; He established it without any pattern; He set it up without there being any need on His part to do this for the purpose of either deriving benefit or avoiding harm. Our Creator is far exalted above this. He did it in His goodness and love, and seeing that His love was great and His wisdom was made visible, He desired to benefit His creatures and servants. Desiring this, He considered that it was not possible for men to obtain the benefits intended for them except by knowing the will of the Creator so as to do what He wanted them to do, and become worthy of receiving His reward and requital for serving Him. But it was again impossible to obtain ⟨the knowledge of⟩ the will of the Creator, blessed be He, except through messengers He would send them so as to make known to them His will as it affected them. For it is not becoming to wisdom to address all and sundry, seeing that some people are ruled by the animal soul, others by the vegetative soul, still others by the rational soul. Furthermore, some are ruled by a combination of vegetative and animal soul, or of animal and rational soul, or of vegetative and rational soul, and in some the rational soul has withdrawn itself and intellect consequently radiates upon them some of its splendour and brilliance.

One who is ruled by the animal soul will be ignorant, confused, daring, arrogant, eager to kill and to avenge himself, shedding blood, and sexually unrestricted. His character resembles that of beasts. One who is
58 ruled by the appetitive, i.e. | vegetative, soul will be stupid, dull, lacking in understanding, bent upon appetites of a low kind, and excessive in food, drink, sexual intercourse, and the begetting of children. He resembles the nature of the plants. One who is ruled by the rational soul will be intelligent, discriminating between things spiritual and corporeal, exceedingly humble, occupied with ⟨the search for⟩ truth and beautiful things, and shunning things which are blameworthy. One who is ruled by a combination of the faculties of the animal and appetitive souls will be a merry fool, occupied with the satisfaction of appetites of a worldly nature, pleasures, and sexual intercourse. One who is ruled by a combination of the faculties of the rational and animal souls will be

daring, stout-hearted, ambitious, and priding himself on victory owing to the influence upon him of the faculties of the animal soul; and owing to the influence upon him of the faculties of the rational soul, he will be whole-hearted, straightforward, discerning, searching, discriminating ⟨between⟩ good ⟨and evil⟩, and will not audaciously undertake fearful things but only what is extremely easy and within his power of accomplishment. One who is ruled by the rational soul in conjunction with the appetitive soul will be subject to appetites, craving for them and pursuing them, excessive in food and drink, and occupied with ⟨the satisfaction of⟩ the natural appetites owing to the influence upon him of the faculties of the appetitive soul; and he will be of a retiring disposition and do all this secretly and quietly owing to the influence upon him of the faculties of the rational soul. One whose rational soul has withdrawn itself [i.e. from the lower souls] and upon whom intellect causes its light and splendour to emanate becomes spiritual, god-like, and longing exceedingly for the ways of the angels, as far as lies within human power.

The Creator, exalted and blessed be He, therefore chose from among His creatures one qualified in this manner to be His messenger, caused him to prophesy, and showed through him His truthful signs and miracles. He made him the messenger and intermediary between Himself and His creatures, and caused His true Book to descend through him. Some of His words therein are unambiguous, self-evident, in no need of elucidation and interpretation. Yet there are others which use corporeal expressions, and are doubtful and in need of elucidation and commentary. Not that the Creator, blessed be He, was incapable of stating everything He wished to say in His Book in unambiguous and
59 | self-evident terms. But He knew that His creatures vary in their intellect, understanding, thoughts, and decisions. For some are animal-like and foolish, who will never allow anything to enter their minds and to occupy their thoughts except what they have perceived with their senses and seen with their own eyes. Others are intelligent, of an inquiring mind, keep their eyes open to the truth of words, and distinguish between their spiritual and corporeal meaning. Still others are of an intermediate type, which includes a variety of shades too numerous to be counted. The Creator, blessed be He, put His message in spiritual, unambiguous words to serve as guide and true teacher to those endowed with intellect and understanding so as to enable them to reach an understanding of the meaning of those messages which are couched in corporeal and ambiguous terms. And He put His message partly in

ambiguous terms for the benefit of those who are dull, deficient in intellect, and bereft of understanding in order that it might impress their imaginative faculty on account of the coarseness and corporeality thereof, and because of the proximity thereof to the sense. For people of this kind are unable to grasp what is conveyed to them in any other way, i.e. without it being brought near to their understanding little by little; being first transposed from a corporeal to a spiritual meaning by instruction commensurate with their understanding; proceeding from there to some higher degree of spirituality; and leading them on to still higher levels until they reach the simple and perfect spiritual meaning. For this reason people who are ignorant and deficient in intellect and morals are in need of a moral teacher endowed with understanding, and of scholars investigating the truth who will speak with everyone in such a way as to cause him to gain understanding according to ⟨the degree of⟩ his nearness to either spiritual meaning and understanding or corporeality and misunderstanding. For it is impossible to obtain an insight into the spiritual meaning of corporeal expressions from books, seeing that books speak in a particular way and express their subject in a particular form, and if the understanding of it eludes the reader, he will remain in his ignorance until he goes to a scholar who interprets its allegorical meaning in a great variety of ways and offers him many explanations. He will teach him first the corporeal aspect of the thing which is close to the senses, and if he notices that his pupil finds it easy and understands it well, he will proceed further; | otherwise, he will further elucidate the corporeal aspect of the matter, and raise his pupil's level of understanding until he arrives at a point where he understands, and the form of the thing is impressed upon his sense. Then he will again explain the matter to him little by little until he reduces the words to their complete spirituality.

Thus, it has been explained and verified that in its activity intellect follows in the footsteps of the Creator, blessed be He, and imitates Him as much as lies within its power. For this reason, the philosophers followed and imitated intellect.

COMMENTS

In the course of his interpretation of prophecy, Israeli touches upon two subsidiary subjects, viz. (1) the functions of the *sensus communis* and fantasy, and (2) the role of 'imaginative forms' in dreams. Israeli calls fantasy (*fanṭāsiya*, *BDef.*, § 4, l. 49; *BEl.*, p. 53;

cf. al-Kindī, pp. 167, 295) a 'spiritual', i.e. internal, sense; for this term see H. A. Wolfson, 'Isaac Israeli on the internal senses', *Jewish Studies in Memory of George A. Kohut*, New York, 1945, p. 583. (Cf. also Comments on *BDef.*, §§ 15 and 32.) While Aristotle does not delimit common sense from fantasy, the commentators (e.g. pseudo-John Philoponus, *CAG* xv. 507) introduce distinctions (cf. S. van den Bergh, *Tahafut*, ii. 187). Israeli's description of the *sensus communis* as 'intermediate between the corporeal sense of sight and the imaginative faculty, which resides in the anterior ventricle of the brain and is called *fanṭāsiya*' (p. 53) follows naturally from this distinction. His explanation of the term *sensus communis* ('It is for this reason that it is called "common sense", for it receives from the corporeal sense, i.e. that of sight, the corporeal aspects of things and transmits them to the spiritual sense mentioned before, i.e. the imaginative faculty') does not, however, agree with pseudo-John Philoponus's designation of common sense as the 'receptacle of the sensible forms through the medium of the particular sense', i.e. the faculty of unifying the various sensations. It remains a 'rather unique' explanation, as Wolfson suggested (p. 583), unless we interpret al-Fārābī's unnamed faculty (the 'common boundary' between the external and internal senses) as common sense (cf. Wolfson, op. cit., n. 11). Avicenna, we may note, identifies the faculty of fantasy with the *sensus communis*. (Cf. F. Rahman, *Avicenna's Psychology*, London, 1952, p. 31; S. van den Bergh, op. cit., p. 188.) The Ikhwān assign the function of 'collecting' the 'images' of sense-perception to the representative faculty. (Cf. Ikhwān, *Anthropologie*, p. 35; see also pp. 55–56.)

Israeli's doctrine of 'imaginative forms' calls for some closer comment. These forms are described as 'intermediate between corporeality and spirituality' (p. 52), 'because they result from the imaginative representations of the corporeal forms, and are more subtle, spiritual, and luminous than the latter' (p. 54). They obviously derive from the activity of imagination or fantasy—hence they are called 'imaginative forms' (p. 53)—yet, at the same time, are said to be impressed upon the *sensus communis* (pp. 52–53) and transmitted by it to the imaginative faculty (p. 55).

It should therefore be clear that they originate not in the normal process of imagination working upon sense data but in a rational activity producing images and presenting them to imagination via common sense. Imagination, it is said, receives them 'in a more subtle way' than the *sensus communis* and transmits them to the memory. All this happens during sleep. On awakening, one 'claims these forms from the memory', and remembering them will endeavour to understand the spiritual meaning which they express in imaginative form.

This doctrine is composed of two elements, which can be related to two distinct literary sources. Firstly, it assumes an activity of imagination prompted by the rational faculty for the purpose of translating 'spiritual forms' into images. Israeli leaves no doubt as to his view that the production of imaginative forms is due to the initiative of intellect. Intellect, he says, wishes to show the soul the spiritual forms present within itself and therefore imparts to them the forms of images (p. 52). What seems somewhat obscure is the part played by intellect in the actual production of imaginative forms. We interpret Israeli's meaning to be that whilst the formation of the images concerned is prompted by intellect, it is carried out by the imaginative faculty. This view would imply that fantasy is not only operating on sense-perception as a faculty of the animal soul but also at the service of the rational soul and working on rational data. As R. Walzer, 'Al-Fārābī's theory of prophecy and divination', *Journal of Hellenic Studies*, 1957, p. 144, has shown, the Neoplatonists (e.g. Plutarch, see pseudo-John Philoponus, *De anima*, iii, p. 515, ll. 12 ff.) speak of a 'double aspect' of φαντασία; being intermediate between perception and reason, it is joined to both; it not only provides reason with material derived from sense-perception, working from below upwards, but also operates the downward way by translating material derived from reason into sensible images. This doctrine goes back to Iamblichus, but has its roots in Aristotle's distinction between φαντασία αἰσθητική and φαντασία λογιστική (see S. van den Bergh, *Tahafut*, ii. 189, n. 334). Walzer has stressed the importance of this tradition for al-Fārābī's theory of prophecy. According to al-Fārābī, imagination 'is capable of an activity of its own, which is no longer dependent on the material supplied by the senses and preserved in the memory, and does not consist in combining and separating this material. This activity comes into play mostly in sleep and in dreams. . . . Through this creative *φαντασία* a kind of access to metaphysical truth with the help of images is open . . . which manifests itself in translating metaphysical truths into symbols' (loc. cit.). Israeli's doctrine of imaginative forms, though less developed than al-Fārābī's, would appear to derive from the same Neoplatonic tradition.

Secondly, Israeli's description of the nature of the imaginative forms seen in dreams can be shown to be influenced by al-Kindī's treatise *On the Quiddity of Sleep and Vision*, which is extant in the Arabic original (al-Kindī, pp. 293 ff.) and in a Latin version, *De somno et visione*, edited by A. Nagy, *Die philosophischen Abhandlungen des Yaʿqūb ben Isḥāq al-Kindī*, Münster, 1897, pp. 12–27. It may be noted that the Karaite author, Yaʿqūb al-Qirqisānī, a contemporary of Israeli's, closely follows this treatise in his chapter (xiv) on dreams in the *Kitāb al-Anwār wa'l-Marāqib* (ed. L. Nemoy), as G. Vajda has shown ('Études sur Qirqisani', *Revue des études juives*, cvi (1941–5), 52 ff.). Israeli, it would seem, is indebted to al-Kindī's treatise to a much lesser degree, but its traces are quite noticeable.

Israeli makes the point that the images seen in dreams as a result of the activity of intellect are 'more subtle, spiritual, and luminous' than the corporeal images produced in our waking state by sense-perception, the latter being 'full of darkness and shells' (p. 54). Similarly, he says in *BSubst.* (v. 12^{r-v}) that 'one sees things in sleep in a simple form without matter and without organs, because one sees colours without the eye, hears sounds without the ear, and perceives things without the senses; this is the manner of the angels'. This valuation of images seen in dreams as being superior to those of sense-perception is based on the fact that dream images (1) are divorced from matter; and (2) derive from a rational activity of fantasy. Both points are stressed in al-Kindī's treatise. Having dealt with the function of the 'representative faculty' (*al-muṣawwira*) or fantasy, which consists in preserving the individual forms of things without matter when their substances are absent from our senses, al-Kindī continues

For the difference between sense and that representative faculty is that sense causes us to find the forms of what it perceives as carried by their matter, whereas that faculty causes us to find individual forms despoiled, without substrata, yet with their features and all their qualities and quantities. And that faculty indeed performs its operations in the sleeping and the waking state. Nevertheless, it is more pronounced in sleep than in waking. . . . When cogitation so completely takes hold of someone who cogitates that it does not employ any of the senses at all, then cogitation brings him to sleep and the representative faculty becomes more capable than ever of causing its operations to become manifest. . . . He will see them, like the sense [*sic*], despoiled of the senses without any difference whatever between them. Nay, in cogitating about what he cogitates, the form of cogitation will appear despoiled, purer, more manifest, and in clearer form than what is conveyed by the senses. (Arabic, pp. 295–7; Latin, pp. 13–15.)

It should be clear from the passage quoted that al-Kindī distinguishes between two kinds of forms despoiled of matter, viz. one produced by fantasy, which here assumes the function of the faculty of representation, and one created by the cogitative faculty. The forms of the second kind are described as 'stronger, more manifest, and better', which recalls Israeli's characterization of the imaginative forms created by the influence of intellect as 'more subtle, spiritual, and luminous' than the corporeal images. Moreover, there is a close correspondence between Israeli's view of the corrupting influence of matter ('darkness and shells'), which is responsible for the inferiority of corporeal images, and al-Kindī's account of the reasons why images (forms) received by the soul without the senses are superior, without 'disturbance' or 'corruption'. As he explains, where there is no matter, there is no corruption (op. cit., Arabic, pp. 298–9; Latin, pp. 16–17).

Finally, Israeli's examples of what the soul may see during sleep (p. 54) may also be drawn from al-Kindī's *On the Quiddity of Sleep and Vision* (Arabic, pp. 299–300; Latin, p. 17). The passage concerned reads as follows:

Again, it [cogitation] finds what sense does not find at all. For it can itself compose forms, whereas sense cannot compose forms, because it cannot mix matter or its operations (?). Indeed, sight cannot cause us to find a man possessing horns or wings or anything similar which man does not naturally possess, or an irrational animal that speaks. . . . But it is not impossible for cogitation to imagine a man flying, or having wings, although he is un-winged, and a wild beast [Latin: wolf] speaking. . . . For this reason we find in sleep sensible forms which we do not find at all in sense-perception.

The difference between al-Kindī's and Israeli's treatment of the subject is chiefly this: that the former attributes dream images to the power of cogitation, whereas the latter ascribes them to intellect. The difference should, however, not be overstressed, because Israeli regards cogitation as an intellectual faculty (p. 55; *BDef.*, § 15; cf. Wolfson, op. cit., pp. 586–9). Al-Kindī, on the other hand, may have considered it as a special kind of imagination, as did al-Fārābī and Ibn Sīnā (cf. Wolfson, op. cit., p. 587).

PART II

THE PHILOSOPHY OF ISAAC ISRAELI

PART TWO

THE PHILOSOPHY OF ISAAC ISRAELI

THE texts and comments presented in Part I of this volume will have acquainted the reader with the tenets of Israeli's philosophy and the principal sources from which it derives. It now remains for us to attempt a coherent picture of the more or less scattered features of his Neoplatonic doctrine and to relate it to the context of kindred types of Neoplatonism in tenth-century Islam and, wherever possible, to the Jewish theological tradition inherited by Israeli. We have chosen for our frame of reference the Neoplatonic scheme of the Downward and Upward Ways, viz. the tracing of the process of emanations from the Divine source down to the world of the corporeal substances and, in the reverse direction, of the return of the human soul from its entanglement below to its origin on high. It will become clear from our account that this scheme was very much in Israeli's mind when dealing with the *disjecta membra* of his system from a variety of viewpoints and, apparently, without a unity of ultimate purpose. To his contemporaries as well as to his successors in medieval Jewish Neoplatonism this unity of approach was much more obvious and noticeable than it is to us who are no longer under the spell of the Neoplatonic *ethos* and have to reconstruct the meaning of its terms and concepts by way of analysis and by comparison with literary parallels.

The main parallels utilized for a clarification and appraisal of Israeli's thought are the following:

(1) The compilation, or compilations, from Plotinus's *Enneads* and some additional pseudepigraphical material which were current in the tenth century and bore the name of al-Shaykh al-Yūnānī ('the Greek sage'). As F. Rosenthal has proved, there existed a source common to the *Theology of Aristotle* and al-Shaykh al-Yūnānī (cf. *Orientalia*, xxi (1952), 447, 473).

(2) The vulgate version of the *Theology of Aristotle* (ed.

F. Dieterici) and the Fragments of the Long Version discovered by A. Borisov (see above, p. x).

(3) The Epistles (*Rasā'il*) of the Sincere Brethren (*Ikhwān al-Ṣafā'*) which seem to have been written in the middle of the tenth century and represent a fusion of Islam (with Ismā'īlī leanings) and Greek philosophy, notably Neoplatonism. Though later than Israeli they may be justifiably used for an elucidation of his thought, seeing that they draw on many Neoplatonic texts which were in circulation in his own period. In fact, they are nearest to Israeli as far as their spiritual outlook is concerned. (See *Encyclopaedia of Islam*, s.v. *Ikhwān al-Ṣafā'*; 'A. 'Awā, *L'Esprit critique des 'Frères de la Pureté'*, Beyrouth, 1948; A. L. Tibawi, 'Ikhwān aṣ-Ṣafā and their Rasā'il', *The Islamic Quarterly*, London, ii (1955), 28–46; S. M. Stern, 'The Authorship of the Epistles of the Ikhwān al-Ṣafā'', *Islamic Culture*, 1946, pp. 367–72; 1947, pp. 402–3.)

(4) The pseudo-Empedoclean *Book of the Five Substances*, parts of which are preserved in excerpts from a Hebrew translation (ed. D. Kaufmann) and reflect a great deal of Neoplatonic doctrine. (On the part played by pseudo-Empedocles in other Islamic works see S. M. Stern's article *Anbaduḳlīs* in the *Encyclopaedia of Islam*, 2nd edition.) According to Shēmṭōb ibn Falaquera (*c.* 1225–95), Solomon ibn Gabirol's *Fountain of Life* is largely based on the *Book of the Five Substances* (cf. S. Munk, *Mélanges de philosophie juive et arabe*, p. 3). Joseph ibn Ṣaddīq (*Microcosm*, ed. Horovitz, p. 54) writes that 'One who wishes to understand the true nature of this [the Will of God] and similar subjects should study the book of Empedocles or other works by other scholars written on this subject'. Israeli does not seem to have known the *Book of the Five Substances*, yet it is of interest to compare his own particular kind of Neoplatonism with that of pseudo-Empedocles.

It goes without saying that our account of Israeli's philosophy will be based chiefly on the results of the researches presented in the first part of this volume, some of which reappear in an expanded form; but we shall also have an opportunity of pointing out further sources which were used by our author.

A. THE DOWNWARD WAY

I

THE CREATOR

THE concept of God is nowhere clearly expounded in the extant Israeli texts. It may be assumed that the *Book of Substances* contained a section dealing at some length with the subject, for what is left of fragment ii indicates a discussion of the problem how creation in time can be reconciled with the unchanging power and will of God. A discussion of this kind clearly presupposes some introductory statement concerning the nature of God. Fragment vi probably also commenced with a disquisition on God as the First Cause before describing in the extant section the degrees of being in terms of their nearness or remoteness from the First Cause. In the absence of a coherent treatment of the theme we have to trace Israeli's theological doctrine from scattered references in the available texts.

God is described as 'the Creator' (*al-bāri'*) who 'is acting perpetually and in acting is in no need of things outside Him' (*BSubst.* v. 12^{v}); His 'generosity and bestowal are perpetual, as He has no need of others, and want and dependence are absent from Him' (*BSubst.* vi. 14^{r}). Goodness and love are the sole motives of His act of creation since He does not need the world nor does He derive any benefit from it (*BEl.*, p. 57). His power is 'infinite'; 'its scope has no limits, and intellects do not encompass it with their knowledge' (*BSubst.* vii. 15^{r}). 'It is clear that what the Creator, may He be exalted, does is the most faultless and excellent' (*BSubst.* iv. 9^{r}). He is 'not affected by passivity in any sense, but He is the agent of everything which is acted upon and the cause of everything caused' (*BDef.*, § 34). He is 'the cause of causes, the First without beginning, the Agent who is not acted upon' (*Mant.*, § 8). He has 'appointed and ordained' the power of the sphere or nature 'for the sake of influencing coming-to-be and passing-away', i.e. for the creation of animals and plants (*BDef.*, § 6, ll. 22–24; § 9, ll. 5–7; § 44). 'Creation' as an activity of nature means 'the passing of corporeal substances from privation to existence'. It does not signify creation out of nothing. This the Creator alone is capable of doing. His action is 'innovation' and 'making-anew', i.e. 'making existent existences from the non-existent', and 'there is no innovator and maker-anew except the Creator, may He be praised and may His name be sanctified' (*BDef.*, § 44). He created the 'first substance' and the 'truly first genus' without mediator (*BDef.*, § 2, ll. 107–8; § 3, ll. 10–11). They came into being by His 'power' (ibid.) or by His 'power and will' (*BSubst.* iv. 5^r). The simple substances and the sphere are generated from the power and will of the Creator, whereas the bodies are made by nature (*BSubst.* v. 12^v).

This account will have conveyed an impression of the rather complex nature of Israeli's concept of God. Aristotelian, Neoplatonic, and Jewish elements are blended in it. Israeli was by no means original in his attempt to reconcile the conflicting notions inherited from the Greek and Jewish traditions. As has been shown in the Comments on the *Book of Definitions* (§§ 42–45), his insistence on creation from nothing—a fundamental concept in orthodox-rabbinic Judaism[1]—could be based on al-Kindī, who in turn may be indebted to earlier Islamic Neoplatonists. Israeli's refutation of an argument obviously directed against the doctrine of creation in time (*BSubst.* ii. 17^{r-v}) is likewise modelled on earlier discussions. It points out that if the object of an action does not pass from potentiality into actuality at all times, this is not due to the impotence of the agent to effect this but to the intrinsic impossibility of this happening except at the time it does happen. Thus Moses could not have appeared at the time of Adam, not because of God's impotence to effect this but because of the natural order of procreation ordained by God's wisdom. Only by an act of *creatio ex nihilo* could Moses have been brought into being at the time of Adam. Similarly, John

[1] Cf. A. Altmann, 'A Note on the Rabbinic Doctrine of Creation', *Journal of Jewish Studies*, vii (1956), 195–206; G. Scholem, 'Schöpfung aus Nichts', *Eranos-Jahrbuch*, xxv (1957), 87–119.

Philoponus (*De aeternitate mundi*, ed. Rabe, pp. 567–8) argues that it was not in the nature of Socrates to be created before Sophroniscos; but before Sophroniscos came into being God had willed that Socrates should exist, not absolutely, not always, but when it should be possible. Israeli clearly reflects this passage, although his argument misses the point. Philoponus distinguishes between God's eternally willing something and God's willing it to be eternal,[1] whereas Israeli merely draws a line between the operation of the natural order and creation from nothing, which still leaves unexplained why the world should have been created in time if God's will and power do not change.

If our interpretation of the Israeli passage is correct—unfortunately the fragment at our disposal is lamentably short—the author upholds not only the doctrine of *creatio ex nihilo* but also that of creation in time. This latter notion ill accords with the doctrine that God is 'acting perpetually'. The passages relating to this view bear striking witness to Israeli's Neoplatonic background. The image behind them is that of emanation, of an eternal flow from the Divine source which is never exhausted and gives itself ungrudgingly. It also explains the motive of creation as stated by Israeli. 'Why did the Creator make the world?', Plato asks in the *Timaeus* (29E), and he gives the answer, 'He was good and therefore not jealous, and being free from jealousy He desired that all things should be like Himself'. Plotinus alludes to this passage and adds that, being perfect, the One spontaneously creates (*Enn.* v. 4. 1). Perfection cannot help being creative. Moreover, 'He does not need the things which have come into being from Him but leaves them altogether alone, because He needs none of them, but is the same as He was before He brought them into being; and if anything else could be derived from Him, He could not grudge its existence' (v. 5. 12). 'There is nothing which is good for the One, nor does It wish for anything. It transcends good, and is good not for Itself, but for the others, if any of them can participate in It' (vi. 9. 6; vi. 7. 41).

[1] Cf. S. van den Bergh, *Averroes' Tahafut al-Tahafut* (*The Incoherence of the Incoherence*), translated from the Arabic with Introduction and Notes, London, 1954, ii. 3.

A point in Israeli's doctrine deserving of special attention is the emphasis it puts on the 'power and will' of God. We may note that the Long Version of the *Theology* also uses these terms, but does so with a difference. In Israeli, 'power' and 'will' do not represent any kind of hypostasis but are obviously aspects of God identical with His essence or being, whereas the Long Version of the *Theology* seems to regard them, at least occasionally, as identical with the hypostatic 'Word' (*kalima*): 'In this way, intellect unites essentially with the Word, also designated as the Power (*qudra*) of God, His Will (*irāda*), His Command (*amr*), or His Knowledge (*'ilm*). . . . I speak of intellect which God created by His Command and Will' (Fragment B, 15v. 5 ff.; Borisov, p. 763). Israeli's use of the terms 'power' and 'will' seems to go back to older Islamic sources which for theological reasons felt it necessary to stress the aspects of power and will in the concept of Divine creation. The voluntaristic theology expressed by the emphasis on the Will of God appears *prima facie* to be a foreign element in the context of Neoplatonism and to stem from the biblical tradition rather than from Plotinus. But it should not be overlooked that the notions of both power and will figure largely in the *Enneads*, especially in the treatise *On the Freedom and Will of the One* (vi. 8). According to Plotinus, the will (βούλησις) of the One is nothing distinct from His essence. 'What is there in Him which would not be will? He is all will; there is nothing in Him which He does not will. Firstly, therefore, His will is He Himself. That which He willed to be, the manner willed by Him in consequence of His will, all this has been engendered by the will' (vi. 8. 21). This will, Plotinus assures us, 'is neither arbitrary nor accidental: a will (θέλησις) which tends towards the Best is not arbitrary' (vi. 8. 16). 'The nature of the Good is its will.' Its will and its essence are one (vi. 8. 13). The acts flowing from the One are therefore expressions of an essential necessity which is perfect freedom.[1] At the same time, Plotinus stresses the 'infinite power' of the One (vi. 9. 6), and describes it as superior to His will (vi. 8. 9).

The Plotinian doctrine of the power and will of the One carries the implication that things have come into being not as a result of

[1] Cf. W. R. Inge, *The Philosophy of Plotinus*, 1948, ii. 113–14.

deliberate choice or planning but by the necessity which is God's freedom. The One is like the centre of a circle which engenders by its power the radii and the circle but remains itself unmoved (vi. 8. 18). He is the source of all movement but Himself before movement and rest (vi. 9. 3). Both the *Theology of Aristotle* and the Arabic Plotinus (al-Shaykh al-Yūnānī) stress this aspect of the One. The *Theology* describes the series of emanations as a movement proceeding from the motionless God (Dieterici, p. 4) and declares that the First Creator did not create anything by thought (*ra'y*) and cogitation (*fikr*), for as He creates solely by virtue of His being and essence the thing created need not be preceded by any act of planning (pp. 55–57). The Arabic Plotinus quoted by al-Shahrastānī (*Religious and Philosophical Sects*, p. 337) reflects this very passage in his statement that 'the First Agent requires for His innovation of things neither thought (*ra'y*) nor cogitation (*fikr*),[1] and in another source (al-Shaykh al-Yūnānī, Rosenthal, i, p. 477), 'The First Agent must be stationary and motionless. . . . His action must be without reflection, motion, and volition which would be inclined towards the action produced.' There is nothing in the available Israeli texts to suggest that the will and power of God were understood to exclude the necessity of reflection and deliberate choice. Most probably Israeli's voluntaristic concept of creation ignored the Plotinian tradition in this respect and interpreted the Will in a less paradoxical and less subtle way than Plotinus did. But in the absence of any clear testimony we can only guess as to his exact opinion.

We are, however, on safe ground in assuming that Israeli did not regard the Will as a distinct hypostasis as is the case in the Long Version of the *Theology* and in later Jewish Neoplatonism, notably Ibn Gabirol and Judah Ha-Levi. In this connexion, we may note a terminological point of some significance. In the *Theology of Aristotle*, both in the Long Version and the vulgate recension, we meet the term 'the First Creator' (*al-bārī' al-awwal*). The same term appears in the Arabic Plotinus (Rosenthal, i, p. 479) and in the

[1] Joseph ibn Ṣaddīq, *Microcosm* (ed. Horovitz, p. 56), likewise says that 'The Creator, blessed be He, created His creatures without thought (*'iyyūn*) and cogitation (*maḥăshābhā*)'.

pseudo-Empedocles Fragments (Kaufmann, pp. 31, 51). Israeli never uses this expression but refers to God simply as 'the Creator' (*al-bārī*). We suggest that the term 'First Creator' was originally introduced in order to distinguish between the One and intellect. Plotinus designates intellect as 'reason and cause' (λόγος καὶ αἰτία), and describes the One as 'cause of the cause', or 'cause in an eminent and truer sense than intellect' (vi. 8. 18). Since, then, intellect assumes the role of the immediate cause of all subsequent generation, the One came to be called not only the 'cause of the cause' as in Plotinus but also the 'First Creator'. In the Long Version of the *Theology* the justification of this term is even more clearly pronounced, and it may be that the term originated there and was borrowed later by circles which did not share the particular theology which necessitated it. It seems obvious that the term was framed in this context in order to distinguish between God and the Word. The 'Word' (*kalima*) is designated as 'the cause of causes', since it created the first intellect: 'from this point of view the Word is called cause of causes, whereas from the first point of view it is the First Creator [who merits this title]: for all things proceed from Him and come-to-be through Him: He made and created them' (Fragment C, 6; Borisov, p. 764). The function of the 'Word' in this probably Ismāʿīlian version of the *Theology*[1] comes so close to that of the Creator that the term 'First Creator' for God is indeed called for. Moreover, some of the attributes of the One mentioned by Plotinus are transferred to the Word: 'It is neither rest nor movement, and it is because of this that it is described as "nothing" (*laysa*)' (Borisov, ibid.). The description of the Word as 'nothing' goes back to the Plotinus passage (*Enn.* vi. 9. 5) which says that 'in reality no name fits It [the One]'. The Greek text, ᾧ ὄνομα μὲν κατ' ἀλήθειαν οὐδὲν προσῆκον, was obviously interpreted in the sense that in reality the name 'nothing' (οὐδέν) befits It, an interpretation which is certainly incorrect yet can claim the approval of a modern Plotinus scholar of note.[2] The

[1] Cf. S. Pines, 'La longue recension de la Théologie d'Aristote dans ses rapports avec la doctrine ismaélienne', *Revue des études islamiques*, 1954, pp. 7 ff.

[2] A. H. Armstrong in his *The Architecture of the Intelligible Universe in the Philosophy of Plotinus*, Cambridge, 1940, pp. 15, 17. See, however, É. Bréhier,

doctrine of the Word is expressly rejected in the Arabic Plotinus: '. . . the intellect is no *logos* (*kalima*), nor is there a *logos* in it, because it was created by a Creator who did not possess an attribute or form, so that He could have put that attribute as *logos* into it' (Rosenthal, i, p. 487). Israeli, we have noted before, holds a similar view, seeing that the notion of the Word does not figure in his doctrine of creation. In his case, however, the position is more complicated because he interposes first matter and first form or wisdom between God and intellect (see below, pp. 159 ff.).

Finally, we miss another important feature of the Plotinian doctrine in Israeli. The negative aspect of the One which Plotinus derived from his exegesis of Plato's *Parmenides*[1] is almost completely absent, except for the statement that the intellects cannot encompass God's power (see above, p. 151) and that assimilation to the Creator can only mean assimilation to His works (*BDef.*, § 2, ll. 15–16). Plotinus had taught that the One 'exists in and by Himself without any attribute' (vi. 9. 5–6; v. 3. 13; v. 8. 11) and even without essence (vi. 8. 12, 19). Yet none of the extant treatises of Israeli offers a negative doctrine of the Divine attributes. Only in the *Yĕṣīrā Commentary* by his pupil, Dūnash ibn Tamīm, do we come across a decidedly negative theology. Speaking of the tetragrammaton ('the great name of the Creator'), Ibn Tamīm says that this term 'does not signify that the Creator possesses a denomination, for a name is an accident, designating something superadded to the named, whereas in the Creator nothing is accidental; but men are incapable of conceiving His essence . . . which is why they attribute to God denominations borrowed from His most beautiful qualities and actions, such as Creator, Generator, &c.' (Vajda, *Commentaire*, cx, pp. 75–76). This statement clearly reflects the Plotinus passage quoted above, in which the One is said to bear no name.[2] Seeing that Ibn Tamīm's

Plotin, Ennéades, vi. 2, Paris, 1938, p. 178, and V. Cilento, *Plotino, Enneadi*, iii. 1, p. 426.

[1] Cf. E. R. Dodds, 'The *Parmenides* of Plato and the origin of the Neoplatonic One', *The Classical Quarterly*, xxii, 1928; Armstrong, op. cit., pp. 16 ff.

[2] Philo, *Somn.* I. ii. 62, describes God as 'unnameable' (ἀκατονόμαστος) and 'ineffable' (ἄρρητος), which, however, does not imply that God has no name. He

Commentary is greatly indebted to his master's teaching, one may safely assume that his statement represents Israeli's view also.

refers to the 'most holy and divine name of God', i.e. the tetragrammaton, as one 'which only those whose ears and tongues are purified may hear or speak in the holy place, and no other person, nor in any other place at all' (*Moses*, ii. 23. 114; *De decalogo*, 19. 93–94). Cf. H. A. Wolfson, *Philo*, ii. 110–26.

II

FIRST MATTER AND FIRST FORM (WISDOM)—INTELLECT

In Plotinus, intellect (*Νοῦς*) emanates direct from the One. Israeli, following the pseudepigraphical source, interposes two simple substances—first matter and first form or wisdom—between the Creator and intellect. First matter is described as 'the first substance which subsists in itself and is the substratum of diversity' (*Mant.*, § 1), 'the universal substance, which is one in number, exists by itself, and is the substratum for diversity absolutely' (*BSubst.* iv. 5^v), 'the truly first genus which is created by the power of the Creator without mediator' (*BDef.*, § 3, ll. 10–11). It is known amongst the philosophers as 'the root of roots' (*Mant.*, § 1).

First form or substantial form is described as impregnating first matter, and is identified with 'the perfect wisdom, the pure radiance, and clear splendour' (*Mant.*, § 1). In the *Book of Substances* (iv. 5^r) it is spoken of as 'the perfect wisdom, pure science, and unmixed knowledge'. The *Book on Spirit and Soul* (§ 9), paraphrasing the Neoplatonic source, refers to it as 'the absolute brilliance, i.e. the perfect wisdom'. The *Book of Definitions* (§ 2, l. 59) speaks of 'the beauty and splendour of wisdom' as something distinct from 'the light of intellect'. 'The light created by the power of God without mediator' mentioned in *BDef.* (§ 2, ll. 61–62) is identical with wisdom. Like first matter, it is created 'by the action, without mediation, of the power and the will [of God]' (*BSubst.* iv. 5^r).

Intellect is defined as 'the specificality (*naw'iyya*) of things', i.e. the totality of forms, a definition which, as shown in the Comments on the *Book of Definitions* (§ 4), derives from al-Kindī, as does the division of the intellect into (1) the intellect which is always *in actu*, (2) the potential intellect in the soul, and (3) the 'second intellect' which passes in the soul from potentiality to actuality. Obviously

Israeli combines the Aristotelian concept of the Divine intellect which is always *in actu*—al-Kindī's 'first intellect'—with Plotinus's *Νοῦς* or 'universal intellect'. The term 'second intellect', used by Israeli but absent in al-Kindī, refers to the actualization in the soul of the potential intellect by way of sense-perception and is distinct from the intuitive knowledge of intellect. For intellect is described by Israeli as knowing what it knows 'without cogitation and consideration because it finds its own essence eternally without change'. In other words, Israeli conceives the intellect exactly as Plotinus understands *Νοῦς*, as the universal mind which in thinking the ideas or *νοητά* thinks itself (*Enn.* v. 3. 5). Like Plotinus, he describes the intellect as being 'like the light of the sun' (*BSubst.* iii. 3^v; *Enn.* v. 6. 4), a metaphor which Plotinus as a rule applies to the One,[1] and which Israeli might have reserved for the superior hypostasis of wisdom.

It is not quite clear how Israeli differentiates the nature of wisdom from that of intellect. Seeing that intellect contains the totality of forms and knows them by an act of intuitive self-knowledge, one fails to discern the possibility of a level of knowledge superior to it. We are not very much helped by Israeli's description of wisdom as 'the true knowledge of the eternal, everlasting things' (*BSubst.* iv. 6^r) or as 'the true knowledge of the first and everlasting things . . . which are eternal by their nature' (*BDef.*, § 3, ll. 5–8). What, then, is the relationship between wisdom and intellect according to Israeli?

Intellect, it is said, comes-to-be from the conjunction of first matter and form, as it is composed of them. From the account in the Mantua Text it would appear that matter and form are not only the constituent elements, as it were, of intellect but rank as the first two hypostases and intervene between God and intellect. This interpretation is borne out by the fact that first form is described as 'wisdom', which suggests a stage higher than intellect, and is spoken of in terms of the most perfect light. Moreover, it is

[1] A. H. Armstrong suggests that Plotinus's fondness for the simile of the sun has for its background the 'solar theology' of Posidonius (developing Plato's image of the Sun in *Republic*, vi–vii) and such a conception as expressed in the *Hermetica*, xvi. 6 (Scott), where the light of the sun is said to be 'the receptacle of νοητὴ οὐσία'. Cf. *Architecture*, pp. 55–57.

clearly stated that 'The beginning of all roots is two simple substances', i.e. first matter and form. On the other hand, the discussion of the subject in the *Book of Substances* (iv. 4^{v} ff.) suggests that matter and form or wisdom have no existence except in intellect. It is said that ascending from the vegetative to the animal and thence to the rational soul, we find that our next step leads us to 'the perfect wisdom' which 'is the property of the intellect'. For, it is argued, it is impossible that intellect should exist except in wisdom or that wisdom should be created anywhere except in intellect, the existence of one implying that of the other, the abolition of one likewise that of the other. In other words, wisdom is but the 'form and perfection' of the intellect's substantiality' (ibid.), and as there does not exist, in this view, a distinct hypostasis called first matter or one called form or wisdom, Israeli is quite consistent in stating that 'this being so, it is clear that intellect is the most noble of all substances, of the highest degree and loftiest rank', a statement which does not tally with the accounts given in the Mantua Text and in the *Book on Spirit and Soul.* It should, however, be added that even in the *Book of Substances* Israeli reverts to the position of his pseudepigraphical source which he unreservedly adopts in the Mantua Text and in the *Book on Spirit and Soul.* The final conclusion he reaches in the *Book of Substances* is not merely to the effect that 'intellect is composed of matter and form' as proved in the course of an elaborate discussion, but goes beyond this result: 'As intellect is composed of matter and form, it is clear that matter and form precede it by nature; thus it is clear and manifest that the first of created things are two simple substances and that intellect is composed of them.' In fact, the whole discussion is introduced in fulfilment of a 'promise' 'to bring proof for the statement that the first of created things are two simple substances out of which is established the nature of the intellect'. Israeli obviously had the pseudepigraphical source known to us from the Mantua Text and the *Book on Spirit and Soul* before him when he wrote the *Book of Substances*, and our passage is no doubt intended as a commentary on the statement quoted. In the course of his discussion he temporarily loses sight of the hypostatic character of matter and form or wisdom which the source so clearly announces, and gives matter and form a purely functional meaning as constitutive elements of intellect. In the end, he re-establishes their character as 'the first of created things' and as 'preceding' intellect 'by nature'.

What makes a clear demarcation between the hypostatic and merely functional character of the various stages of the spiritual realm rather difficult—and this applies to Israeli as much as to Plotinus—is the fact that the levels of being concerned imply no temporal sequence. The higher is not prior in time to the lower. It is only prior 'by nature'. This is clearly stated by Israeli (cf. *Mant.*, § 7; similarly *LTheol.* x. 2). If, therefore, matter and form precede intellect only 'by nature', i.e. from the logical aspect, not in time, the whole conception of their distinct hypostatic character is in jeopardy, unless one admits from the outset the Plotinian doctrine of hypostases as valid within an eternal emanationist system.

The interposition of first matter and form or wisdom between God and the intellect is a characteristic feature of Israeli's metaphysical doctrine. It goes back to the pseudo-Aristotelian source which is quoted *in extenso* in the Mantua Text, paraphrased in the *Book on Spirit and Soul*, and commented upon in the *Book of Substances* (cf. Comments on *BSubst.*, p. 96; and Comments on *Mant.*, p. 127). It sets Israeli's doctrine apart from another pseudepigraphical variant of Neoplatonism, viz. the pseudo-Empedoclean scheme known from the Hebrew fragments of the *Five Substances*, where matter alone is interposed between God and intellect. 'When the Creator, blessed be He, created the world, He created the world of matter, alive with eternal intellectual life. Matter draws this life from the Creator . . . and in that matter are all forms of that world in the most subtle, simple, glorious, and beautiful manner possible. . . .. After He created this matter, He created intellect.' (Kaufmann, p. 19.) Notwithstanding the fact that matter is said to harbour the totality of forms, the single hypostasis preceding intellect in this pseudo-Empedoclean scheme is matter. The position is somewhat confused in a passage of unknown origin in the *Ghāyat al-Ḥakīm*: 'God created five substances, putting one above the other, and making the higher more excellent than the one beneath it, so that it gives it wisdom, virtue, and light. These five are: first matter (*al-hayūlā al-ūlā*), which is the highest world and the first form, and this is the first element (*al-'unṣur al-awwal*); then intellect; then soul; then nature, which is the heaven; then corporeal matter, which is bodily matter. He put first matter in the horizon of His throne, and made it draw light and wisdom and virtue from it by powers belonging to it [the throne] which are similar to it [matter], and bestow these things upon it. He put intellect in the horizon of first matter . . .' (p. 286, ed. Ritter). The reference to first matter and first form places this scheme close to Israeli's. (The possibility of the passage depending on Israeli is not excluded. Cf. the conjecture concerning another passage in the *Ghāyat al-Ḥakīm* in the Comments on *BDef.*, § 9.) On the other hand, no further mention is made of first form in the context of this passage, and intellect is said to come-to-be in the horizon of first matter only, which would seem to indicate a pseudo-Empedoclean background. We need not, however, pursue the analysis of this passage. The difference between the Israeli source and the pseudo-Empedoclean writings may be traced to different interpretations of the original Plotinian doctrine.

The assumption of a double hypostasis of matter and form prior to intellect, which we meet in the Israeli source, seems at first sight to be irreconcilable with Plotinus's teaching. No trace of it can, in fact, be found either in the vulgate version of the *Theology of Aristotle* or in the quotations from Plotinus which have been preserved under the name of 'the Greek Sage' (al-Shaykh al-Yūnānī) in Arabic texts. The introduction of a hypostasis following God and preceding intellect may have been stimulated by theological considerations. It may be partly due to a desire to facilitate the adoption of the concept of creation within the framework of Neoplatonic metaphysics. We shall return to a discussion of this point later. But such a modification might have been impossible without certain clues provided in Plotinus's own doctrine. Such a clue is in fact offered in Plotinus's treatise *On the Two Kinds of Matter* (*Enn.* ii. 4. 4), where the 'intelligible ὕλη' is described as the substratum informed and differentiated by the εἴδη. As A. H. Armstrong[1] has observed, this account of the intelligible world is

[1] *Architecture*, pp. 66 ff.

difficult to reconcile with Plotinus's ordinary account of the world of *Νοῦς*. Whereas *Νοῦς* in the ordinary sense functions as Mind and represents the interpenetration of the intellectual and intelligible, *Νοῦς* in the sense discussed here stands for the union of matter and form. Is it too far-fetched to assume that the Neoplatonist responsible for the Israeli source tried to solve the discrepancy by postulating two kinds of intellect, one composed of matter and form, and one functioning as Mind and designated as intellect *par excellence*? The two primary hypostases would thus reflect Plotinus's doctrine of intellect as intelligible matter endowed with form. Intellect, on the other hand, would represent Plotinus's concept of intellect as Mind. This would also answer the question which we raised concerning the relationship between wisdom and intellect.

The assumption of spiritual matter as a single hypostasis prior to intellect in the pseudo-Empedoclean writings may similarly go back to a suggestion contained in authentic Plotinian teaching. Armstrong points out that Plotinus occasionally describes the One as a root or seed and as the potentiality from which all things evolve into actuality. The implications of this idea, which has its source in the Stoic notion of the *σπέρμα* or *σπερματικὸς λόγος*, and which is hardly compatible with the Platonic-Aristotelian tradition,[1] need not detain us here. What interests us is the fact that Plotinus applies the metaphor of 'root' and 'seed' and the conception of potentiality to the One, and also to intellect and soul (*Enn.* iii. 3. 7; iv. 8. 5, 6; v. 9. 6). It need not therefore surprise us to find that in the pseudo-Empedoclean writings matter signifying potentiality stands at the fountain-head of the spiritual substances, following immediately upon God. It should also be noted that the term 'root' (*Enn.* iii. 3. 7) plays a conspicuous part in the terminology of the Israeli source—first matter there being called 'the root of roots'—and in a pseudo-Platonic treatise quoted by the thirteenth-century Jewish mystic Azriel of Gerona[2] where 'root' is synonymous with matter.

[1] Cf. Armstrong, op. cit., pp. 62–63.
[2] *Pērūsh ha-Aggādōth*, ed. J. Tishby, Jerusalem, 1945, p. 82.

III

THE THREE SOULS—NATURE

In the Plotinian triad of hypostases, intellect is followed by soul, soul itself being divided into a higher and lower phase, the latter amounting, in fact, to a fourth hypostasis called nature. Israeli, once again following his pseudo-Aristotelian source, assumes three distinct hypostases of soul (i.e. rational, animal, vegetative)—transferring Aristotle's tripartite division of the individual soul to the universal soul—and adds as a final quasi-spiritual substance the 'sphere' or heaven, representing the Plotinian hypostasis of nature. This scheme is adopted throughout Israeli's writings (*Mant.*, § 1; *BDef.*, § 5, ll. 45 ff.; *BSubst.* iii; *BSpirit*, § 9; *BEl.*, Fried, pp. 56–61, where the typology of men is based on it), and presents another characteristic feature of his version of Neoplatonism. It also occurs in Ibn Ḥasdāy (cf. the passage reproduced in the Comments on *BSubst.*, above, pp. 98–99) and in the Long Version of the *Theology of Aristotle*, where it is due to the influence of the same source.

In *BSubst.* v. 12^{r}, the three souls are described as the specificalities, i.e. forms, respectively of the three stages of living beings (men, animals, plants), analogous to intellect which is the 'specificality of all things'. They are 'intelligibilia of the Creator' (ibid., 12^{v}), the archetypes, as it were, of all living souls which must be assumed to draw their life from them. Strangely enough, Israeli does not shed much light on the nature of the three universal souls beyond making them mere replicas, on a macrocosmic scale, of the tripartite division of the particular souls familiar from Aristotle's *De anima*. Not that one should find serious fault with the implied obliteration of the border-line between the universal and the particular souls. It has been said of Plotinus's cosmic psychology that it is 'simply an application of Platonic individual psychology to the universe',[1] and warrant for this latitude lies in the very

[1] Cf. Armstrong, op. cit., p. 88

nature of the Neoplatonic doctrine which sees in the soul of man not only a microcosm but an actual participant in the universal soul and intellect. But whilst Plotinus gives due consideration to the difference between the cosmic soul and the individual, especially the human soul,[1] Israeli is content to project Aristotle's individual psychology on to the cosmic plane.

The rational soul, being distinct from intellect and inferior to it, has no intuitive, only discursive, knowledge. It is 'ignorant and needs instruction and memory' (*Mant.*, § 1), and has the property of 'reason, investigation, and discrimination' (*BSubst.* iv. 5^r). Plotinus, too, teaches that the discursive reason of the soul is no longer intuitive like intellect (*Enn.* v. 1. 3–4). The animal soul is still less endowed. It possesses only estimation and fantasy in addition to locomotion and sense-perception (*Mant.*, § 1; *BSubst.* iv. 10^r; *BSpirit*, § 9; *BDef.*, § 5, ll. 55 ff.). The vegetative soul, being the lowest of the three, is capable only of nourishment, growth, and generation (*Mant.*, § 1; *BSubst.* iv. 10^v, 11^v; *BSpirit*, § 9). Details of this Aristotelian psychology and the exact meaning of the terms employed need not occupy us here as the subject has been dealt with elsewhere.[2]

The sphere or heaven, the last of the 'simple substances', holds an intermediate position between the higher substances and the sensible world. In his elaborate discussion of the sphere in *BDef.*, § 6, Israeli is at pains to justify its inclusion in the spiritual realm in spite of the fact that it is a body. He argues that 'it is not really body in so far as its matter is concerned'—a reference, no doubt, to the 'fifth element' of which Israeli holds the sphere to consist (see Comments on *BDef.*, § 9). Not being composed of the four elements like the sensible world, it is 'unaffected by growth and decrease, coming-to-be and passing-away', and has a 'lasting existence'. Moreover, on account of its close proximity to the vegetative soul, it is 'in its shape, spirituality, and sublimity still near to the order of the higher souls' and therefore 'moves with a perfect movement, i.e. a circular movement, which is more complete and

[1] *Enn.* iv. 3. 12–18; iv. 8. 8 *et passim*; cf. Armstrong, op. cit., pp. 90–91.

[2] Cf. H. A. Wolfson, 'Isaac Israeli on the internal senses' (see above, pp. 55, 141), pp. 583 ff.

perfect, and farther removed from attrition and change than the others'. The simple, perfect, circular movement of the sphere is also stressed in the Mantua Text (§ 1) and the *Book of Substances* (iii. 2^r). At the same time, the sphere is no longer purely spiritual. It is 'coarse and bulky' (*BDef.*, § 6, l. 34). 'Its light is the least bright and that farthest removed from spirituality. . . . Its powers are dispersed, and the matter which carries it acquires bodily shape, and receives length, width, and depth' (*BSubst.* iii. 2^r). Standing at the gateway of the corporeal world and yet sharing to some extent in the glory of the spiritual substances, its function is to start the process of generation and corruption in the lower world. It is 'the celestial power ordained in nature by the Creator, may He be exalted, and appointed over the action of coming-to-be and passing-away' (*BDef.*, § 6, ll. 22–24; § 9, ll. 5–7; § 44; *Mant.*, § 1, end). The reference to nature in the sentence quoted makes it clear that the equation of the sphere with nature, which we have seen is characteristic of Israeli's metaphysical schema, is due to the function which the sphere is held to exercise. Discussing the various meanings of the term 'nature', Israeli says that 'Nature in reality is the spheric power appointed by its Creator for influencing coming-to-be and passing-away' (*BSubst.* iii. 2^v; see also *BDef.*, § 9). The parallel text in the Long Version of the *Theology* reads, 'Out of its light came-to-be nature. On account of the distance of that substance from the unmixed light, it became dense and coarse; it lacked the pure refinement and acquired corporeality. It is confined by circumferences and dimensions such as length, width, and depth, and moves with a circular, simple, and fixed movement, which is the spherical movement appointed by the first Creator for the sake of coming-to-be and passing-away.' The manner in which the activity of the sphere operates is not clearly indicated, except that we are told that from the movement of the sphere the four elements arise, from which all beings in the corporeal world are composed and to which they return (*Mant.*, § 4; *BSubst.*, iii. 3^v; *BDef.*, § 6, ll. 18 ff.; § 44; § 45; *BSpirit*, § 7, §§ 9–10).

The doctrine of the three universal souls is not found in other Neoplatonic pseudepigraphs, except the Long Version of the *Theology of Aristotle*, where it derives from Israeli's pseudepigraphical source.[1] The vulgate version of the *Theology* (Dieterici, p. 32, ll. 9 ff.) does not offer an exposition of the theme of the three universal souls.[2] The reference to the tripartite division of the soul (p. 6, ll. 16–17) concerns the individual human soul only. The *Ghāyat al-Ḥakīm* describes the soul as standing midway between first matter and intellect on the one hand and nature and matter on the other. There follows the sentence, 'He also created an animal, a vegetative, and a mineral soul . . .', which does not seem to imply a doctrine of three universal souls; for it is clearly stated that these souls 'draw no force from intellect' and 'their destiny and dwelling place is dust from which they emanated [*sic!*]' (p. 286). In the Hebrew fragments of the *Five Substances*, the splitting up of universal soul into three hypostases is missing altogether. The term 'animal soul' is used only to denote the phase of the soul at which it becomes entangled in the passions of the body. In itself the soul is pure, descended from the higher, spiritual world. There is no scope in this metaphysical scheme for a division of universal soul into a series of hypostases. In a passage quoted in the name of Empedocles, and reading almost like an attack on the doctrine of the Israeli source, it is said, 'The philosopher explained this by saying that in that world there is no shadow, for it is a world of light. Now, animal soul is a shadow of the rational soul but there is no shadow yonder. . . . From this it should be clear that in that world beyond there is no animal soul' (Kaufmann, p. 49; see also pp. 36, 43).

The division of the universal soul into three hypostases, though alien to the Plotinian schema, is not entirely without precedent in Plotinus. We suggest that the importation of Aristotle's psychology into the Neoplatonic system of the Israeli source may have been encouraged by a passage in the *Enneads* (v. 2. 1) which describes the emanation of the lower soul from the higher: 'The soul looking there, whence it came, is fertilized, but going on to another and

[1] As G. Vajda (*Commentaire*, cxxii, p. 31) has shown, the doctrine of the three hypostases of the soul occurs in the Latin version of the *Theology*, Book 10, ch. 2, fols. 46v–47 of the 1517 edition. The authenticity of the text is now confirmed by *LTheol.*, book X; moreover, it can now be established that the doctrine is derived from Israeli's pseudo-Aristotelian source.

[2] Cf. Vajda, op. cit., n. 1.

opposite movement generates an image of itself which is sensation and in plants nature . . . it is not fully present in plants, but it has come-to-be in plants because in advancing so far into the lower region it has made another hypostasis by its going forth and its eagerness for its inferior.' This passage clearly speaks of the two levels of the animal and vegetative soul as part of the lower phase of the universal soul, leaving it open to identify the higher aspect of the universal soul with the rational soul. From here it was not difficult to go farther in identifying the three aspects of soul with Aristotle's psychology. It should be noted that the Plotinus passage which we have quoted is paraphrased in the vulgate version of the *Theology* (Dieterici, p. 140).

The identification of the Plotinian hypostasis of nature with the sphere is found not only in Israeli and the Long Version of the *Theology* but also in the pseudo-Empedoclean writings. There, however, the Plotinian term 'nature' is not yet completely ousted and replaced by 'sphere'. Thus the fragments of the *Five Substances* use the phrase 'universal nature, which is the heaven' (Kaufmann, p. 32). In other places, either 'nature' or 'heaven' is used (heaven, pp. 19, 25, 39; nature, pp. 20, 24, 34).

There seems to be no warrant in Plotinus for this equation of nature with the sphere. As we have already noted, Plotinus distinguishes between two phases of the soul, a higher and a lower or secondary one. Their respective functions have been described by A. H. Armstrong as 'a transcendent principle of form, order, and intelligent direction' on the one hand, and as 'an immanent principle of life and growth' on the other. The lower soul is, in fact, a fourth distinct hypostasis, and bears the closest analogy to the 'world soul' in Plato's *Timaeus*.[1] Mackenna terms it 'All-soul' and Pistorius 'soul of the universe'.[2] The name most often given it by Plotinus is that of *φύσις*, 'nature', designating an unconscious immanent life-force, which 'does not know, but only acts' (*Enn.* iv. 4. 13), and which produces the universe without reasoning or planning in a kind of dream-like contemplation (*Enn.* iii. 8. 4). Obviously, the conception of nature employed here is different from

[1] Cf. A. H. Armstrong, op. cit., pp. 84–86; id., *Plotinus*, London, 1953, p. 37.
[2] P. V. Pistorius, *Plotinus and Neoplatonism*, Cambridge, 1952, p. 76.

the one used in the previously quoted passage (*Enn.* v. 2. 1.), where it is said that the lower soul 'generates an image of itself which is sensation and in plants *nature*'. In fact, Plotinus often uses 'nature' in the sense of vegetative soul only (*Enn.* iii. 6. 4; v. 2. 2; vi. 7. 11), and this particular usage became fairly widespread in medieval philosophical terminology.[1] Israeli's adoption of the term 'nature' for the sphere and his identification of the last Plotinian hypostasis with the sphere goes back to his pseudo-Aristotelian source, and is, as we have shown, completely at variance with Plotinus. For whilst Plotinus conceives of nature as the immanent life-force of an animated cosmos (*Enn.* ii. 4. 7), Israeli regards it as the generating power belonging to the heavenly bodies which produce the four elements, not without adding an astrological colouring by the assertion that the sphere is 'in charge of the contingencies of this world, such as influencing the appearance of religions, the limits of the reigns of kings, their share in good and ill fortune' (*BDef.*, § 6, ll. 49 ff.).[2]

It may be added that Israeli's disciple, Dūnash ibn Tamīm, in his *Commentary on Sēfer Yĕṣīrā* comes nearer to the original Plotinian doctrine by joining a fourth soul, i.e. 'the soul of the sphere' (*ha-nefesh ha-galgalīth*), obviously a kind of world-soul, to the three universal souls (Vajda, *Commentaire*, cxii, pp. 28–29). His doctrine is, however, further complicated by the distinction of three degrees in each of the four souls (ibid.).

[1] Cf. Klatzkin-Zobel, *Thesaurus Philosophicus*, Berlin, 1928, ii, 12, no. 3. Further passages are *Kuzari*, i. 31 and v. 10. Ibn Gabirol (*Fons Vitae*, iii. 46–47) distinguishes 'nature' from the vegetative soul from which it originates. The faculty of nature consists of the four forces of attraction, retention, assimilation, and expulsion.

[2] On the astrological beliefs of al-Kindī, the *Ghāyat al-Ḥakīm*, the Ikhwān al-Ṣafā', and Jābir (*Textes choisis*, ed. Kraus) cf. G. Vajda, 'La doctrine astrologique de Juda ben Nissim ibn Malka', *Homenaje a Millás-Vallicrosa*, Barcelona, 1956, ii. 499. The Jābir text quoted by Vajda as a summary of the prolific treatment of the subject in the *Epistles* of the Ikhwān entirely agrees with Israeli's view: The epochs of the philosophers and periods of the prophets are determined by the position of the celestial bodies.

IV

CREATION, EMANATION, AND NATURAL CAUSALITY

ISRAELI draws a clear line between the way in which intellect comes into being from first matter and form or wisdom, and the manner in which the subsequent hypostases originate. The difference is, in brief, one between creation 'by the power and the will', on the one hand, and emanation, on the other. The light of wisdom and first matter, he repeatedly states, are 'created' by power and will (see above, p. 152). Only occasionally is it said that the first light 'emanates' from the power and will (*BSubst.* iv. 8^{v}), a phrase which must be taken *cum grano salis*, for in the same treatise it is expressly stated that intellect 'is nearest to *creatio ex nihilo*' because wisdom is its form and the perfection of its substantiality (*BSubst.* iv. 5^{r}). Wisdom is therefore clearly conceived as called into being by a *creatio ex nihilo*, and the same must apply to first matter. Moreover, the *Book of Substances* fully explains the difference between the two kinds of causality. Refuting an imaginary opponent, Israeli explains why the power and will of God cannot be held to have created the specificalities of the substances below intellect; in other words, why *creatio ex nihilo* ends with intellect, and emanation does the rest. The reason, he explains, lies in the difference between 'influence and action', on the one hand, and emanation, on the other. 'The light of wisdom is brought into being from the power and the will by way of influence and action, while the light which emanates from the intellect is essential and substantial, like the light and shining of the sun, which emanate from the sun's essence and substantiality.' The salient point of this distinction must be seen in the stress on the nature of emanation as 'essential' causality. 'Specific form is not brought into being from an influencing and acting thing but from an essential one.' The illustration offered is that of reason which establishes the nature of man essentially, not by way of influence and action (ibid. iii. 3^{v}). This can only mean that Israeli regards the procession of the simple substances from intellect as being of a logical and necessary order in contrast to the coming into being of intellect which is due to an act of power and will. The distinction between essence and existence in Ibn Sīnā would seem to be foreshadowed by this differentiation. Its theological motive is obvious. Israeli seeks to introduce the concept of creation into the framework of an emanationist metaphysics, and thus to relieve it of its more or less pantheistic character. Instead of assuming a necessary efflux of all grades of being from One, he postulates a primary act of *creatio ex nihilo*, followed by emanation. How much Israeli was concerned with the problem of creation can be seen from his distinction between 'innovation' (*creatio ex nihilo*) and creation from existing things in the sense of natural causality ('coming-to-be'), a distinction for which he is indebted to al-Kindī, as shown in the Comments on *BDef.*, §§ 42–45. He is most emphatic in differentiating between God's activity of 'innovation' and the causality of nature which is operated through the sphere (*BSubst.* v. 12^{v}). 'Innovation' is a creation 'from nothing', whilst 'creation' is defined as the production of a thing from something existent, and is identical with 'coming-to-be'. As we have noted, Israeli is equally emphatic in keeping apart *creatio ex nihilo* and emanation. The cosmological process therefore falls into three parts: (1) The first two substances are created *ex nihilo* by the power and will of God; (2) The spiritual substances come into being by way of emanation; (3) The corporeal substances are 'created' by the causality of nature, i.e. through the operation of the sphere.

It would appear that the distinction between creation and emanation was not a feature of the pseudo-Aristotelian source from which Israeli took the broad outline of his metaphysical doctrine. The text of the source quoted in the Mantua Text contains no reference to it. It simply states, 'The beginning of all roots is two simple substances' (*Mant.*, § 1). No inference can be drawn from Israeli's paraphrase of the passage in *BSpirit*, § 9, which states, 'God created . . .',[1] because Israeli could have easily adapted the

[1] The sentence as it stands in our text reads, 'God created the intellect as a splendour'. We suggest that the passage is corrupt (see Comments on *BSpirit*,

account to his own view. The same applies to the text in the *Book of Substances* (iii. 2^v; iv. 8^r), using the term 'the first created things'. But the Long Version of the *Theology* and the parallel text in Ibn Ḥasdāy, both of which go back to Israeli's pseudepigraphical source, also use similar phraseology. The former says: 'The first created thing is the first intellect',[1] and Ibn Ḥasdāy states: 'The beginning of creation was two simple substances.' It is therefore likely that Israeli found the description of the first cosmological act in terms of 'creation' already in his source, and that the text quoted in the Mantua Text is incomplete. Moreover, his distinction between *creatio ex nihilo* and emanation in terms of 'action and influence', on the one hand, and essential causality, on the other, is not entirely novel. It is to some extent foreshadowed in the vulgate version of the *Theology*. There we read: 'The first light is not a light in a thing but light as such, subsistent in itself; hence it illumines the soul by the mediation of intellect, being devoid of such qualities as those possessed by fire and other agents. In fact, all agents act by virtue of qualities inherent in them, not by virtue of their ipseity, whereas the First Agent [God] creates the things without any quality, for there is no quality in Him, but He acts by His ipseity. This is why He is the First Agent, who made the first beauty [i.e. wisdom] which is in intellect and soul' (Dieterici, p. 51). Ibn Sīnā, commenting on this passage, mistook the first light for God.[2] But a careful reading of the text of the *Theology* makes it clear that God is the First Agent who made the first beauty, i.e. the first light. This light is said to be a substance ('subsisting in itself'), which recalls the description of the first

p. 114, where attention is drawn to the omission of the opening sentence) and that there is a lacuna between 'God created' and 'intellect as a splendour'. The missing sentence must have referred to the creation of first matter and first form or wisdom, because the subsequent account takes it for granted that 'the perfect wisdom and the pure brilliance'—also called the 'light of the Creator, the absolute brilliance'—precedes intellect. 'God created' may therefore be assumed to refer to wisdom, not intellect.

[1] The 'first intellect' in *LTheol.* corresponds roughly to Israeli's 'wisdom', although Israeli describes wisdom as the first form whilst *LTheol.* attributes to first intellect the characteristics of first matter (genus of genera, &c.). In other respects ('possessing the pure brilliance and the unmixed light') it is, however, closely reminiscent of Israeli's 'wisdom'.

[2] Cf. G. Vajda, 'Les Notes d'Avicenne sur la Théologie d'Aristote', *Revue Thomiste*, Paris, 1951, no. 2, pp. 379 ff.

substance by Israeli, the important difference being that matter does not figure here at all. The stress on the absence of 'qualities' from the causality of the creative act of God, and the comparison of 'essential' causality with the activity of fire, are reminiscent of Israeli's distinction between the two kinds of causality. As has been shown in the Comments on *BDef.*, §§ 42–45, similar speculations are already found in Ammonius's *On the Opinions of the Philosophers.* According to the view attributed to Thales, the concept of creation implies the denial of 'forms' co-eternal with God. Israeli's insistence that in creation only power and will (excluding 'form') are at work reflects the same theology.

The creation of first matter and form is invariably described as 'by the power and the will' (*BSubst.* iii. 2^r; iv. 5^r) or simply 'by the power of the Creator' (*BDef.*, § 2, ll. 107–8; § 3, ll. 10–11). It may be noted that the *Book of Definitions* uses the shorter phrase, the *Book of Substances* the longer one. But one need not read any significance into this variation. What does require some elucidation is the exact meaning of the phrase 'without mediation' which as a rule accompanies the formula. One is tempted to suggest that this phrase has a polemical significance and implies the rejection of a school of thought which interposes a mediating power between God and the first two substances. Thus the Logos doctrine of al-Nasafī and the Ismā'īlī sect postulates the Word (*amr*) as such an intermediary, and the Long Version of the *Theology*, probably reflecting the Ismā'īlī doctrine, as Pines suggested,[1] describes the first intellect as 'united with the word of the Creator'. Israeli's repeated emphasis on the unmediated character of the creation of first matter and form could therefore be said to have a polemical ring. But it can easily be shown that this interpretation is not correct. The simple meaning of the phrase is that the first substances are more perfect than the subsequent ones because nothing stands between them and the Creator. Intellect, too, is said to 'receive the light from the power and will without mediation' because it 'receives the light of wisdom without the mediation of any other substance between itself and wisdom' (*BSubst.* iv. 9^v), whereas the rational soul receives it through the intermediacy of

[1] Cf. above, p. 156, n. 1.

intellect, the animal soul through the intermediacy of intellect and rational soul, &c. The term 'mediation' is therefore equivalent to 'intervening stage', and the phrase 'without mediation' simply means without intervening, light-obscuring stages. Only occasionally does it signify the sole agency of God, as in the statement that 'the sphere and the substances above . . . are generated by the power and will without the mediation of any agent except the Creator, while the compound and sensible bodies under the sphere are made by nature' (*BSubst.* v. 12[v]). The vulgate version of the *Theology* uses the phrase in exactly the same sense in which it is generally employed by Israeli. We quote a few passages which will show this clearly. 'Although all beings emanate from Him alone, it is the first being, i.e. the being of intellect, which emanates from Him in the beginning without mediation; thereafter, all beings in the higher and lower worlds emanate from Him by the mediation of intellect and the supernal world.' The passage goes on to explain that everything mediated and remote from the source is deficient, and that only the unmediated is perfect (Dieterici, pp. 136–7). Only intellect is unmediated in an absolute sense. 'From the Divine realm, a power of light radiates upon intellect, and from it, by the mediation of the intellect, upon the universal, celestial soul, and from intellect, by the mediation of the soul, upon nature' (p. 3; see also pp. 6, 13, 38–40). In a relative sense, i.e. compared with the lower world, the entire spiritual world may be called unmediated. 'Know thou that intellect, soul, and all spiritual things . . . neither deteriorate nor perish because they go forth from the First Cause without mediation. But nature and the sensible and natural things are liable to corruption and deterioration as they are caused by causes which are themselves caused, i.e. come forth from intellect by the mediation of the soul' (p. 141). As we have seen, Israeli too applies the term 'without mediation' in its relative sense to all spiritual substances. In the Hebrew fragments of the pseudo-Empedoclean *Five Substances* (Kaufmann, p. 19), the term 'without mediation' (*bĕlī 'emṣā'ūth*) is used in the same sense.

Israeli's concept of emanation calls for some closer investigation. We have already noted that Israeli defines emanation as an 'essential' causality distinct from 'influence and action', and that he regards the spiritual substances as each emanating from the light or 'essence and substantiality' of the preceding one. This view (which, as we shall see, is not consistently maintained) accords with the account of the series of emanations in the pseudo-Aristotelian source quoted in the Mantua Text (§ 1), where emanation is described in terms of a 'radiance and splendour' going forth in turn from intellect and the three souls. At each successive stage the radiance becomes 'less and dimmer' because of the growing distance from the source. This view of emanation is in the direct line of the Plotinian tradition. The metaphor of 'radiance' and the comparison with the sun which frequently occurs in Israeli (*Mant.*, § 1; *BSpirit*, § 9; *BDef.*, § 5, ll. 36–42) go back to Plotinus (*Enn.* i. 7. 1; v. 1. 6; v. 3. 12; vi. 8. 18), who, in addition, also employs the metaphors of a spring overflowing with water (*Enn.* iii. 8. 10), and of the effusion of heat from fire, cold from snow, and scent from perfume (*Enn.* v. 1. 6). These latter images do not occur in Israeli, though they are found in the quotations from Plotinus transmitted in the name of al-Shaykh al-Yūnānī (Rosenthal, i. 476–7). The strange simile of the rays of the sun 'falling on glass mirrors set in the windows of baths and palaces' has been discussed in the Comments on *Mant.*, § 1.

We meet with an entirely different conception of emanation in writings of Israeli other than the Mantua text. Its keynote is the assumption that each successive hypostasis acquires not only light but also 'shadow' and 'darkness' from the preceding one, and that the shadow and darkness grow more dense at each stage, thus accounting for the progressive lessening of the spiritual force. The *Book of Definitions* uses the formula describing the lower substance as coming into being 'in the horizon and shadow' (§ 5, l. 49) or 'in the horizon and out of the shadow' (§ 6, ll. 6–7) of the higher one. The use of the term 'horizon' (*ufq*) in this connexion is familiar from the vulgate version of the *Theology*, which describes the soul as placed 'within the horizon' of the spiritual world (Dieterici, p. 20, ll. 2–3), and from the *Liber de causis* (§ 2).[1] The

[1] Cf. Guttmann, *Israeli*, p. 18. Dūnash ibn Tamīm's *Commentary on Sēfer Yĕṣīrā* (p. 70, Grossberg) borrowed the term, no doubt, from Israeli.

motifs of 'shadow' and 'darkness' as concomitants of emanation may have been known to Israeli from the pseudo-Aristotelian source, although the text quoted in the Mantua Text omits all reference to them. They occur, however, in Ibn Ḥasdāy and the Long Version of the *Theology*, both of which are based on pseudo-Aristotle, and also in Israeli's own quotation from the pseudo-Aristotelian source in *BSpirit*, § 9, where the terms used are shadow and exhaustion, i.e. 'darkness'. The metaphor of 'shadow' is found also in the *al-Mudkhal al-Ṣaghīr* (attributed to al-Rāzī the physician), where it is stated that intellect projected a shadow, from which God created the rational soul;[1] that the latter projected a shadow from which God created the animal soul, &c. Israeli cannot therefore be regarded as the originator of this motif. The frequent use he made of it was noted already by Albert the Great, who describes it as an 'elegant' saying and quotes it in many places.[2]

In the *Book of Substances* Israeli makes an interesting attempt at combining the two metaphors of light and shadow by introducing the formula 'ray and shade': the form of nature is brought into being 'from the shade of the vegetative soul and its ray'; the latter 'from the shade of the animal soul and its ray', &c. 'Thus it is evident that the ray and shade of the intellect are the specificality of the rational soul; the ray and shade of the rational soul are the specificality of the animal soul', &c. (iii. 3^{r}).

How does Israeli conceive the nature of emanation under the aspects of 'shadow' and 'ray and shade' respectively? The only text offering something like a conceptual analysis of the imagery used is a passage in the *Book of Definitions* (§ 6) where the difference between the higher and the lower substances is discussed. The passage explains why the former remain unaffected by what issues from them, i.e. by the emanant substance, whilst the latter, viz. the elements and composite bodies, are changed by what derives from them. The answer given is that 'the lights . . . of the higher substances, viz. the three souls, are not increased or

[1] Quoted by Vajda, *Revue des études juives*, N.S., xii (1935), 30, n. 1, from a manuscript in the Bibliothèque Nationale, Paris.

[2] Cf. Jakob Guttmann, *Die Scholastik des dreizehnten Jahrhunderts*, Breslau, 1902, p. 57; id., *Israeli*, p. 42.

decreased by the issue of what is derived from them, as these come from the shadow of their light, not from their light itself in its essence and substantiality'. The elements and bodies, on the other hand, are themselves changed, increased, and decreased. The point which interests us here is Israeli's theory that emanation is not really an efflux of the very light or substance of the source but the casting of a shadow by the light, and the coming-to-be of a new substance out of the shadow. More precisely, the shadow *is* the new substance. In a less radical sense, the lower substance is said to originate from both the light and the shadow, or 'in the horizon and shadow', or 'from the ray and shade' of the higher one. The radical interpretation is, however, borne out by Israeli's statement, 'it is clear that in every brilliant thing the light in its essence and substantiality is brighter and has a greater splendour than the light of its shadow; thus it is clear that the brilliance of the vegetative soul is greater and stronger than that of the sphere which is derived from its shadow' (*BDef.*, § 6, ll. 28–33). This view implies that emanation is no longer an 'essential' causality in the sense that the light which emanates proceeds from the essence of the source, 'like the light and shining of the sun, which emanates from its essence and substantiality' (*BSubst.* iii. 3^{v}). It distinctly affirms that emanation is but the casting of a shadow and that the emanant substance originates in the shadow cast, not in the substance or essence of the source. Israeli does not seem to have been aware of the contradiction. For in the same treatise (*BSubst.*) in which he describes emanation as 'essential' causality, he also speaks of emanation in terms of 'light which issues from the shadow of a substance' (iv. 9^{r}). The formula 'ray and shade' may, however, be due to an attempt at harmonizing the two conceptions.

Israeli's insistence that emanation does not imply any change, decrease, or increase in the source reflects a well-known Plotinian doctrine. It is one of the functions of the metaphor of radiation (περίλαμψις) in Plotinus to illustrate the fact that emanation leaves the source unaffected (*Enn.* iii. 8. 10).[1] It also implies a more or less

[1] Cf. Armstrong, *Architecture*, p. 52; id., *Plotinus*, p. 33; Pistorius, op. cit., p. 55.

pantheistic metaphysics.[1] Israeli, we have seen, obviates any such interpretation by introducing the idea of an act of creation from nothing prior to the stage of emanation (see above, p. 172). For this very reason he is unable to use the concept of emanation for explaining, as Plotinus did, how multiplicity could have arisen from the absolute unity of God (*Enn.* v. 3. 16). He differs in this respect from the Arabian philosophers who, following Plotinus and Porphyry (*Sententiae*, ed. Mommert, xi), see in the idea of gradual emanation the means of explaining how from the One the many could have been derived.[2] It may be mentioned that Maimonides (*Guide of the Perplexed*, ii. 12) adopts, on the one hand, Plotinus's metaphor of the water-spring (*Enn.* iii. 8. 10), which expresses the idea of an eternal creation without volition, and, on the other hand, opposes the very same idea, insisting as he does on creation in time and by will. Israeli at least tries to harmonize *creatio ex nihilo* and emanation by assigning them to two different stages of the cosmological process.

The progressive reduction of the light in the course of emanation is made the subject of a special discussion in the *Book of Substances* (iv. 8^{r} ff.). The question posed concerns 'the reasons for the difference of the substances, and the precedence of one substance to another'. Israeli suggests three reasons. (1) The light—in this instance the reference is not to intellect but to the light created by power and will, i.e. wisdom, also described here as 'caused to emanate from the power and will'—met no shadow at the beginning, while its end met various imperfections and obscurities. This represents a certain variation of the motif of 'shadow', since it is no longer maintained that the light is unaffected by the issue of what derives from it, and that the lower substance is but the shadow of a higher one. Instead, it is suggested that the light itself is vitiated by what it meets on its way, i.e. by being mixed with darkness. (2) The reception of the light by one substance from the other varies according to the degree of 'mediation', i.e. intervening stages. Only intellect receives the light without the mediation of another substance; the others receive it through one, two, three, or more intermediaries. This adds yet another motif in

[1] Cf. Armstrong, *Architecture*, p. 62; id., *Plotinus*, p. 33.
[2] Cf. S. van den Bergh, *Tahafut*, ii. 63.

explaining the progressive lessening of the light. In *BSpirit* (§ 9) it appears jointly with that of 'shadow and exhaustion': the splendour and brilliance of the rational soul 'are less than the splendour and brilliance of intellect; the reason being that the degree of intellect is intermediate between the soul and its Creator, so that the soul acqqired shadow and exhaustion, i.e. darkness, as the intellect intervened between it and the light of the Creator'. The two motifs of 'shadow' and 'mediation' are joined also in *BDef.*, § 5, ll. 55 ff., where it is said that 'the animal soul . . . comes into being from the shadow of the rational soul, on account of which it is removed from the light of the intellect and acquires shadow'. (3) A third reason is 'the difference between that which bestows and that which is bestowed, the bestowing and the reception of the bestowal'. This reason is not, however, further explained in the available text, as our fragment breaks off before the discussion of this point is reached.

Our analysis of Israeli's concept of emanation has shown that whilst it preserves, and develops, features of the original Plotinian doctrine, it falls short of some of its profounder aspects. One of the most significant traits of Plotinus's concept of emanation, viz. the doctrine of the two 'moments' in the generative process, is completely obliterated. According to Plotinus, the first moment of emanation is one of pure, uninformed potentiality, and the second one of turning back to the source in contemplation, resulting in the substantiality and full reality of the emanant. As Armstrong remarks: 'Here we meet another of the great principles of the philosophy of Plotinus; that all derived beings depend for their existence, their activity, and their power to produce in their turn, on their contemplation of their source.'[1] This doctrine has been preserved in the Arabic quotations from al-Shaykh al-Yūnānī ('After its emanation from the First Agent, it turned to its Cause and looked at it according to its potency; it thus became intellect and substance'; Rosenthal, i. 475; *Enn.* v. 1. 7), in the vulgate version of the *Theology* (Dieterici, pp. 137–8), and in the Hebrew fragments of the *Five Substances* (Kaufmann, pp. 20–21). No trace of this doctrine is found in Israeli.

[1] Cf. Armstrong, *Plotinus*, p. 34.

V

THE ELEMENTS AND COMPOSITE SUBSTANCES

FROM the motion of the sphere the four elements come into being. Israeli describes the origin of the elements in a number of passages: 'As the nature of the sphere is movement, one part collided with the other, and fire came into being from its movement, and from fire air, from air water, from water earth' (*BSpirit*, § 9). This passage represents a shortened version of the section dealing with the genesis of the elements in the pseudo-Aristotelian source quoted in full in the Mantua Text (§ 2). The *Book of Definitions* (§ 5, ll. 13–14) states similarly that 'through the movement of the sphere the four matters, which are the elements of the bodies, come into being'. A different view is expressed in the *Book of the Elements* which attributes the origin of the elements to the power of God: 'In reflecting on the elements, you will find that nothing preceded them from which they could justifiably be assumed to have come into being, except the power of their Creator' (Fried, pp. 7, 10).[1] The elements are in this context described as the 'truly first principles of natural beings' and as 'simple' in contrast to composite beings. It may well be that this latter view does not mean to contradict the former one but is directed against the doctrine asserting the origin of the elements from the four qualities (warm, cold, moist, dry). For there follows a lengthy repudiation of this particular view (pp. 11–13, 28–29, 36–37, 51; see also *Mant.*, § 2, end). Israeli may therefore be said to hold the opinion that the elements owe their existence to a process of generation caused by the motion of the sphere. The reference to the 'power of God' may be a shorter and more popular version of the phrase by which Israeli repeatedly describes the function of the sphere as the 'power ordained by the Creator, and appointed by Him, over the action of coming-to-be and passing-away' (see above, p. 167). Occasionally,

[1] Cf. Guttmann, *Israeli*, p. 58.

Israeli also describes the genesis of the elements as due to an 'emanation' from the sphere (*BSpirit*, § 7), but this is undoubtedly a slipshod expression and not to be taken seriously.

Israeli's doctrine of the primacy of the elements needs some further elucidation. In two passages, he describes corporeal substance as 'the long, broad, and deep body' (*BDef.*, § 2, ll. 99–100; § 3, l. 15). This term is familiar from the Epistles of the Ikhwān, where it denotes the so-called 'absolute body' (*jism muṭlaq*), i.e. the matter underlying the four elements.[1] It is also designated as 'universal matter' as distinct from three more kinds of matter, viz. (1) the matter underlying artificial objects; (2) the matter underlying natural objects, i.e. the four elements; and (3) prime matter, which is the substance underlying the absolute body. Prime matter represents the lowest grade of the spiritual substances, and stands at the gateway, as it were, of the sensible world. The Ikhwān—as later Ibn Gabirol and Joseph ibn Ṣaddīq—insist that prime matter itself is a simple spiritual substance which emanates from the soul and which cannot be perceived by the senses.[2] If it receives quantity, it becomes the 'absolute' or 'long, broad, and deep body'.[3] The history of this concept, which goes back to Plotinus and Simplicius and plays an important part in medieval philosophy, has been traced by H. A. Wolfson,[4] and need not be restated here.

Israeli nowhere elucidates the meaning of the term 'the long, broad, and deep body' used by him, but it may be tacitly assumed that he accepted it in its full technical sense. He must therefore have shared the Neoplatonic view that there is a common substratum or matter, i.e. the absolute body which underlies the four elements. It may be noted that the Ikhwān followed Aristotle (*De gen. et corr.* ii. 1–4) and Plotinus (*Enn.* ii. 4. 6) in deducing from the reciprocal transformations of the elements their composition from matter and form.[5] Israeli, on the other hand, describes the

[1] Ikhwān, ii. 46 (*Naturanschauung*, p. 55); iii. 187 (*Weltseele*, p. 13).

[2] Ikhwān, iii. 187 (*Weltseele*, p. 13); Ibn Gabirol, *Fons Vitae*, ii. 1; Joseph ibn Ṣaddīq, *Microcosm*, ed. S. Horovitz, p. 9.

[3] Cf. Ikhwān, ii. 46 (*Naturanschauung*, pp. 2–3).

[4] *Crescas' Critique of Aristotle*, 1929, pp. 100, 572–3, 580–90.

[5] Cf. Ikhwān, ii. 6, 46, 50 (*Naturanschauung*, pp. 5, 55, 61).

elements as 'simple' (*BEl.*, Fried, p. 38). This need not, however, be taken as a rejection of the view that they are composed of matter and form. For the spiritual substances, too, are described as 'simple' and, at the same time, composed of matter and form. The Ikhwān hold the relationship between the elements and their qualities to be one of matter and form. They distinguish between forms which constitute the essence of a thing, e.g. the upward movement of fire, and forms which merely perfect and complete a thing, e.g. the heat of fire. Israeli echoes this distinction but prefers to speak of the second group as 'accidents' rather than 'forms'. The natural qualities are said by him to be only 'natural accidents' inherent in the substance of the elements because they do not constitute their essence. Heat, for example, does not constitute the essence of fire because there are hot things which are not fire. The statement 'fire is hot' cannot be reversed. Fire is, however, properly defined as 'a subtle, light, luminous body, tending to rise upward' (*BEl.*, Fried, pp. 29–31). In thus admitting form, Israeli necessarily implies that the elements are composed of matter and form.

Israeli distinguishes between the 'body' (*jism*) of the celestial sphere and the 'body' (*jirm*) of substances in the lower world, a distinction which goes back to al-Kindī, as shown in the Comments on *BDef.*, § 5. Whereas Plotinus rejected the Aristotelian notion of a fifth element and held the bodies of the stars to consist of fire (*Enn.* ii. 2. 3), Israeli stresses the essential difference between the immutable substance of the sphere and the coming-to-be and passing-away which is the destiny of the bodies composed of the four elements and returning to them. It may, however, be safely assumed that he regarded the sphere and the sublunar bodies as sharing in a common matter, i.e. the 'absolute body'. Seeing that the sphere possesses quantity, it must have the 'long, broad, and deep body' for its substratum in common with the elements from which the sensual bodies are said to originate as a result of the mixture and interpenetration of the elements (*BEl.*, Fried, pp. 38–39; *Mant.*, § 2).

The description of the origin of the elements in the Mantua Text (§ 2) is based on Aristotle's account of the transformations of one element into another (*De gen. et corr.* ii. 4), but presents the process as a gradual dissipation of the original warmth, and thus co-ordinates it with the general metaphysical scheme of the 'downward way' which operates also in the realm of the spiritual substances. There is, however, in Israeli no distinct treatment of matter as found in Plotinus. Nor do we meet in him the ambiguity and inconsistency which characterizes Plotinus's evaluation of matter as 'a purely negative conception, absolute potency', on the one hand, and as 'a positively evil, anarchic force',[1] on the other. The demonic function of matter is taken over in Israeli by the mysterious force of 'darkness' and 'shells', anticipating, if not actually influencing, the use of the latter term in Jewish mystical thought. 'Shells' and 'darkness' are said to 'obscure' man's cogitative faculty and to militate against the illumination of the soul by the light of intellect (*BEl.*, p. 56). The shells are also described as the 'corporeal' aspect of images which are meant to convey a spiritual truth in allegorical form (ibid.). One is not wide of the mark in suggesting that the 'shells' stand for the corporeal or sensual mode of experience as opposed to the intellectual or spiritual. The term is obviously taken over from pseudo-Empedoclean writings. It occurs in al-Shahrastānī's account of Empedocles' doctrine, where the lower is said to be the 'shell' (*qishr*) for the higher, and the remark is made that 'Sometimes he [sc. Empedocles] uses for shell and kernel (*lubb*) the expressions "body" (*jasad*) and "spirit" (*rūḥ*) respectively' (*Religious and Philosophical Sects*, p. 262). In a subsequent chapter, al-Shahrastānī reports similarly in the name of Proclus the doctrine that after the combinations of the elements had taken place 'shells' originated, and that the world may be divided into two realms, i.e. 'the world of purity and kernel', on the one hand, and 'the world of filth and shells', on the other (p. 341). The motif does not occur in the genuine Empedocles fragments but may be traced to a passage in Plato's *Republic* (x. 611D), where philosophy is said to perform the task of 'scraping off the shells and weeds which have overgrown the soul'. It should be noted that the pseudo-Empedocles fragments frequently use this motif.[2]

[1] Cf. Armstrong, *Architecture*, p. 86.
[2] Noted already by S. Horovitz, *Microcosm*, p. iii, n. 10.

B. THE UPWARD WAY

VI

PURIFICATION—ILLUMINATION—UNION

THE philosophy of Plotinus bears a twofold aspect. In its description of the downward way, setting out the series of emanations from the One, it is dominated by what has been termed an 'objective' or 'philosophical' view. In its outline of the upward way, prescribing the purification of the soul, its ascent to the level of intellect, and final union with the One, it expresses a 'subjective', 'actual', or 'religious' concern.[1] The religious aspect comes increasingly to the fore in post-Plotinian Neoplatonism. Proclus holds a particularly prominent place in that development. In his Commentary on Plato's *First Alcibiades*,[2] he describes the soul's 'ascent to the Divine' (ἡ ἐπὶ τὸ θεῖον ἀναγωγή) in three stages. The first step is that of 'self-purification' (ἡ ἑαυτῶν κάθαρσις).[3] In this way the soul is freed from the impediments of things sensible and ready to receive the light of intellect from above. At the second stage, intellect 'illumines' (ἐπιλάμπει)[4] the soul, and at the third, the soul, having reached the level of intellect, becomes 'full of God', i.e. inspired or possessed (ἔνθεος),[5] and achieves 'union' (ἕνωσις)[6] with Him. In tracing the ascent to the Divine in these three stages, Proclus follows Iamblichus's division of the theme of Plato's *Alcibiades*.[7]

As A. Nygren[8] has pointed out, Proclus's scheme of purification, illumination, and union was adopted, through the intermediacy of

[1] The terms are those used by E. Zeller, P. O. Kristeller, and É. Bréhier respectively. Cf. H.-R. Schwyzer, 'Die zwiefache Sicht in der Philosophie Plotins', *Museum Helveticum*, 1944, pp. 89–90.

[2] Proclus Diadochus, *Commentary on the First Alcibiades of Plato*, Critical Text and Indexes by L. G. Westerinck, Amsterdam, 1954.

[3] Op. cit. 5. 2; 7. 8; *et passim*.

[4] Op. cit. 30. 17; 52. 4; 318. 8.

[5] Op. cit. 161. 7; 183. 17 *et passim*.

[6] Op. cit. 34. 3, 5; 50. 15 *et passim*.

[7] Cf. V. Cousin, *Nouveaux fragments philosophiques*, Paris, 1828, p. 296.

[8] *Agape and Eros*, authorized translation by P. S. Watson, London, 1953, pp. 573–4.

pseudo-Dionysius, into Christian mysticism, where it appears as the threefold way of *via purgativa*, *via illuminativa*, and *via unitiva*. Its traces in Islam can be found in the Epistles of the Ikhwān al-Ṣafā' and in al-Kindī. We quote a passage from the Ikhwān which clearly reflects Proclus's doctrine of the three stages of ascent:

> When the soul awakens from the sleep of negligence and the slumber of foolishness and makes an effort and throws off the shell and veil of the body, i.e. the natural habits, beastly dispositions, and foolish opinions, and is cleansed from material appetites, it escapes and experiences its resurrection, it becomes luminous, and its substance will be brilliant, and its gaze will be sharpened.
>
> It will then behold this spiritual form, contemplate the eternal substances of light, and behold the hidden things and secret mysteries which cannot be perceived by the corporeal senses and by corporeal impressions.
>
> Having contemplated these hidden things, it will cling to them, even as the lover clings to the beloved. It will become one with them, as light unites with light, and will eternally remain with them in a bliss which speech cannot describe and which thought is unable to grasp.[1]

Al-Kindī re-echoes Proclus's theory of the three stages in a passage describing the 'Divine science' (*al-ʿilm al-ilāhī*) which the prophets attain by the will of God upon (1) purification (*taṭhīr*) of the soul, (2) its illumination (*ināra*) by the truth, and (3) the help, inspiration (*ilhām*), and messages from God.[2] The third stage is described here as one of 'inspiration' (corresponding to Proclus's ἔνθεος), without achieving 'union' with God. It should, however, be noted that even in Plotinus mystical union is sometimes represented as a purely passive 'inspiration' by God, as A. H. Armstrong has shown.[3]

Isaac Israeli adopts the Neoplatonic tradition of the three stages of the upward way which we have traced, and which he may have known from a variety of sources. In the *Book of Elements* (p. 58) he describes the highest type of man as one 'whose rational soul is withdrawn', i.e. from the influence of the lower souls; 'upon

[1] Ikhwān, iii. 28–29 (*Anthropologie*, p. 102).

[2] Cf. M. Guidi and R. Walzer, *Studi su Al-Kindī, uno scritto introduttivo allo studio di Aristotele*, Rome, 1940, pp. 395, 409.

[3] Cf. *Architecture*, pp. 71–74.

whom intellect has caused to shine some of its light and splendour', and 'who has become spiritual and divine and longing exceedingly for the ways of the angels'. This clearly reflects Proclus's scheme: (1) the withdrawal of the rational soul must be understood in terms of the soul's purification (see below), (2) the shining of the light and splendour of intellect upon the soul corresponds to Proclus's 'illumination', and (3) the soul's 'becoming spiritual and divine' corresponds to the stage of 'union'. The three stages are even more clearly marked in a passage in the *Book of Definitions* (§ 2, ll. 56–62), where the final purpose of man is described in the following terms: 'That he may avoid beastly and unclean actions in order thereby to obtain . . . the illumination by the light of intellect and by the beauty and splendour of wisdom; when attaining this rank, he becomes spiritual and will be joined in union to the light which is created, without mediator, by the power of God.'

The first stage, i.e. that of purification, is portrayed by Israeli as a turning away from the passions and appetites of the two lower souls. The classification of men according to the prevalence in them of one soul or two souls combined is a favourite theme of his (cf. *BEl.*, pp. 57–58; *Mant.*, § 6). The 'withdrawal' of the rational soul therefore means its disentanglement and purification from 'beastly and unclean' actions. The motif of 'darkness' and 'shells' also plays a part in this concept of purification. Israeli says that when a man's 'cogitation becomes spiritual, pure, luminous, and contains but little in the way of shells and darkness, then intellect will cause some of its light and splendour to emanate upon it' (*BEl.*, p. 56). The stage, therefore, preparatory to the 'illumination' by intellect is a cathartic process by which darkness, shells, and impurities of all kinds are removed from the rational soul. The virtues resulting from this purification are invariably described as the 'pursuit of truth' (*BDef.*, § 1, l. 54; *BSubst.* vii. 15^v; *Mant.*, § 6) and the 'practice of what corresponds to the truth' (*BDef.*, § 1, ll. 50–51) or 'doing what is dictated by the intellect' (*BSubst.* vii. 15^v). The practical virtues are therefore termed 'intellectual precepts' (*BDef.*, § 2, l. 75), and their enumeration follows a more or less stereotyped pattern, to which parallels exist in the Long Version of the *Theology* (ch. x) and in Ibn Ḥasdāy's *The Prince and the Ascetic* (ch. xxxiii).[1] The catalogue of virtues includes the worship of God (*BDef.*, § 2, ll. 55–56, 73; *BSubst.*, loc. cit.; *Mant.*, loc. cit.), holiness (*Mant.*, loc. cit.), justice (*BDef.*, § 2, l. 78; *BSubst.*, loc. cit.), rectitude (*BDef.*, loc. cit.), equity (*BSubst.*, loc. cit.), lovingkindness and mildness (*BDef.*, § 2, l. 79), and, generally speaking, 'seeking the things which are good and true' (*Mant.*, loc. cit.), 'always doing good' (*BSubst.*, loc. cit.), 'following the good and keeping away from evil' (*BDef.*, § 1, ll. 51–52).

The 'illumination' of the soul by the intellect, which marks the second stage of the upward way, is not further described by Israeli but we shall not be amiss in suggesting that it corresponds to what he terms 'wisdom' as distinct from 'philosophy'. The role of philosophy within the scheme of ascent will be separately discussed in the following chapter. As for wisdom, it is defined as the 'true knowledge of the first, enduring, and everlasting things' (*BDef.*, § 3, ll. 5–6). Similarly, Iamblichus in his *Life of Pythagoras* says that 'Wisdom, truly so called, is a certain science conversant with the first beautiful objects which are divine, imperishable, and possessed of an invariable sameness of substance', whereas philosophy is 'the striving for a thing of this kind'.[2] Al-Kindī, from whom Israeli took his 'description' of wisdom (see Comments on *BDef.*, § 3), does not differentiate between wisdom and philosophy. Israeli, on the other hand, clearly distinguishes between the philosopher's aspiration towards the knowledge of the eternal substances and wisdom's possession of that knowledge.

The final stage, i.e. that of 'union', is described by Israeli as one at which the soul 'becomes spiritual' or 'becomes intellectual'. The phrase goes back to Plotinus who says that when the soul has completed its purification, 'itself becomes intellect' (*νοῦς γενομένη αὐτή*, vi. 7. 35) and at this level 'each one of us is an intelligible world' (*καί ἐσμεν ἕκαστος κόσμος νοητός*, iii. 4. 3). Israeli seems to be rather fond of this phrase. We have already quoted above the passages from the *Book of Elements* and *Book of Definitions* in which it occurs. To these three more may be added. The *Book on Spirit and*

[1] Cf. the present writer's article, 'Isaac Israeli's *Chapter on the Elements*', *Journal of Jewish Studies*, vii (1956), 37–38.

[2] Cf. Iamblichus, *Life of Pythagoras*, translated by T. Taylor, London, 1818, p. 39.

Soul (§ 6) says of the rational soul that when 'inclined towards the highest excellence', it 'becomes intellectual'; and the *Book of Substances* (vii. 15^{v}) describes the rational soul which is 'near to perfection' as 'spiritual'. Finally, the *Yĕṣīrā Commentary* by Israeli's disciple, Dūnash ibn Tamīm, describes the souls which withdraw from the body and achieve union with the upper world as 'becoming intellect' (Vajda, *Commentaire*, cvii, p. 150). This stage is also called 'divine' (*BEl.*, p. 58)—a term which reflects the doctrine of philosophy as 'assimilation to God' (see below, pp. 197 ff.)—and 'angelic' (*BEl.*, loc. cit.; *BSubst.* vii. 15^{v}). The union achieved at this stage is the union of the rational soul raised to the level of intellect with the supernal light of wisdom, thereby completing its ascent from bondage in the flesh and the two lower souls to the highest spiritual substance. This is clearly stated in the passage of the *Yĕṣīrā Commentary* to which reference has already been made: 'Intellect unites with the divine light in a spiritual, not corporeal, union (*ittiḥād*)'. The *Book of Definitions* (§ 2, ll. 60–62) says similarly that having become spiritual, man 'will be joined in union to the light which is created, without mediator, by the power of God'. There is no suggestion here of a final union with God Himself. All that the soul of man can hope to achieve is union with the supernal wisdom created by God. In the Ikhwān passage quoted above (p. 186) the same view prevails: The soul's union is said to be one with the eternal substances only. One may also note that both in Israeli and in the Ikhwān the concept of 'union' is more or less synonymous with that of 'attachment'. Israeli speaks of the soul as being 'joined in union', and the Ikhwān employ both the simile of the lover clinging to the beloved and the phrase 'it will become one with them'. It is, however, possible that the term 'attachment' is used by Israeli in a sense different from that of 'union' when, in another passage, he characterizes the soul in its perfect state as pursuing that which 'attaches' the creature to the Creator, like the souls of the prophets which are 'attached' unto Him (*Mant.*, § 6). The catalogue of virtues listed in this context ('knowledge and understanding, purity and holiness, the worship and nearness of his Creator') and the statement that these and similar virtues 'attach the creatures to God' are reminiscent of the biblical and rabbinic terms of 'cleaving unto God', with which Israeli must have been familiar. They do not imply any mystical notion of union but suggest an adherence of the soul to God by following in His 'ways', i.e. imitating His attributes of love and mercy.[1] Israeli's stress on the virtuous life as a condition of 'attachment' to God would seem to reflect the Jewish traditional outlook rather than the Neoplatonic notion of union. On the other hand, the comparison he draws between the 'adherence' of the pious and that of the prophets points in the direction of mystical union, seeing that the highest degree of prophetic experience is conceived by him as one of union (see below, p. 214). It is therefore only fair to interpret this particular passage in accordance with Israeli's view as stated elsewhere, and to take it to mean that the virtuous life is a stepping-stone to man's attachment to, viz. union with, God (more exactly, the supernal wisdom). This concept of 'attachment' (*dĕbhēqūth*) goes far beyond the biblical and rabbinic teachings, and represents the first attempt to link the biblical use of the verb *dbq* ('to cleave' unto God) with the Neoplatonic notion of mystical union. Israeli's bold step was of far-reaching significance. It paved the way for the extensive employment of the term *dĕbhēqūth* in the Neoplatonic sense[2] in medieval Jewish literature, both philosophical and kabbalistic.

Mystical union with the supernal light of wisdom is regarded by Israeli as a stage which the rational soul can achieve even while still joined to the body, provided it 'withdraws' from the influence of the flesh and of the lower souls. This view is clearly attested in the *Yĕṣīrā Commentary* (Vajda, *Commentaire*, ibid.), where the highest degree of prophecy is interpreted as a mystical union, and

[1] Cf. Deut. iv. 4; xi. 22; xiii. 5; xxx. 20. In rabbinic literature the stress is not on 'adherence' but on 'walking in God's ways'. See *Sifrē*, Deut. 49; Babylonian Talmud, *Sōṭā*, 14*a*. Cf. A. Marmorstein, *Studies in Jewish Theology*, ed. J. Rabbinowitz and M. S. Lew, 1950, pp. 112–14.

[2] For the history of the concept of *dĕbhēqūth* in medieval Jewish thought and in Hasidism cf. G. Scholem, *Major Trends in Jewish Mysticism*, revised edition, pp. 377–8, nn. 5–7; id., 'Devekut in Early Hassidism', *Review of Religion*, xv (1950), 115–39; H. Chone, *Sōd ha-dĕbhēqūth 'ēṣel ha-Ramban*, *Sinai*, ed. J. L. Fishman, xi (1942–3), 86–99; J. G. Weiss, 'Contemplative Mysticism and "Faith" in Hasidic Piety', *Journal of Jewish Studies*, iv (1953), 24 ff.; id., 'R. Abraham Kalisker's Concept of Communion with God and Men', ibid. vi (1955), 87 ff.

the general statement is added, 'In fact, when the souls withdraw from the body, the latter being still alive, this withdrawal is a union with the upper worlds'. Israeli puts the 'true teachers' on the same level as the prophets (*BSubst.* vii. 15^{v}; *BDef.*, § 2, ll. 76–77), and obviously regards them too as capable of achieving mystical union. He could hardly have ignored the testimony provided by Plotinus's famous passage (*Enn.* iv. 8. 1.) describing his own personal experience of *unio mystica.*[1] The *Theology of Aristotle* (Dieterici, p. 8) reproduces that passage. The text in the *Theology* reads as follows:

Sometimes, I was as it were alone with my soul: I divested myself of my body, put it aside, and was as it were a simple substance without a body. Then I entered into my essence by returning into it free from all things. I was knowledge, knowing and known at the same time. I saw in my essence so much of beauty, loveliness, and splendour that I remained astonished and confused, and I knew that I was a part of the exalted, splendid, divine upper world, and that I was endowed with an active life. When this became clear to myself, I rose in my essence from this world to the divine world, and I was as it were placed there and attached (*muta'alliq*) to it. I was above the whole intelligible world and saw myself as if I stood in that exalted divine position, and beheld there such light and splendour as tongues are unable to describe and ears are impotent to hear.

It should be noted that the final stage of the experience described here is one of 'adherence' to, not union with, the divine world, whilst the original Plotinus passage clearly expresses the soul's identity with the Divine (καὶ τῷ θείῳ εἰς ταὐτὸν γεγενημένος). But the point need not be unduly stressed. The portrayal of the supreme mystical experience essentially agrees with the picture drawn by Israeli: the soul ascends above the level of intellect and unites with the supernal substance, becoming a part of it.

The passage quoted seems to have been extremely popular in

[1] Porphyry, *Life of Plotinus*, § 23, distinctly says of Plotinus that he was capable of *unio mystica*, and Marinus, *Life of Proclus*, § 22, describes the ecstatic states produced by theurgy. Cf. R. Walzer, 'Al-Fārābī's theory of Prophecy and Divination', *Journal of Hellenic Studies*, 1957, p. 144.

Islamic and Jewish Neoplatonism. Al-Fārābī quotes it at length from the *Theology*.[1] Moses ibn Ezra quotes its opening sentence,[2] most probably from the Epistles of the Ikhwān,[3] and Shēmṭōb ibn Falaqēra renders the whole passage in Hebrew.[4] Solomon ibn Gabirol's chapter on ecstasy in the *Fons Vitae* (iii. 56–57)[5] is clearly modelled on the passage in the *Theology*.[6] It can hardly be doubted that Israeli knew it in some form or other.

The 'return' of the soul is a theme which assumes its full religious significance under the aspect of the after-life. The Epistles of the Ikhwān contain a great number of passages admonishing the soul to prepare for its return to the world above from which it is descended. The Islamic ceremonies and customs of pilgrimage are said to be symbolic of man's descent and return. 'Therefore behold, brother, and consider how thy soul's return can be achieved.'[7] Israeli, too, sees the consummation of the soul's return in the blissful union with the supernal light of wisdom in the after-life. One who has achieved the three stages of purification, illumination, and union 'will become one that exalts and praises the Creator for ever and in all eternity'. Moreover, 'this, then, will be his paradise and the goodness of his reward, and the bliss of his rest, his perfect rank and unsullied beauty' (*BDef.*, § 2, ll. 62–64). In this remarkable passage, Israeli links the traditional Jewish eschatology with Neoplatonic mysticism: 'Paradise' he interprets as the bliss experienced by the soul in its final union with the supernal light. In the rabbinic tradition (Babylonian Talmud, *Bĕrākhōth*, 17*a*) the future world is described in spiritual terms as one in which 'The righteous sit with crowns on their

[1] Cf. *Alfārābī's Philosophische Abhandlungen*, ed. Dieterici, Leiden, 1892, p. 50.

[2] *Al-Ḥadīqa* (cf. above, p. 7, MS. Sassoon, p. 21; Hebrew version, *Sēfer 'Ărūgath ha-Bōsem*, ed. L. Dukes, in *Zion*, ed. M. Creizenach and J. M. Jost, ii, Frankfurt a. M., 1842–3, 121.

[3] As M. Steinschneider suggested in *HebrÜb.*, p. 243, n. 971.

[4] *Sēfer ha-Ma'ălōth*, ed. L. Venetianer, Berlin, 1894, pp. 22.

[5] Reproduced in Ibn Falaqēra's *Liqqūṭīm*, iii. 37–38.

[6] Cf. Jakob Guttmann, *Die Philosophie des Salomon ibn Gabirol*, Göttingen, 1889, p. 165, n. 2.

[7] Ikhwān, ii. 118–19 (*Naturanschauung*, pp. 148–9). In al-Shaykh al-Yūnānī, iii. 47, 51–55, the same theme is stressed.

heads, enjoying the splendour of the Shekhinah'.[1] Israeli was therefore in a sense on traditional ground in his own interpretation of 'paradise'. The reward promised in the after-life is, again, considered by him as identical with the bliss of union. 'This world is the place of labour, the next the place of reward' (*BSpirit*, § 12). In the *Book on Spirit and Soul*, where the doctrine of reward is fully dealt with, Israeli distinguishes between 'two kinds of bliss: one which occurs without delay, the other remote' (§ 13). By immediate bliss he obviously understands the blessings of this world, whilst the 'remote' one is explained as 'the union with the excellent splendour' (ibid). The theme of reward must have been particularly dear to Israeli, as is evidenced by the frequency with which it is touched upon in his various writings (*BDef.*, § 1, l. 52; § 2, l. 57; § 5, ll. 53–55; *BSubst.* iv. 9^r; *BEl.*, p. 57; *Mant.*, § 6; *BSpirit, passim*).

The counterpart to Israeli's doctrine of paradise and reward is his concept of hell. He who 'perseveres in his injustice, sinfulness, coarseness, and in the evil of his ways, will be rendered unclean by his impurities, and they will weigh him down, and prevent him from ascending to the world of truth' (*BDef.*, § 2, ll. 83–86). A soul 'weighed down' by its impurities will not only be unable to 'attain the light of intellect and the beauty of wisdom', but 'will remain contained under the sphere, sorrowful, in pain without measure, revolving with the revolution of the sphere in the great fire and the torturing flame' (ll. 86–89). The notion of the 'hell and fire' which God 'has prepared for the wicked and sinners' (ll. 89–90) is thus interpreted in terms of the soul's inability to ascend and pass beyond the sphere.[2] More precisely, hell is the consuming fire beneath the sphere and revolving with it (see

[1] Interpreted by Maimonides (*Hilkhōth Tĕshūbhā*, viii. 2) to mean: 'They know and comprehend concerning the true essence of God what they do not know whilst still in the dark and lowly body.'

[2] Similarly, al-Shaykh al-Yūnānī, iii. 47, 51–55, says of 'the stupid souls which were soiled by the human bodies and their coarseness' that they 'are prevented by that fact from ascending to their world'. They descend 'into deep pits, from which they ascend only after long periods'. The punishment of those who 'knowingly did evil' is said to consist in a series of transmigrations. According to the *Epistles* of the Ikhwān, a soul which cares only for the pleasures of this world 'remains blind in its folly below the lunar sphere and submerged in the sea of matter'. Cf. Ikhwān, iii. 93 (Dieterici, *Anthropologie*, p. 155).

Mant., § 2), in which the souls of the wicked are caught. This conception goes back to two sources. In the rabbinic tradition, hell is described as the heat of the sun which burns the wicked or as a strange heat in their bodies which consumes them (Babylonian Talmud, *'Abhōdā Zārā*, 3*b*; *Nĕdārīm*, 8*b*); and Plato speaks of the corporeal element as 'burdensome and weighty and earthy', hampering, depressing, and dragging down the soul into the visible world (*Phaedo*, 81C–D). Israeli combines these two traditions against the background of his own cosmology.

Note. It has been observed by S. Horovitz[1] that Israeli's concept of hell is reflected in Joseph ibn Ṣaddīq's description of the soul's fate after death (*Microcosm*, p. 77), and Julius Guttmann has traced its influence on Jewish Neoplatonists, especially Ibn Gabirol.[2] It can, however, be shown that many more features of Ibn Ṣaddīq's eschatology are borrowed, almost word for word, from Israeli's *Book of Definitions* and *Book on Spirit and Soul.* We quote the relevant passages from the final chapter of the *Microcosm* (pp. 76–79), which deals with 'The true meaning of reward and punishment'.

'The wise soul . . . will after its separation from the body remain perpetually and eternally in the upper world, and this will be its bliss and paradise and reward, i.e. its attachment to its world, and its return to its origin. It will be illumined by the true light which emanates from [Israeli: is created by] the Creator, blessed be He, without intermediary. This is the final purpose of the human soul' (p. 76, ll. 14–18; see also p. 77, ll. 2–5). Cf. *BDef.*, § 2.

'This will be its reward for its good work, and it [the soul] will be of the rank of the higher spiritual substances, as it is written, "I will give thee free access among those that stand by" (Zech. iii. 7) . . . moreover, "The soul of my lord shall be bound in the bundle of life with the Lord thy God" (1 Sam. xxv. 29)' (p. 76, ll. 18–22). Cf. *BSpirit*, § 8; cf. p. 117.

'At the hour of death everything composed returns to its constituent elements, earth to earth and air to air. The spiritual substances likewise

[1] S. Horovitz, *Die Psychologie bei den jüdischen Religionsphilosophen des Mittelalters*, Heft III, B: Josef Ibn Ṣaddik, Breslau, 1906, pp. 204–5.

[2] Cf. Julius Guttmann, 'Zu Gabirols allegorischer Deutung der Erzählung vom Paradies', *Monatsschrift für die Geschichte und Wissenschaft des Judentums*, 1936, p. 182. See also Jakob Guttmann, *Die Scholastik des dreizehnten Jahrhunderts*, p. 58, on the influence of Israeli's doctrine on the Latin schoolmen, notably Albert the Great.

return to their upper world at the hour of reward, as it is written, "Then shall the dust return to the earth as it was, and the spirit shall return to God who gave it" (Eccles. xii. 7)' (p. 77, ll. 19–23). Cf. *BSpirit*, § 8.

The description of the soul which is weighed down by its impurities and caught in the rotation of the sphere and in the elemental fire (*BDef.*, § 2) recurs in the passage (*Microcosm*, p. 77, ll. 30–32), as has already been shown by Horovitz, loc. cit. There follows the moving simile of the returning traveller who finds his way barred:

'It [the soul] is in the position of one who went out with a convoy and returns from his journey, but when approaching the place of his relatives and friends does not succeed in reaching them, and remains in sorrow and pain perpetually, without rest' (p. 77, ll. 32–34). Cf. *BSpirit*, § 14.

VII

THE ROLE OF PHILOSOPHY

As has been shown in the Comments on the *Book of Definitions* (§ 2), the three 'descriptions' of philosophy offered by Israeli are borrowed from al-Kindī and derive, with the exception of the last one, from the traditional list of definitions of philosophy contained in the Alexandrian commentaries on the *Isagoge*. The Neoplatonic background of Israeli's concept of philosophy is equally pronounced in the case of the third description which can be shown to reflect the influence of Proclus, and was probably included in some lost Alexandrian commentary which served as al-Kindī's immediate source. All the three descriptions assign to philosophy a role intimately connected with the 'upward way' or 'return' of the soul.

(1) Philosophy is first 'described' 'by its name', 'love of wisdom' (*BDef.*, § 2, ll. 8–9).[1] It is not 'wisdom' itself but merely the aspiration towards it, as Iamblichus characterized it (see above, p. 188). Israeli clearly distinguished between wisdom and philosophy, for his descriptions of 'wisdom' (*BDef.*, § 3) follow those of philosophy, and are not, as in al-Kindī, put together with those of philosophy under the common name of philosophy. The character of philosophy as a striving for wisdom is well brought out in Ḥunayn ibn Isḥāq's preface to his anthology of Greek wisdom,[2] in which he expressed the hope that his work might be 'a true guide to future adepts of philosophy' and enable them 'to uphold philosophy and *strive* to live in the spiritual world, in the angelic realm, and to become attached to it'. The goal of philosophy may therefore be said to be the illumination of the soul by the intellect and its attachment to the spiritual world. The function proper to philosophy

[1] The etymology of φιλοσοφία (*falsafa*) was commonly known amongst Islamic philosophers. Cf. the passages in A. Müller, *Die griechischen Philosophen in der arabischen Überlieferung*, Halle, 1873, p. 9; al-Shahrastānī, *Religious and Philosophical Sects*, p. 251; Shēmṭōbh ibn Falaqēra, *Sēfer ha-Maʿălōth*, ed. Venetianer, p. 48, quoting al-Fārābī.

[2] *Sēfer Mūsērē ha-Pilōsōfīm*, ed. A. Loewenthal, Berlin, 1896, p. 51.

is obviously a cathartic one: to turn the soul away from the world of sense-perception and towards the contemplation of the spiritual substances. The Epistles of the Ikhwān enjoin those 'who love science and wisdom' to shun the pleasures of this world so as to strengthen their capacity for 'the contemplation of things Divine'.[1] One has to see Israeli's description of philosophy as 'love of wisdom' against this Neoplatonic background in order to appreciate its pregnant meaning.

(2) Philosophy is, in the second place, described as 'assimilation to the Creator according to human capacity' (*BDef.*, § 2, ll. 15–16), a definition which we also meet in al-Fārābī,[2] al-Baṭalyawsī,[3] in the Epistles of the Ikhwān,[4] and other Islamic authors.[5] It goes back to the famous passage in Plato's *Theaetetus* (176B): 'Wherefore also we should fly away from earth to heaven as quickly as we can: and to fly away means to become like God, as far as this is possible: and to become like Him, means to become holy, just and wise' (B. Jowett's translation).

Plato does not elucidate the term 'becoming like God' (ὁμοίωσις θεῷ). It may suggest a mere 'imitation' of God, which would still leave a gulf fixed between God and man: or it may imply that man can 'become like God' in the sense that his nature is raised to a Divine level. Philo of Alexandria, who quotes the *Theaetetus* passage (*De fuga*, 12. 63), seems to waver between these two possible interpretations. On the one hand, he urges good rulers and other men to 'imitate' (μιμέομαι) God's actions (*De spec. leg.* iv. 36. 188; *De virt.* 31. 168)—a concept which he could have borrowed from rabbinic sources.[6] On the other hand, he speaks of our true end as

[1] Cf. Ikhwān, ii. 17 (*Naturanschauung*, p. 19), and Shēmṭōb ibn Falaqēra, loc. cit.

[2] In his *Prolegomena to the study of Aristotle's philosophy*, § 4 (F. Dieterici, *Alfārābī's philosophische Abhandlungen*, Leiden, 1890, p. 53).

[3] Cf. the Arabic original in *Al-Andalus*, 1940, p. 92, and the Hebrew translation in D. Kaufmann, *Die Spuren Al-Batlajusi's in der jüdischen Religionsphilosophie*, Budapest, 1880, p. 47.

[4] Cf. Ikhwān, ii. 386, iii. 58 (Dieterici, *Anthropologie*, pp. 97, 125); ii. 8 (*Naturanschauung*, p. 7) *et passim*.

[5] F. Rosenthal, 'On the knowledge of Plato's philosophy in the Islamic World', *Islamic Culture*, 1940, p. 409, mentions Abū Zakariyyā' al-Rāzī and Ibn Sab'īn in illustration of the fact that this definition was 'well-known to the Arabs'.

[6] Cf. H. A. Wolfson, *Philo*, ii (1947), 195–6. On the rabbinic doctrine of

'likeness to God' (*De opif.* 50. 144) and of our 'goal of happiness' as 'becoming like God' (*De decal.* 15. 73).[1] A clarification of this and other issues involved in Plato's concept of ὁμοίωσις θεῷ is offered in Plotinus's treatise 'On the virtues' (*Enn.* i. 2), from which we quote the salient points.

Plotinus poses the problem, Does God possess virtue? and answers that God certainly does not possess the civil virtues (prudence, justice, temperance, courage). Yet, paradoxically enough, we may be said to become like Him through acquiring those virtues (i. 2. 1). For there are two kinds of resemblance (ὁμοίωσις), i.e. one based on a common identical element (constituting reciprocal resemblance), and one which is achieved by assimilation to a model which is primary and different from the thing which seeks to approximate to it. Resemblance to God is of the second kind. The civil virtues impose a limit and measure upon the soul, and receive their own limit and measure from an ideal norm. The more a being shares in that ideal pattern and by achieving 'form' removes itself from the anarchy of 'matter', the more it becomes similar to the Divine Being, which itself is without form (i. 2. 2). Similarity to God, according to Plato's view in the *Theaetetus*, is of yet another kind. It no longer involves the civil virtues (dealt with in the *Republic*), but the 'higher virtues', from which the former are derived. Plato speaks of our 'flying away from earth to heaven', and he calls the virtues 'purifications'. In what sense, Plotinus asks, are the virtues purifications, and how is it that by purification we become similar to God in a pre-eminent sense? He answers,

As the soul is evil by being interfused with the body, and by coming to share the body's states and to think the body's thoughts, so it would be good and possessed of virtue if it threw off the body's moods and devoted itself to its own act—the state of thought and prudence; never allowed the passions of the body to affect it—the virtue of temperance;

imitatio Dei cf. S. Schechter, *Some Aspects of Rabbinic Theology*, pp. 199 ff.; A. Marmorstein, *Studies in Jewish Theology*, London, 1950, pp. 106 ff.

[1] The *Letter of Aristeas* nowhere speaks of ὁμοίωσις but stresses the duty of imitating (μιμούμενος) God, 'the benefactor of the whole world'. Cf. *Aristeas to Philocrates* (*Letter of Aristeas*), ed. Moses Hadas, New York, 1951, §§ 210, 281. For Hellenistic parallels cf. H. G. Meecham, *The Oldest Version of the Bible: 'Aristeas' on its traditional origin*, London, 1932, p. 306, n. 1.

knew no fear at the parting of the body—the virtue of courage; and if reason and intellect ruled—in which state is justice. Such a disposition in the soul, become thus intellective and immune to passion (ἀπαθής), it would not be wrong to call likeness to God; for the Divine too is pure and the Divine Act is such that *imitating* it is prudence (ὡς τὸ μιμούμενον ἔχειν φρόνησιν) (i. 2. 3).

The 'resemblance' to God is here linked with the 'imitation' of God, because the virtues concerned are no longer the civil virtues (which God does not possess and which cannot therefore be imitated), but the higher virtues which flow from impassivity (which, in a sense, God possesses, since 'the Divine too is pure'). Plotinus defines the higher virtues as the result achieved by the soul's turning away from what is alien to it. They are said to be identical with the contemplative life, in which we allow the intellect to illumine the 'impress' upon the soul of the intelligible world, which the rule of the body temporarily obscures (i. 3. 4). In the degree to which the soul withdraws from the body it becomes similar to God (i. 2. 5). A man who is completely controlled, even in his involuntary movements, by the rational soul is no longer a 'dual being' or 'demon' but 'becomes God' (θεὸν εἶναι), 'he is purely and simply a god' (i. 2. 6).

Plotinus's treatise 'On the virtues' exercised a considerable influence on the school.[1] It is reflected in Porphyry's Ἀφορμαί,[2] and may have been responsible for the definition of philosophy in the Alexandrian commentators as assimilation to God. There is no evidence that the treatise was known to the Islamic philosophers. The extant texts of the Arabic Plotinus contain no reference to it, and the subtlety of its treatment of the theme is nowhere reechoed. Yet its influence can be discerned in two respects. Firstly, like Plotinus, the Islamic Neoplatonists and Israeli understand by 'assimilation to God' not merely the act of 'imitating' God but an actual 'becoming spiritual and divine', which merges into a union with the supernal world (see above, pp. 185–91). A passage in the Epistles of the Ikhwān, after quoting the definition of philosophy as 'assimilation to God according to human capacity', goes on

[1] Cf. É. Bréhier, *Plotin, Ennéades*, i. 50.
[2] *Porphyrii Sententiae ad Intelligibilia ducentes*, ed. B. Mommert, pp. 17 ff.

to explain: 'The angelic virtues of the soul have to be developed here below in order that it may be able to rise from the world of generation and corruption to the world of the spheres and stars in the amplitude of the heavens, and to live there eternally together with like-minded people of previous generations in the company of the prophets and saints.'[1] Secondly, the aspect of purification which Plotinus (and Porphyry) connected with the higher virtues and the imitation of God became a commonplace in Islamic and Jewish Neoplatonism. At the same time, the definition of philosophy as 'assimilation to God' is interpreted without specific reference to the theme of purification. The Ikhwān describe the effort required to become similar to God in terms of moral and intellectual qualities: 'In this sense the learned philosophers say that philosophy is an assimilation to God as far as this is possible to man, i.e. his science must be truthful, his action wise and well balanced, his character noble, his opinions true.'[2]

Israeli quotes the traditional formula, and, like the Ikhwān, elaborates it by explaining that assimilation to God according to human capacity means two things, viz. 'acquiring true knowledge' and 'doing what corresponds to the truth' (*BDef.*, § 2, ll. 18–19). He appends a lengthy excursus on the meaning of 'understanding the truth of things' which need not be examined in detail. In the course of his exposition he develops his doctrine of the soul's ascent and union with the supernal wisdom, which has been analysed above (p. 187), and adds: 'For this reason Plato said that philosophy is a zeal, a striving, an effort, and concern for death' (§ 2, ll. 65–66). He obviously regards this fresh definition, which figures separately in the Alexandrian lists and in al-Kindī, as intimately connected with the previous one. For, he explains, 'By vivifying animal desires and lusts and by strengthening them, men of intellect are

[1] Cf. Ikhwān, ii. 386 (*Anthropologie*, p. 97).

[2] Cf. Ikhwān, iii. 348 (*Weltseele*, p. 164); see also iii. 58 (*Anthropologie*, p. 125). The Arabic Summary of Galen's περὶ ἠθῶν (*De moribus*, ed. Kraus, in *Bulletin of the Faculty of Arts of the University of Egypt*, vol. v. 1, 1937, Arabic Section, p. 41) contains the following passage: 'But there exists no greater honour to your soul than to imitate God according to human capacity. This goal is reached by disregarding present pleasures and giving preference to the noble.' Cf. R. Walzer, 'A diatribe of Galen', *The Harvard Theological Review*, xlvii (1954), 246.

drawn away from that which is due to God' (§ 2, ll. 70–72). Hence it is necessary to 'kill' those passions, 'For in their mortification and avoidance is the highest rank, the supernal splendour and the entry into the realm of truth' (§ 2, ll. 69–70). In thus linking the theme of 'assimilation to God' with that of the mortification of the body, Israeli stands solidly on Plotinian ground.

Israeli's definition is based on the famous passage in *Phaedo*, 64–68:

The philosopher desires death. . . . What is the nature of that death which he desires? Death is the separation of soul and body—and the philosopher desires such a separation. He would like to be freed from the dominion of the bodily pleasures and of the senses, which are always perturbing his mental vision. . . . All the evils and impurities and necessities of men come from the body. . . . Why then should he repine when the hour of separation arrives? Why, if he is dead while he lives, should he fear that other death, through which alone he can behold Wisdom in her purity? (B. Jowett's translation).

From his source which derived from the Alexandrian commentators Israeli learned that the definition went back to Plato.

Apocryphal sentences epitomizing this passage were widely current in medieval Islamic and Jewish literature.[1] Ḥunayn ibn Isḥāq[2] quotes it in the name of Socrates in the short formula, 'Pursue death, and thou wilt live.' Al-Fārābī, Ibn Sīnā, and many other Islamic authors cite in Plato's name the saying, 'Die voluntarily, and thou wilt live by nature.'[3] Judah ben Nissim ibn Malka (fourteenth century) describes himself in his *Uns al-Gharīb* (*Consolation of the Exiled*) as 'one who seeks life in his death', and quotes in support the apocryphal saying (attributed to Plato), 'Cause ye the living to live and the dead to be put to death', which he explains to mean, 'Cause ye the living, immortal soul to live, and put to death the body which is composed of mortal elements.'[4] Joseph ben Meir ibn Zabāra's *Sēfer Shaʿăshūʿīm* (*Book of Delights*)

[1] For Hellenistic references see M. Schedler, *Die Philosophie des Macrobius*, Münster, 1916, pp. 6–7.

[2] *Sēfer Mūsěrē ha-Pilōsōfīm*, ed. A. Loewenthal, Berlin, 1896, p. 88.

[3] Cf. F. Rosenthal in the article quoted above, p. 197, n. 5.

[4] Cf. G. Vajda, *Juda ben Nissim Ibn Malka, philosophe juif marocain*, Paris, 1954, p. 12.

quotes Plato as saying: 'The body is a destroyer of the spirit, and the latter will not be at rest until the former is destroyed. Hence apply yourselves to the destruction of the body in order to put your spirit at rest, and remove the dead from its grave for the sake of the living, but do not kill the living for the sake of the dead.'[1]

The theme, though alien to the main stream of Jewish religious thought, is not entirely absent from classical rabbinic literature. In a Talmudic passage (Babylonian Talmud, *Tāmīd*, 32*a*), Alexander the Great is alleged to have asked the 'Scholars of the South', 'What should a man do in order to live?' They are said to have replied, 'He should mortify himself.' He then asked, 'What should a man do in order to die?', to which question the answer was given, 'He should vivify himself', i.e. indulge in bodily pleasures. The same idea is epitomized in a passage in the minor tractate *Derekh Ereṣ* which is missing in the extant texts[2] but preserved in a quotation by Jonah Gerondi (*Shaʿărē Tĕshūbhā*, ii. 17), 'If it be thy will not to die, die thou before thou diest.'[3] This saying is almost identical with the formula, *mūtū qabla an tamūtū*, which occurs frequently in Ṣūfī literature.[4] It is apparent from these references that the ascetic outlook of Neoplatonism had penetrated into rabbinical circles, and Israeli's effort to introduce the Neoplatonic ethos into Jewish thought could therefore claim to be in line with a tradition already established. He nowhere voices such a claim but we may tacitly assume that he felt himself entitled to it.

(3) Philosophy is, thirdly, described as 'man's knowledge of himself' (*BDef.*, § 2, l. 93). As shown in the Comments (see above, p. 28), this description also derives from al-Kindī but has no precedent in the extant Neoplatonic commentaries. It may be assumed that al-Kindī found it in some text now lost, which offered a slightly different list of definitions of philosophy. Israeli, again following al-Kindī, explains this definition as meaning that one who knows himself 'in both his spirituality and corporeality'

[1] Cf. I. Davidson, *Sēfer Shaʿăshūʿīm*, New York, 1914, p. 92.

[2] It does not appear in M. Higger's critical edition, *The Treatise Derekh Ereṣ*, New York, 1935.

[3] Cf. N. Brüll, *Jahrbücher für Jüdische Geschichte und Literatur*, ii (1876), 129.

[4] Cf. Vajda, loc. cit. As shown in the Comments on *BDef.*, § 2, the notion of the 'twofold death' is found in the al-Kindī passage from which Israeli derived his definitions of philosophy, and goes back to Porphyry.

knows 'everything', i.e. 'the spiritual and corporeal substance', and, he adds, also knows 'the first substance which is created by the power of God without mediator'. Thus comprising as he does 'the knowledge of everything', he 'is worthy to be called a philosopher' (*BDef.*, § 2, ll. 105–13).

The theme of self-knowledge, we may note from the outset, is one well known in tenth-century Islamic and Jewish thought. The idea that by knowing oneself one knows 'everything' has an exact parallel in a passage in al-Masʿūdī (d. 957/8), who attributes to Aristotle the saying: 'Whosoever recognizes himself, recognizes, by this, everything.'[1] The motif underlying this particular concept of self-knowledge is that of man as a 'microcosm', as distinctly stated by al-Kindī (see above, p. 28). In the Epistles of the Ikhwān this motif plays a most conspicuous part, both in its own right and in connexion with the theme of self-knowledge. We are told that 'Self-knowledge consists of four points: Man must know (1) that he is a totality of a sensual body and a spiritual soul; (2) how soul and body are joined together, and why this happens; (3) what was the condition of the particular soul prior to its union with the body; and (4) what will be the condition of the soul after death, i.e. its separation from the body.'[2] The statement found in al-Kindī and Israeli explaining that substances and accidents are either spiritual or corporeal, and that man comprises both (*BDef.*, § 2, ll. 98–106, and Comments, p. 28), occurs also in the Ikhwān:

> Because man is a totality, composed of the corporeal body and the spiritual soul, they [sc. the wise] found in the structure of his body similitudes for everything that exists in the corporeal world . . . and they also found in the various spiritual beings . . . similitudes to the human soul. . . . And since this had become clear to them . . . they called him a microcosm. We say that the existing things are either substances or accidents or a totality of both or matter and form or their composition. . . . Accidents are either corporeal or spiritual. . . .

[1] Cf. F. Rosenthal, loc. cit.

[2] Cf. Dieterici, *Mikrokosmus*, pp. 148 ff. In Ikhwān, iii. 9 (*Anthropologie*, pp. 46–47) and iii. 319, 349 (*Weltseele*, p. 165), self-knowledge is said to comprise three aspects, viz. the states of the body, of the soul, and of both in their union. The Epistles of the Ikhwān furnish a wealth of detail in drawing analogies between the microcosm and the macrocosm. Cf. Ikhwān, iii. 4 ff. (*Anthropologie*, pp. 41 ff.); iii. 211 ff. (*Weltseele*, pp. 27 ff.).

Man is a totality in which two substances are joined. One of them is the corporeal long, broad, and deep body, which perceives by the senses. . . . The other is the spiritual soul, which knows and perceives by intellect.[1]

It is a fair assumption that al-Kindī, the Ikhwān, and possibly al-Mas'ūdī derived their respective statements from a common Neo-platonic source, in which self-knowledge was interpreted in the sense of the microcosm motif. It is by no means certain that the source also contained the definition of philosophy as self-knowledge, seeing that it is not found in the Epistles of the Ikhwān, who might otherwise have quoted it. On the other hand, the definition embodying the microcosm theme occurs in Porphyry's treatise, 'On *Know thyself*' (in Stobaeus' *Florilegium*, ed. A. Meineke, i. 332), from which we quote the relevant passage:

Others who assert that man has been well described as a microcosm claim that the saying is an exhortation to know man, and that since man is a microcosm it commands him only to philosophize. If, therefore, we are eager unerringly to philosophize, we shall desire earnestly to know ourselves, and we shall attain a true philosophy, proceeding from our own perception towards the contemplation of the Whole. It is rightly said that we draw inferences from those things which are within us and concerning those things which are in the Whole, and, by examining and finding ourselves, we pass the more easily to the contemplation of the Whole.

It would seem that this passage represents the ultimate source for the interpretation of self-knowledge found in al-Kindī and the other texts. It can also be regarded as one of the sources for the definition of philosophy as self-knowledge, notwithstanding the fact that the definition is only implied, not explicitly offered, in the sentence, 'If, therefore, we are eager . . . to philosophize, we shall desire . . . to know ourselves'.

A further source of the definition 'Philosophy is man's knowledge of himself' is Proclus, whose Commentary on Plato's *First Alcibiades*[2] comes very near to defining philosophy as self-knowledge:

[1] Ikhwān, iii. 4 (*Anthropologie*, pp. 41–42).

[2] Proclus Diadochus, *Commentary on the First Alcibiades of Plato*, Critical Text and Indexes by L. G. Westerink, Amsterdam, 1954. For an earlier edition cf. *Procli Opera*, ed. V. Cousin, vol. ii, Paris, 1820.

'we hold the knowledge of our own essence (τὴν τῆς ἑαυτῶν οὐσίας διάγνωσιν) to be the pre-eminent and safest starting-point (ἀρχήν) of the Platonic dialogues and, as it were, of the entire philosophical contemplation (καὶ πάσης, ὡς εἰπεῖν, τῆς φιλοσόφου θεωρίας)' (1. 3–5; see also 4. 19–22). Philosophy, in Proclus's view, is the vehicle and expression of the soul's ascent, and self-knowledge assumes its importance from the role it is destined to play in that ascent:

For whence else does it befit our self-purification and perfection to start than from the point where the Delphian god has commanded us? For to those entering the Eleusinian temple a notice was shown, 'Let none of the uninitiated and unexpiated enter here.' Indeed, the inscription 'Know thyself' upon the entrance to the Delphian temple likewise, I believe, indicated the manner of the ascent to the Divine and of the readiest way of purification, evidently as if to say to those capable of understanding that he who knows himself, starting as he does from the right beginning, can achieve union with God, the interpreter of all truth and leader of the purgative life; and whosoever does not know himself and is uninitiated and profane is unable to participate in Apollo's providence. This then, i.e. self-knowledge, will be the beginning of philosophy and of Plato's doctrine (5. 3–14; see also 5. 16–6. 3).

As we have noted in the preceding chapter (pp. 185 ff.), Proclus's scheme of the soul's ascent was adopted by the Ikhwān, al-Kindī, and Israeli. It is therefore not unlikely that his description of self-knowledge as 'the starting-point of all philosophical contemplation' was also known to tenth-century Neoplatonic thought. There is evidence to suggest that the Ikhwān were familiar with it. Their statement that 'All science begins with man's knowledge of himself'[1] would seem to reflect it. Moreover, Proclus's insistence that 'Nothing is nearer to us than we ourselves' and that, in the words of the *Phaedrus* (22A), 'To be curious about that which concerns others, while I am still ignorant of my own self, would be ridiculous' (6. 13–15) is elaborated by the Ikhwān: One who claims to know other things but does not know himself is like one who feeds others, whilst he himself is hungry; who seeks to heal others, whilst he himself is sick; who clothes others, whilst he himself is naked; who guides others on their way, whilst he does not know the ways of his

[1] Ikhwān, iii. 9 (*Anthropologie*, p. 46).

own house. In such things, a man must begin with himself and turn to others afterwards.[1] Finally, Proclus's interpretation of self-knowledge as 'the contemplation of our own substance' (τὴν θεωρίαν τῆς οὐσίας ἡμῶν, 2. 4; 14. 3–4, 10; 22. 11) is re-echoed in the Ikhwān passages describing self-knowledge as the knowledge of our true substance, i.e. the soul. Proclus clearly understands by 'our own substance' the soul. He refers to Plato's *Alcibiades* as a dialogue in which 'it is shown what our substance is' (6. 9–10), having in mind, no doubt, such passages as 130A ff., where it is said that 'Man is not body but the soul in man.' The Ikhwān likewise say that 'Every man who does not know his soul and fails to understand the difference between body and soul is concerned only with the welfare of his body and the enjoyment of this world. He wants to remain there for ever and is forgetful of the return. If, however, a man knows his soul and *its true substance*, he will give special care to the soul, its well-being and condition after death.'[2] These passages bear the stamp of Proclus's teaching, since they combine a number of features peculiar to it, such as the interpretation of self-knowledge as knowledge of the soul, the use of the term 'substance' for the soul, and the role assigned to self-knowledge in the scheme of return. The characteristic pattern provided by this combination of features is also found in the pseudo-Empedoclean Fragments (Kaufmann, p. 36), where it is said:

It is necessary for us to investigate the soul which is within us, and to speculate as to its nature. Such investigation should not relate to the soul as it is in this body of ours, a soul full of passions and held in the grip of animal pleasures . . . but we must investigate the soul which has abandoned all this and which is cleansed of all filth. In it we shall know what it really is. . . . For the soul which has abandoned those evils and is pure even while still in the body is, as it were, no longer in it nor tied to it. Once we know what this soul is, what its substance

[1] Ikhwān, ii. 318–19 (*Anthropologie*, p. 1); iii. 349 (*Weltseele*, p. 165). Philo of Alexandria, *De somn.* i. 55–57, and *De migr.* 195, likewise suggests that before examining the universe we should first make a thorough investigation of our own 'tenement', of 'all that existeth of good and ill in the halls of thy homestead' (*Odyssey*, iv. 392), a quotation which Socrates is reported to have applied to his own inquiries (Diogenes Laertius, ii. 21). Cf. Philo, translated by F. H. Colson and G. H. Whitaker, Loeb Classical Library, v. 598.

[2] Ikhwān, iii. 277–8 (*Weltseele*, p. 86).

and attributes are, we shall not be mistaken in our statements nor in whatever we ascribe to it. . . . When the soul receives the Divine and exalted virtues which were created by Him without anything intermediate, it becomes apparent without doubt that the soul is an exalted substance of the genus of the upper world which is spiritual, divine, and simple.

In al-Kindī and Israeli self-knowledge is not explicitly connected with the scheme of purification and ascent, as we find it in Proclus, the Ikhwān, and pseudo-Empedocles. One might even say that by interpreting self-knowledge as the knowledge of the microcosm, i.e. soul and body, al-Kindī and Israeli are completely at variance with Proclus's stress on the soul as the only worthwhile object of introspection. But one need not go to any such lengths in assessing the implications of their statements, particularly in view of the fact that the Ikhwān seem to see no contradiction in combining both interpretations. As we have seen, they follow both Porphyry in elaborating the microcosm motif ('man is a totality of body and soul') and Proclus in giving prominence to the soul as the true object of self-knowledge. Al-Kindī and Israeli would have likewise agreed that the ultimate purpose of self-knowledge is to understand the true nature of the soul and its ascent to the upper world.

According to Israeli, self-knowledge implies not only the knowledge of the macrocosm but also of the 'first substance, which is created by the power of God without mediator, which is appropriate to serve as a substratum for change; as well as the first generic accident, which is divided into quantity, quality, and relation, together with the remaining six compound accidents, which derive from the composition of substance and the three accidents' (*BDef.*, § 2).[1] The reference to the first substance obviously suggests that self-knowledge eventually leads to the union with the supernal wisdom and thus to the final goal of the soul's ascent. Israeli does not assert that self-knowledge finds its consummation

[1] The division of the ten Aristotelian categories into a primary group of four (substance, quantity, quality, relation) and a secondary one of the remaining six, resulting from the combinations of the first four, goes back to the Alexandrian commentators. Cf. M. Guidi and R. Walzer, op. cit. (above, p. 186, n. 5), pp. 384–5. See also Dieterici, *Alfārābī's philosophische Abhandlungen*, pp. 150 ff.

in the knowledge of God. It is significant that he does not quote the famous saying, 'He who knows himself, knows his Lord', which is well attested in tenth-century Islamic and Jewish sources.[1] The omission is undoubtedly due to the fact that in Israeli's view the highest knowledge open to man is the knowledge of first matter and first form. God, like Plotinus's 'One', is unknowable (see above, pp. 157–8).

Note. Israeli's definition of philosophy as self-knowledge is quoted in Joseph ibn Ṣaddīq's *Microcosm* (p. 2, ed. S. Horovitz):

'Concerning this subject, the philosophers when laying down the definition and description of philosophy said that philosophy was man's knowing himself; for by knowing himself he knows everything, i.e. the corporeal world and the spiritual world. And this is the science of philosophy, which is the science of sciences and their final purpose.'

Ibn Ṣaddīq concludes his description of philosophy as the 'science of sciences and their final purpose' by explaining that 'it is the preliminary step and road to the knowledge of the Creator and Initiator of everything, blessed and exalted be He'. This theme is amplified in the Introduction to Book 2 of the *Microcosm* (pp. 20–22), which quotes Job xix. 26 as *locus probans* for the idea that self-knowledge leads to the knowledge of God. Unlike Israeli, Ibn Ṣaddīq adopts the doctrine, if not the actual formula, of the Islamic *ḥadīth*, 'He who knows himself, knows his Lord.' (See also *Microcosm*, p. 37, where the same Scriptural verse is quoted in support of the doctrine of the spiritual nature of the soul.)

[1] Cf. F. Rosenthal, op. cit. (above, p. 197, n. 5), pp. 409-10 (quoting al-Mas'ūdī, 'Alī ibn Rabban al-Ṭabarī, and the Ikhwān); G. Vajda, *Archives d'histoire doctrinale et littéraire du moyen âge*, xv (1946), 193 (quoting al-Qirqisānī and Joseph al-Baṣīr). The extraordinary popularity of this saying in medieval Jewish literature is illustrated by the long list of authors using it which Steinschneider, *Hebräische Bibliographie*, xv (1875), 43, has drawn up. See also L. Dukes, *Philosophisches aus dem zehnten Jahrhundert*, Nakel, 1868, p. 59; D. Rosin, 'Die Religionsphilosophie des Abraham ibn Ezra', *Monatsschrift für Geschichte und Wissenschaft des Judentums*, 1899, xliii (N.F. 7), 231; D. Kaufmann, *Gesammelte Schriften*, ed. M. Brann, Frankfurt a. M., 1910, ii. 15–16.

VIII

THE ROLE OF PROPHECY

ISRAELI nowhere offers an elaborate doctrine of prophecy comparable to those appearing in later phases of medieval Jewish philosophy. His scattered references to the prophets in the *Book of Definitions* and elsewhere are fortunately not our only clue to his views on the subject. There is a lengthy excursus on prophecy in the second chapter of the *Book on the Elements* (see above, pp. 135–40), and a passage elucidating three types of prophecy occurs in the *Yĕṣīrā Commentary* of his disciple, Dūnash ibn Tamīm, reflecting, no doubt, the master's own theory.

The doctrine of prophecy which emerges from the sources at our disposal has a decidedly Neoplatonic flavour. It belongs to the same climate of opinion as the references to prophecy in the *Epistles* of the Ikhwān. There is no sharp dividing line between prophet and philosopher. Both share in the common task of guiding mankind towards the same goal: both are concerned with the ascent of the soul, its liberation from the bondage of matter, and its eventual union with the supernal Light. It is characteristic of Israeli as well as of the Ikhwān that the prophets and philosophers are as a rule bracketed together. Thus Israeli says of the 'intellectual precepts' that God reveals them to 'the elect among His creatures, meaning thereby the prophets and messengers and the true teachers'—the latter obviously denoting the philosophers (*BDef.*, § 2, ll. 75–77). In another passage he describes the rank of the rational soul as 'spiritual', 'near to perfection', and 'resembling the spirituality of the angels', and adds, 'like the souls of the prophets, peace be upon them, and the teachers guided aright' (*BSubst.* vii. 15^{v}; see also *Mant.*, § 6).

The function of God's elect, i.e. the prophets and true philosophers, is to 'guide His creatures towards the truth' and to 'prescribe justice and equity', &c. (*BDef.*, loc. cit.). Similarly, the Ikhwān declare the souls of the philosophers to be 'of the same kind' as the souls of the prophets and diviners,[1] and philosophy and prophecy both to be 'divine' and aiming at the same thing, i.e. 'to guide aright the human soul; to establish its welfare; and to lead it forth from hell, the world of generation and corruption, into the paradise which is in the amplitude of the spheres'.[2]

The difference between philosophy and prophecy according to the Ikhwān lies in the difference between the 'acquired intellect' and revelation as their two respective sources of knowledge. There are, we are told, five sources of knowledge altogether, viz. (1) sense-perception; (2) tradition; (3) the *lumen naturale*; (4) revelation and intuition; and (5) analogy and reasoning. Of (4) it is said that 'this kind cannot be acquired by man, nor does it depend on his free will; it is a gift from the exalted God'; and of (5) that 'this is the acquired intellect: the scholars take pride in it, and the philosophers vie with one another concerning it'.[3] In another place we are told that certain things transcending human knowledge such as the history of primeval times or the events of the distant future can be known only by tradition from the prophets who in turn received it by 'inspiration' or 'from the angels'.[4]

The distinction between acquired and revealed knowledge is also stressed by al-Kindī. The 'Divine science' or 'science of the prophets', he says, 'is obtained without research, without effort, without human industry, and without time'. It does not require the employment of the 'preliminary and logical sciences'. It is obtained 'by the will of God, may He be exalted, upon the purification of their [sc. the prophets'] souls and their illumination concerning the truth, by means of His help, His assistance, His inspiration and message'.[5]

To be sure, Israeli differentiates between 'two kinds of knowledge', i.e. the knowledge of the intellect which 'knows without cogitation and consideration' and the knowledge derived by 'cogitation, consideration, investigation, and distinction' (*BDef.*,

[1] Ikhwān, ii. 7 (Dieterici, *Naturanschauung*, p. 6).

[2] Ikhwān, iii. 49 (Dieterici, *Anthropologie*, p. 117; cf. also *Einleitung*, pp. 129–30).

[3] Ikhwān, iii. 291 (Dieterici, *Weltseele*, p. 99). Saadya Gaon, *Kitāb al-Amānāt wa'l-I'tiqādāt*, ed. Landauer, pp. 12–14, has a similar list, from which he omits, however, revelation.

[4] Ikhwān, iii. 41 (Dieterici, *Anthropologie*, pp. 112–13).

[5] Guidi–Walzer, op. cit., pp. 395–6, 409–10.

§ 4, ll. 9 ff.). But he nowhere describes the difference between philosophy and prophecy as one between acquired and revealed (or intuitive) knowledge. He may have felt that this distinction hardly established a criterion of prophecy, seeing that the illumination of the soul by intellect is achieved by the philosophic quest and represents the stage of wisdom as its goal (see above, p. 196). In his view, the prophet is not merely an illuminate but one who has reached the final aim of the soul's ascent and achieved union with the supernal Light. There is also, he holds, a lesser degree of prophecy, i.e. the foreknowledge of the future by way of prophetic dreams. Israeli does not explicitly distinguish between the ecstatic and the dream type of prophecy but his meaning may be inferred from the fact that Dūnash ibn Tamīm lists them as two separate grades, adding a third one, and relating the three types to the three mystical terms, 'voice' (*qōl*), 'spirit' (*rūaḥ*), and 'speech' (*dibbūr*) of the *Sēfer Yĕṣīrā* (i. 9). We propose to analyse these three conceptions of prophecy outlined in the Ibn Tamīm passage[1] and treated more fully in Israeli's *Book on the Elements* (see excerpt, above, pp. 135–40), where, however, no reference occurs to the type of prophecy termed *qōl*.

(*a*) The lowest form of prophecy (*qōl*) is 'a voice which God creates in the air and which He directs towards the ear of him who merits to hear it'. It manifested itself not only in biblical times but also during the period of the Second Temple and was then called *bath qōl* (lit. 'daughter of a voice').[2] This concept goes back to Philo who explains the biblical term, 'God spoke', by suggesting that God created an 'invisible sound' (ἦχον ἀόρατον), which was something incorporeal, living, rational, and sounded forth as an 'articulate voice' (φωνὴ ἔναρθρος), which was also incorporeal, yet visible (*Moses*, ii. 39. 213; *De decalogo*, 9. 32–35).[3]

[1] Vajda, in *Revue des études juives*, cvii. 55–58, gives a translation (in French) of the passage and valuable comments on the Hebrew text. Cf. his edition of new fragments of the Arabic original from the Genizah Collection in Cambridge, ibid. cxiii. 37–61. The Arabic text of our passage is found on p. 40.

[2] Passages recording the experience of *bath qōl* in Talmudic literature are collected in Nahum N. Glatzer, 'A Study of the Talmudic Interpretation of Prophecy', *The Review of Religion*, New York, 1946, pp. 122 ff.

[3] For a full analysis of Philo's doctrine of prophecy by the Divine voice see H. A. Wolfson, *Philo*, ii. 36–43.

Saadya Gaon, Israeli's younger contemporary, also interprets the biblical phrase 'God spoke' to mean that God 'created a speech which, through the medium of the air, reached the ear of the prophet or the people'.[1] In his *Commentary on Sēfer Yĕṣīrā*, Saadya suggests that the 'created voice' is produced in the subtle rarefied air called by him 'second air' (*ăwīr shēnī*), from which all things emanated, and which he identifies with the Divine 'glory' (*kābhōd*), the 'throne of God', the *Shĕkhīnā*, and the 'Holy Spirit'.[2] Both to Philo and Saadya revelation by the 'created voice' represents the highest form of prophecy,[3] whereas Ibn Tamīm regards it as the lowest, as is clear from the fact that he identifies it with the notion of *bath qōl*, the post-biblical remnant, as it were, of prophecy.

(*b*) The second type of prophecy (*rūaḥ*) is said by Ibn Tamīm to be the one most commonly found among the biblical prophets and to include the category of 'vision' (*ḥāzōn*). 'All these passages and those resembling them represent prophetic dreams.' Ibn Tamīm affirms that if a man of sound faith and opinions frees himself from the pursuit of worldly pleasures and becomes 'endowed with a superior soul', the majority of his dreams will be veridical. He adds that the dreams which occur towards the morning when the stomach has completed the work of digestion are as a rule veridical and foretell future events. 'For this reason our Sages have said, The dream is a sixtieth part of prophecy.'[4]

Israeli concludes his account of dream prophecy (see above, p. 136) with a similar statement: 'From this point of view, there is agreement between all authors of books on religion and all who believe in prophecy that dreams are a part of prophecy.' He is

[1] Saadya Gaon, op. cit., p. 105.

[2] *Commentaire sur le Sefer Yecirah*, ed. M. Lambert, pp. 72–94. For a full treatment of Saadya's doctrine of 'created voice' and 'created glory' cf. the present writer's article, 'Saadya's Theory of Revelation', *Saadya Studies*, ed. E. I. J. Rosenthal, Manchester, 1943, pp. 4–25.

[3] As for Philo, cf. Wolfson, op. cit., pp. 51 ff.; as for Saadya, cf. Altmann, op. cit., p. 23.

[4] Babylonian Talmud, *Bĕrākhōth*, 54*b*. For Talmudic discussions on dream interpretation cf. Babylonian Talmud, *Bĕrākhōth*, 55*a*–57*b*. See also R. J. Z. Werblowsky, 'Kabbalistische Buchstabenmystik und der Traum', *Zeitschrift für Religion und Geistesgeschichte*, viii (1956), 164–9, where a medieval text (by Joseph ben Abraham Jiqatilla) using Talmudic material in connexion with a Kabbalistic theory of dreams is reproduced.

probably aware of the large body of Hellenistic tradition about prophetic dreams, particularly from Stoic sources, which had passed into Islamic thought.[1] He obviously shares the current belief that divination by dreams is one of the media of prophetic knowledge, as Philo did before him.[2] For an elucidation of the mental processes which constitute the prophetic dream he uses the concept of 'imaginative forms' which, as shown in the Comments (pp. 142–5), goes back to pseudo-John Philoponus's notion of creative fantasy in sleep and to al-Kindī's stress on the superiority of images received in dreams over those which come by way of sense-perception. Israeli recognizes that this kind of activity happens not only in prophetic dreams but whenever 'intellect wishes to reveal to the soul what its Creator has caused to emanate upon it, namely an understanding of the spiritual things which it finds in itself'. Intellect 'imparts to them forms intermediate between corporeality and spirituality in order that they may be more readily impressed upon the *sensus communis*'. For the same reason and following the very example of intellect, the ancient philosophers, Israeli says, employed allegorical language for the expression of their thoughts.[3] In prophetic dreams exactly the same thing happens, with the only difference that in this case the initiative lies not with intellect ('when intellect wishes . . .') but with God: 'For when the Creator wishes to reveal to the soul what He intends to innovate in this world, He makes intellect the intermediary between Himself and the soul, even as the prophet is an intermediary between the Creator and the rest of His creatures' (see above, p. 135). Strange and bizarre images such as flying men and talking beasts may occur in dreams other than prophetic. They do 'teach us certain truths', once they are competently interpreted. But they assume a special significance in prophetic dreams, for they exemplify the prophets' 'exalted qualities and their achievement of having passed from the flesh to a spiritual state, since that which they made manifest

[1] Cf. S. van den Bergh, *Tahafut al-Tahafut*, ii. 167–8. As shown by van den Bergh and, before him, by W. Jaeger, *Aristotle*, Oxford, 1934, pp. 162–3, the Stoic notion of prophetic dreams goes back to Aristotle's early treatise, *On Philosophy* (fragm. 10, ed. Rose), from which Posidonius took it, and which is quoted in Sextus Empiricus and Cicero.

[2] Cf. Wolfson, op. cit., ii. 55–59.

[3] *BEl.*, pp. 51–52 (see above, p. 135); *BDef.*, § 5, ll. 32–35.

transcends the natural order' (p. 136). Israeli, like his disciple, Ibn Tamīm, emphasizes the need for turning away from the allurements of the world as a pre-condition for prophetic dreams as distinct from ordinary dream experience. One may assume that the philosopher's dream in which 'certain truths' are imaginatively portrayed also presupposes a measure of spirituality. We understand in this context why Israeli leaves the border-line between philosophy and prophecy rather indistinct. There is obviously only a difference of degree between the two types of persons concerned, whilst the phenomenon of prophecy as such is constituted by a Divine initiative.

(*c*) The highest form of prophecy (*dibbūr*), Ibn Tamīm tells us, was reached by Moses, of whom it is said, 'God spoke unto him face to face' (Exod. xxxiii. 11; Num. xii. 8). The term 'spoke', which Philo interpreted as indicating a 'created voice', is regarded by Ibn Tamīm as a veiled reference to the 'union' (*ittiḥād*) of Moses' soul with the supernal Light.

> We say . . . that Moses' soul was superior to the soul of all other men. It was subtle, light, and united with the world of the rational soul, even prior to its separation from the body. In fact, when the souls separate themselves from their respective bodies, while the latter are still alive, this separation is a union with the supernal worlds, for in that state the soul becomes intellect, and intellect unites with the Divine Light in a spiritual, not corporeal union. This forms part of the third science, and this allusion suffices for the intelligent.[1]

It is clear from this passage that Dūnash ibn Tamīm regards the highest form of prophecy as identical with the ecstatic experience, of which there would seem to exist varying degrees, the highest stage being the one reached by Moses. Again, the transition between philosopher and prophet is one of degree only, seeing that philosophers too are avowed to have experienced mystical union (see above, p. 191). In defining prophecy at its highest level in terms of ecstasy, Ibn Tamīm reflects Israeli's doctrine:

> One whose rational soul has withdrawn itself [from the lower souls] and upon whom intellect causes its light and splendour to emanate

[1] For an interpretation of this passage see above, p. 189.

becomes spiritual, god-like, and longing exceedingly for the ways of the angels, as far as lies within human power. The Creator, exalted and blessed be He, therefore chose from among His creatures one qualified in this manner to be His messenger, caused him to prophesy, and showed through him His veridical signs and miracles. He made him the messenger and intermediary between Himself and His creatures, and caused His Book of Truth to descend through him [see above, p. 139].

This description is clearly designed to fit the prophecy of Moses, although it may be applicable to some extent to other prophets as well.[1] The portrayal in this passage of the perfect man as distinct from the other types does not contain any reference to mystical union as the culmination of his ascent. It substitutes for it the Divine gift of prophecy, the power of performing miracles, and the bringing down from Heaven of the Book. The substitution of these gifts for the experience of mystical union need not mean that in Israeli's view that supreme experience is absent from Moses' prophecy. It would rather seem to indicate that here *unio mystica* takes the form of inspiration or possession, in which the prophet's soul becomes the organ of God. Plotinus himself at times describes mystical union as a mere passive yielding to the entrance of the One, and comes very near to Philo's concept of ecstasy and inspiration, as A. H. Armstrong has shown.[2] True, Plotinus nowhere characterizes ἐνθουσιασμός or inspiration as 'prophecy', but in the final chapter of the *Enneads* (vi. 9. 11), where he describes the enthusiasm of mystical union, he speaks of 'the wisest men among the prophets' as those who 'have explained in riddles what the vision of God is like'. Israeli's doctrine of prophecy as a Divine inspiration at the stage of mystical union has therefore a precedent, although hardly its model, in Philo and, to some extent, in Plotinus. It could have derived from al-Kindī who replaces mystical union by inspiration (see above, p. 186). The doctrine that Divine books

[1] When quoting Scriptural proof in *BSpirit*, Israeli hardly distinguishes between Moses and the other prophets. *Loci probantes* from the Torah as well as from the Hagiographa (Prov.; Eccles.) are introduced, 'As the prophet says' (§§ 4, 8). Only once do we find the expression 'A proof from the Torah' (§ 13). Other quotations ranging over the whole of the Bible except the Torah are introduced by the terms 'It is said', 'It is written', or are referred to as 'the words of Scripture'.

[2] Op. cit., pp. 71–74.

originate in a state of enthusiasm and are dictated by God or an angel goes back to Hellenistic sources.[1]

A final word has to be said on Israeli's insistence upon the need for presenting truths and intellectual precepts in an imaginative form. As we have noted, he regards this method of expression as imperative, from a pedagogical viewpoint, even in philosophy. In the case of prophecy he holds this to be all the more important because of the very purpose of the prophetic mission. God created the world, he explains, from the motive of goodness and love, and desiring the 'benefit' of His creatures and their worthiness of reward—by which Israeli understands the bliss of spiritual union in the Hereafter—He had to reveal His will, by the fulfilment of which alone man obtains that reward. In order to reveal His will, He had to send His messengers, the prophets, to mankind, and seeing that the multitude of men, led astray by worldly desires, are incapable of grasping spiritual truths unless presented in some corporeal, i.e. imaginative, form nearer to their understanding, He had to clothe those truths in the form of allegories. To be more precise, not all Divine truths of revelation are stated in a veiled form. The 'Book' also contains messages in 'spiritual, unambiguous words' in order to put into the hands of the intelligent a key, as it were, for the correct interpretation of the symbolic language used therein for the benefit of the less intelligent. It is the privilege of 'scholars' to interpret to the multitude the impressive, yet obscure meaning of those images until they grasp it little by little.

This conception of prophecy as the repository of Divine truth in imaginative form for the benefit of the *profanum vulgus* is closely akin to Philo's notion of the mysteries which lie hidden in Scripture and have to be extracted by means of the allegorical method.[2] But the pedagogical aspect is much more pronounced in Israeli than in

[1] Cf. Festugière, *La Révélation d'Hermès Trismégiste*, p. 318.

[2] Cf. Wolfson, op. cit., i. 49. Philo evolved his allegorical interpretation of Scripture in imitation of Homeric exegesis. It is interesting to find that Christian patristic allegory often harmonized Homer and the Bible by reading the allegorical meaning of the one into the other. Cf. H. Rahner, *Griechische Mythen in christlicher Deutung*, Zürich, 1945, *passim*. The use of the allegorical method in both Hellenistic and medieval Jewish thought has been analysed by I. Heinemann in *Mnemosyne*, ser. iv, vol. v, 1952, Leiden, pp. 130 ff.; and in *The Hebrew Union College Annual*, Cincinnati, xxiii (1950–1), 611 ff.

Philo. How Israeli put his theory into practice we are hardly able to judge, since very little is left of his exegetical Commentary on Genesis.

Note. As is commonly assumed, Saadya Gaon, Israeli's younger contemporary, was the first to introduce into Jewish theology the distinction between two kinds of Divine laws, viz. 'rational' (*ʿaqliyya*) and 'obediential' (*samʿiyya*). We suggest that Saadya's notion of 'rational laws' may be to some extent indebted to Israeli's concept of 'intellectual precepts' (*BDef.*, § 2, l. 75). Saadya deals with the subject in the first place from a Muʿtazilite background, the term 'rational' being tantamount to 'man's natural gift, his mental equipment by birth' (*fiṭra*), and reflecting the Stoic notion of natural reason. In addition, however, Saadya also shows the influence of the Platonic psychology and doctrine of virtues, and is inclined to see in reason the ruling faculty of the soul which is not in a state of automatic harmony with nature but more often in conflict with it. He is not so far removed from the spiritual temper of the Neoplatonic tradition when speaking of the eternal strife between reason and nature, which compels the former to seek all kinds of devices against the 'indolence' and 'greed' of the latter.[1] Viewed from this aspect, the 'rational laws' are guides to wisdom rather than expressions of 'natural' reason, a concept which comes very close to Israeli's notion of 'intellectual precepts', and may have been inspired by it. In discussing how reason is able to control the recalcitrant forces of nature, Saadya again follows a line of thought which places him in close proximity to Israeli. He explains the function of 'images' and 'parables' as designed to move and stir man's nature. An image can achieve what reason by itself is incapable of doing: being an expression of reason in terms of nature, i.e. sense-perception, it can more easily influence nature.[2] This recalls Israeli's description of images as more likely to impress the *sensus communis* and fantasy.

It is not improbable that Saadya's doctrine of 'rational laws' owes something to Israeli, seeing that a brisk correspondence on philosophical matters obtained between the two men prior to Saadya's departure from Egypt,[3] as testified by Ibn Tamīm.[4]

[1] Cf. the present writer's article, 'Saadya's Conception of the Law', *Bulletin of the John Rylands Library*, Manchester, xviii (1944), 4–8.

[2] Loc. cit., pp. 8–9.

[3] According to H. Malter, *Saadia Gaon, His Life and Works*, Philadelphia, 1942, pp. 54 ff., Saadya left Egypt not later than 915.

[4] Cf. Vajda, *Commentaire*, cvii, p. 20; and above, p. xxii, n. 1.

INDEX OF NAMES

INDEX OF SUBJECT-MATTER

PRINTED IN
GREAT BRITAIN
AT THE
UNIVERSITY PRESS
OXFORD
BY
CHARLES BATEY
PRINTER
TO THE
UNIVERSITY